THE POVERTY OF PLENTY

The Poverty of Plenty

Wang Xiaoqiang

and

Bai Nanfeng

Translated by Angela Knox

St. Martin's Press New York

First published in the United States of America in 1991

Printed in Hong Kong

ISBN 0–312–05340–1

Library of Congress Cataloging-in-Publication Data
Wang. Hsiao-ch'iang.
[Fu jao ti p' in k' un. English]
The poverty of plenty/Wang Xiaoqiang and Bai Nanfeng:
translated by Angela Knox.
p. cm.
Translation of: Ju jao ti p' in k' un.
Includes index.
ISBN 0–312–05340–1
1. China—Economic conditions—1976– —Regional disparities.
I. Bai, Nan-feng. II. Knox, Angela. III. Title.
HC427.92.W37713 1991
330.951'058—dc20 90–8948
CIP

Contents

List of Figures

List of Tables

List of Maps

Translator's Acknowledgement

I would like to thank Professor Yin Zhiqi for his considerable support and assistance in this translation project, and also Zhao Yiheng and Liu Bingchang for their painstaking checking of the translation drafts. My thanks too go to Terry Cannon for his interest and encouragement. Finally, I would like to thank the authors for their trust and co-operation.

ANGELA KNOX

Chinese Transliterations

I have in the main followed the official *pinyin* system of Romanisation in use in China today. For Tibetan place names, however, I have used the more commonly known transliterations.

Weights and Measures

1 mu = 0.06 hectares
1 jin (catty) = 0.5 kilograms
1 dan = 50 kilograms

Introduction

Chinese people often refer to China's western borders as New Zealand or Xinxilan; the name is created by the first syllables of Xinjiang in the north-west and Xizang, or Tibet, in the south-west. The name comes from when thousands of urban educated youngsters went west during the Cultural Revolution in the 1960s, following Mao's call for them to temper themselves by working among the peasants. For many, it felt like exile; and New Zealand was an appropriate name for the unfamiliar, un-Chinese region they found themselves in.

The sense of China's far west as being a place apart is also reflected in its economy. In recent years, concern about what is known as the east–west divide has been increasing as the legacy of underdevelopment has been exposed by the startling successes achieved especially in the coastal areas after ten years of reform. For Chinese economists, the 'west' generally refers to China's north-west and south-west regions comprising the autonomous regions and provinces of Inner Mongolia, Ningxia, Gansu, Qinghai and Xinjiang in the north-west and Sichuan, Tibet, Guizhou, Guangxi and Yunnan in the south-west.[1] Between them, these regions cover two-thirds of China's total land area and contain 25 per cent of its population. The reasons behind the contrast between the thriving eastern seaboard provinces and the underdeveloped 'west' (excluding Gansu and Sichuan) and possible solutions to this problem form the subject of Wang Xiaoqiang and Bai Nanfeng's analysis in *The Poverty of Plenty*.

The study is based on fieldwork in Tibet and Guizhou in 1984, and draws on the authors' own personal experiences of life in poor rural areas when they, too, were sent down to the countryside during the Cultural Revolution. Wang Xiaoqiang himself trained as a tractor assembly worker, and worked for several years in a rural factory. Both authors belong to a top-level think tank for economic reforms which advised the pro-reform leader Zhao Ziyang on economic policy before his disgrace following the student protests of June 1989. They have brought to this study an understanding of central government policies and their impact in the different regions.

But what basis is there for the existence of the east–west divide? Chinese accounts cite gross output value figures to show that the western regions trail far behind the east. The gap between the gross value of industrial and agricultural output (GVIAO) of the coastal

Table I.1

	Consumption (yuan per capita)	*Region*
Xinjiang	410	western
Zhejiang	365	coastal
Jiangsu	397	coastal
Guangdong	408	coastal
Qinghai	371	western
Tibet	359	western

Note: 1984 figures from *Statistical Yearbook of China 1986*, p. 558.[3]

provinces and the western regions was 256 billion yuan in 1981 but by 1987 it had reached 679 billion yuan – and is still growing, according to Wang and Bai. Yet this does not mean that the economies of the western regions, which, it must be remembered, contain only 25 per cent of the population, are stagnating or in recession. Average annual growth in GVIAO in the national autonomous regions between 1981 and 1988 was a very respectable 9.7 per cent.[2] And *per capita* consumption figures reveal no clear distinction between east (or coastal regions) and west, as Table I.1 shows.

Wang and Bai, however, believe that the 'healthy' appearance of the economies of western regions, based as they are on aid and imports from the coast, belies underlying problems. They point out that economic indicators such as output value tell us little about infrastructural development and nothing about the underlying economic model in operation.

Seeing the east–west divide in economic terms alone omits a whole range of important issues. One defining characteristic of the western regions which has a major bearing on the divide is the ethnic difference. 'New Zealand' and its neighbouring areas contain over 72 per cent of China's total non-Han population (who only make up 7 per cent of the total population) and consist largely of territories not fully integrated socially, culturally or economically with China proper.

It is important to bear this aspect in mind when considering Chinese strategies for developing the western 'backward regions', as Wang and Bai term them. Wang and Bai prefer to see the ethnic difference in terms of 'quality of human resources', or rather, as a problem of the 'poor' quality of the inhabitants of 'backward regions' which they say inhibits the exploitation of the natural resources of these regions and prevents them from developing a commodity economy. Some have argued that to view the inhabitants of the western regions as lacking the 'quality' required for successful development within China's Han-dominated economy, is to analyse the situation from a Han colonialist perspective.

Historically, China has a long tradition of making vassal states serve imperial aims. Its geopolitical strategy since 1949 with regard to the border regions shows many similarities with previous practice. Where once vassal states provided tribute to the Chinese emperor, they are now expected to provide raw materials and natural resources. Fears of territorial disintegration have always haunted China's rulers, even more so today as ethnic tensions rise in the USSR. The economic and political integration of outlying regions has been and still is crucial. Mao saw China as 'a plate of loose sand', a metaphor he used as a rationale for strong central control. Throughout China's history, the border regions have been populated with soldiers settled on the land as in Xinjiang and Han settlers sent to support the garrisons as in Mongolia and Manchuria.[4] This has served the double purpose of relieving population pressure in China proper and establishing a Chinese presence with a built-in defence force. Today, undisclosed (but presumably large) numbers of People's Liberation Army soldiers are stationed in all the border regions, but most notably in Tibet and Xinjiang. The military has played a major role in developing the regions by building transport infrastructure and by engaging in agriculture and industry through the Production and Construction Corps (PCC), comprising PLA soldiers transferred to civilian work. In Xinjiang, output from PCC factories and farms now makes up nearly a quarter of the region's total output.[5]

China's Seventh Five-Year Plan (1986–91) incorporates elements of past practice. Based on a model of regional comparative advantage, the plan sees the western regions as the providers of energy and mineral resources, to be used by the central provinces where much of China's energy and defence industry is based, while the coastal provinces continue to be the focus of development, the argument being that the wealth created in this region can later be shared with the west. The plan also provides for personnel to be transferred from the east to the west in order to raise the level of technology there. Although in 1985 there were plans to shift the focus of economic construction to the west by the year 2000, and arguments to this effect continue to surface from time to time in the Chinese press, the then party secretary Zhao Ziyang officially stated in April 1988: 'Our goal is to seek common prosperity for all nationalities, but this cannot be achieved simultaneously.' For the time being, he said, the west was to supply the raw materials for the development of the east,[6] and in return provide a ready market for the goods the east produces. Raising incomes, increasing marketisation and exploiting natural resources in the west are clearly of major importance for this strategy.

Wang and Bai's analysis falls very much within the ambit of the Seventh Five-Year Plan. They recognise the natural resource advantages of the regions under consideration and lay great stress on economic viability, criticising previous policies for undue emphasis on political factors. Towards the end of the study the authors include a short section examining the impact of nationalism and religion on economic development, but they do not question the proposition that national minority peoples should remain under the ultimate control of the Han government in Beijing. For Wang and Bai the main problem lies almost wholly within the local, non-Han, population, who, as 'backward' people, 'lack a sense of commodity economy'. As such, their analysis provides a valuable insight into Chinese views on development.

Throughout *The Poverty of Plenty*, Wang and Bai constantly bring the reader back to the question of *who* is doing the developing. They show that although output and incomes have risen in 'backward' regions, the hoped-for development of a commodity economy has not happened. Their examples of the effects of the reforms in underdeveloped Guizhou in the south-west and go-ahead Wenzhou, a coastal city in Zhejiang, bring them to one conclusion: the reforms depend on the quality of human resources which the authors equate roughly with the degree of market entrepreneurship.

For Wang and Bai, the quality of human resources is a function of historical development which is actively hindered by aid and poor infrastructure. Aid, they argue, leads to increasing dependence; and to the emergence of a self-contained economic system in which central government aid pays for imports from the coastal regions while failing to touch the lives of the majority of the self-sufficient inhabitants of the less developed west. Factors conducive to the quality of entrepreneurship, on the other hand, include diversified business activities (e.g. rural enterprises), education, access to the media and mobility.

But in addition to these external factors of the social infrastructure that make for poor quality in human resources, Wang and Bai imply that there are some culturally internal factors which militate against development. This gets uncomfortably close to Han chauvinism. Examples of these factors include cultural/religious taboos such as Tibetans' reluctance to eat fish or their religious beliefs which preclude the use of 'scientific' methods of past or drought control. Moreover, their evidence for the poor quality of teachers in one minority region, Guizhou, fails to take into account that most teachers are working with a second language, and a notoriously difficult written language at that.

Wang and Bai's study of the problems impeding development was widely acclaimed when it appeared in 1986, and many of the ideas and concepts they put forward have been taken up in calls for developing education and raising the quality of human resources in 'backward' regions. How successful have attempts at development been since then?

Great emphasis has been laid on extending education to the indigenous people, and encouraging vernacular teaching, as well as developing other aspects of social infrastructure. In Tibet, 13 of the 43 state-funded key projects begun in 1984 were dedicated to developing the region's scientific, technological, cultural, educational and medical facilities. Education has been seen as important not only in aiding present development, but also in developing local expertise in preparation for the predicted shift to the west in the focus of construction at the turn of the century. Radio reports have enthusiastically noted a shift towards commerce among Tibetans 'who used to look down upon business as beneath their dignity'.[7]

Another new development has been the increase in border trade. Building on the principle of comparative advantage, advocated by Wang and Bai, regions such as Xinjiang have opened up markets with the Soviet Union, Pakistan and Mongolia. Xinjiang's border trade was worth US$16.82 million in 1988, and by September 1989 already stood at over double that figure.[8] A traditionally Islamic region, Ningxia has established strong trade and labour service contacts with the Middle East. By mid-1989, 120 Sino–foreign joint ventures had been established in north-west China, with a total investment of US$300 million.[9] Xinhua reported that Xinjiang and Ningxia were seeking government approval for proposals to set up two special economic zones.[10] Tibet's border trade with India and Nepal amounted to US$12 million, compared with US$7.6 million in 1986. Tibet traded carpets, goats, woollen yarn, cloth and knitwear with Nepal in return for light industrial products such as bicycles and TV sets.

Wang and Bai's proposal to develop tourism has made a particularly profound impact. They see it as a way to build up the infrastructure the western regions so desparately need and promote the flow of 'modern' information required to raise the quality of human resources. Tourism has been seen as the cheap alternative to central government aid, and in Lhasa a massive joint venture hotel has been built in recent years to cater for the influx of tourists. Lhasa's income from tourism in 1988 was nearly US$2 million,[11] making it the fastest growing industry in the region. However, the political impact of tourism in Tibet has been less favourable to the Chinese government. As well as bringing with them modern values and modern patterns of consumption, tourists have also brought a certain appreciation of Tibetan culture and sympathy with nationalist aspirations, which China has perceived as a threat to territorial integrity.[12]

Development in the western regions has its risks as well as its advantages for the Han central government. As always, the problem remains that the unpredictable native inhabitants of these regions may refuse to fall in with plans imposed from far away. The past five years or so have seen increased hostility in 'New Zealand' towards the Han presence and policies. The national liberation uprisings in Lhasa in September 1988 and March 1989, which led to the imposition of martial law in that city, were not isolated expressions of discontent. Elsewhere, in an echo of the Salman Rushdie affair, there were riots in Xinjiang in May 1989 protesting against 'a bad book' which detailed spurious Islamic sexual practices, while attacks on Han settlers have been reported in Kashgar in western Xinjiang and in the regional capital Urumqi. More recently, rising nationalism has spilled over from Soviet Central Asia. In early April 1990 a 'counter-revolutionary rebellion', allegedly fomented by Muslim separatists, was put down in a small town near Kashgar. Until some effort is made to understand the nationalist feelings and grievances of the ethnic minorities, Han plans for their border regions will continue to meet with resistance; both passive and active.

Following the events of June 1989, the Economic Structural Reform Institute of China, the influential think-tank which had advised the former party and government leader Zhao Ziyang on reform policies, was put on ice. Its director Chen Yizi fled to the west and is now one of the leaders of the Paris-based dissident organisation, the Federation for a Democratic China, while deputy director Wang Xiaoqiang has extended his stay as Ford Foundation fellow in the USA. But the strongest indicator that economic change cannot be divorced from internal politics comes from the fact that Wang's co-author Bai Nanfeng, associate research fellow at the institute, was arrested in connection with the pro-democracy movement and was still in detention in May 1990.

ANGELA KNOX

Notes

1. Shi Zhengyi 'Research and Development in the Economies of China's National Minority Regions' in *Explorations into Economic Development in Western Nationality Regions* (*Xibu Minzu Diqu Jingji Kaifa Tansuo*), Central Institute of Nationalities National Minority Economic Research Group, Central Institute of Nationalities Publishing House, 1986, p. 4.
2. *Beijing Review*, 27 March–2 April 1989, p. 4
3. Table adapted from T. Cannon in D. Goodman (ed.) *China's Regional Development*, Routledge, 1989, p. 168.
4. See M. Rossabi, *China and Inner Asia*, Thames, 1975.
5. *Jiefangjun Bao*, 10 March 1989.
6. *Beijing Review*, 16–22 May 1988, p. 17.
7. *Xinhua*, 20 April 1989.
8. *China Daily*, 6 November 1989.
9. *Xinhua*, 30 June 1989.
10. Ibid.
11. *Xinhua*, 12 April 1989.
12. R. Schwartz, 'Reform and Repression in Tibet', *Telos*, no. 80, p. 11.

Map 1   *Per capita* gross value of industrial and agricultural output, 1982

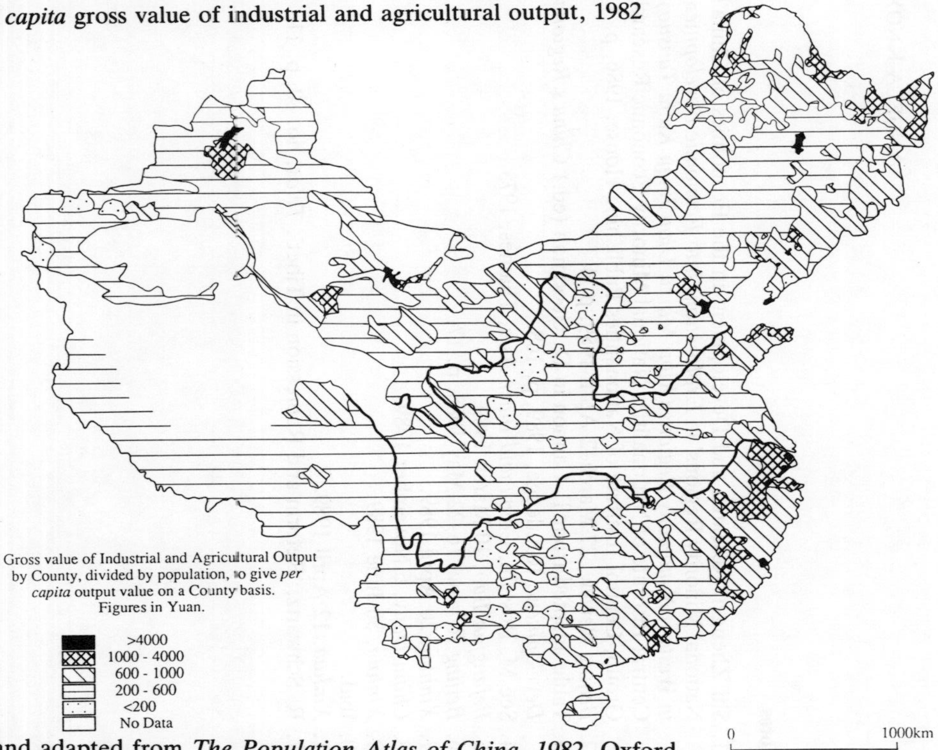

Simplified and adapted from *The Population Atlas of China, 1982*, Oxford University Press, 1988, by courtesy of Terry Cannon

Map 2 Proportion of ethnic minority population, 1982

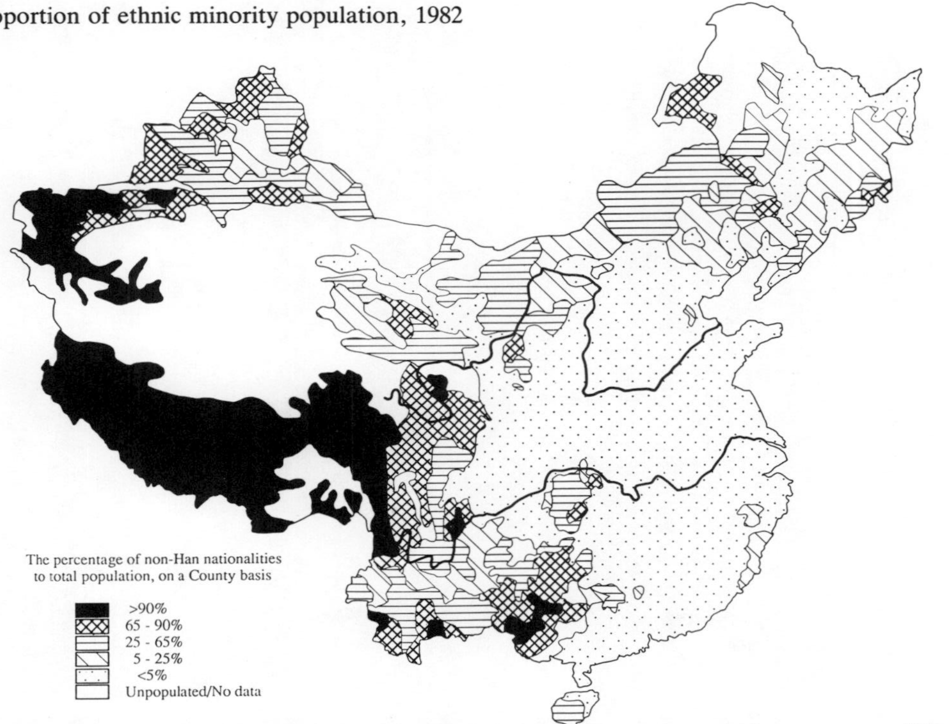

Simplified and adapted from *The Population Atlas of China, 1982*, Oxford University Press, 1988, by courtesy of Terry Cannon

1 Extremes of Poverty and Wealth

The Third Plenum of the Eleventh Party Congress held in 1978 marked the beginning of a second momentous revolution in China's rural areas. The reform of the economic system and the readjustment of economic relations meant a new and more rational alignment of essential production factors. What was not foreseen was that starting in the poorer regions, these new regulations for the realignment of essential factors grew from a mere trickle to a mighty flood, and brought about a new and more alarming inequality in their wake as they spread throughout the country. After the welcome imposition of the household responsibility system (the system introduced nationwide in 1980 whereby individual households contract yearly to deliver an agreed quota of production to the state in return for land, inputs and compensation), this poverty gap between regions became more and more acute, leading to a third-world division within China itself, to a theoretical debate between proponents and opponents of the 'staggered' reform theory, and to increasing concern about the importance of economic development in backward regions.

1.1 THE MATTHEW EFFECT

In St Matthew's Gospel it says 'If a man is rich, gifts will be made to him, and his riches will abound; if he is poor, even the little he has will be taken from him' (Matthew 13, 12). This is known as the Matthew effect in cybernetics, and is used to describe positive feedback. In simpler terms, it is the spiralling effect of the direct ratio of 'more leads to more' which holds between cause and effect. To take an example, as a writer through publishing his works becomes more and more well known, so it becomes easier for him to get his writing published; and similarly as more of his works are published, he becomes more and more famous and naturally finds it even easier to get published.

China is a vast country, and economic growth in all regions has shown serious imbalances, as everyone is aware. One point worth noting is that statistics from the period following the initial implementation of the far-reaching restructuring of the economy are revealing an emerging Matthew effect in the fact that poor regions are getting poorer, while advanced regions are forging ahead. Figure 1.1 shows this effect.

China is at present undergoing the shift from a natural economy towards a commodity economy. In other words, it is changing from an agricultural society to an industrial society. The per capita gross industrial output figures illustrate even more clearly the yawning gulf between advanced and backward regions.

If we compare Jiangsu, which lies above the mean in Figure 1.2, with the provinces and regions below the mean, their per capita GVIO expressed as a percentage of the figures for Jiangsu are as follows: Ningxia – 44 per cent, Xinjiang – 44 per cent, Inner Mongolia – 42 per cent, Qinghai – 40 per cent, Yunnan – 29 per cent, Guizhou – 23 per cent and Tibet – 7 per cent. In 1983 the whole of Tibet, with a population of 1 930 000, achieved a GVIO of 130 million yuan through the combined efforts of state, collective and individual enterprises. That same year Yishan (population 190 000), a district of Cangnan county in the Wenzhou region of Zhejiang Province, urban enterprises apart, achieved a yearly output of over 100 million yuan in rural household sideline ventures of fine synthetic textile reprocessing and plastic woven carrier bag production alone, and all this without a single penny of state investment. These glaring inequalities are by no means new. What is new is their excessive growth.

The different provinces and regions do not exhibit a uniform speed of growth. Logically, only if the backward regions develop much faster than advanced regions will they be able to reduce the gap between them within a short space of time. However the tendency revealed in Figures 1.1 and 1.2 above is not in accord with what we might desire. If we take Jiangsu and Tibet as extreme examples, by a process of simple deduction we can foresee the worst prospect of an increasing gap between backward and advanced regions.

In 1983 Tibet's GVIAO was 0.85 per cent that of Jiangsu. A simple projection based on growth rates in recent years in the two regions anticipates that this percentage will drop to 0.55 per cent in 1990. In absolute terms, the gap in the GVIAO of the two regions will jump from 81 800 million yuan to 180 800 million yuan, an increase of 221 per cent. This represents an average yearly increase of 12 per cent, or 2.26 times the rate of increase in Tibet's GVIAO. It also means that if in 1990 Tibet wants to maintain the gap in GVIAO between itself

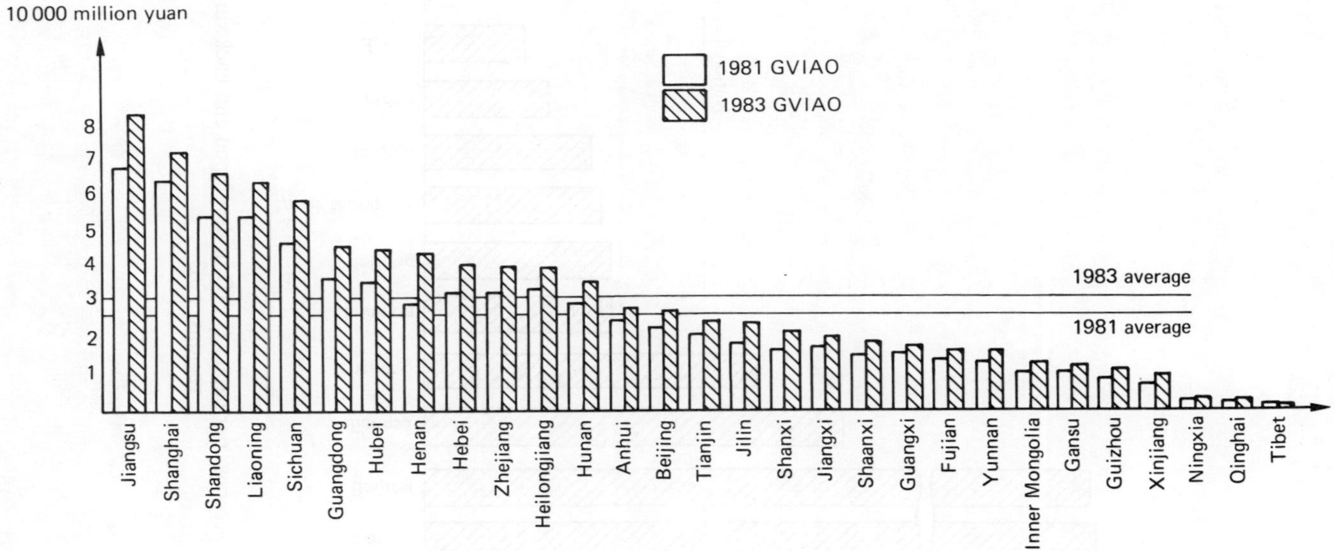

Figure 1.1 GVIAO for 1981 and 1983 in all provinces, municipalities and autonomous regions (Taiwan excepted)

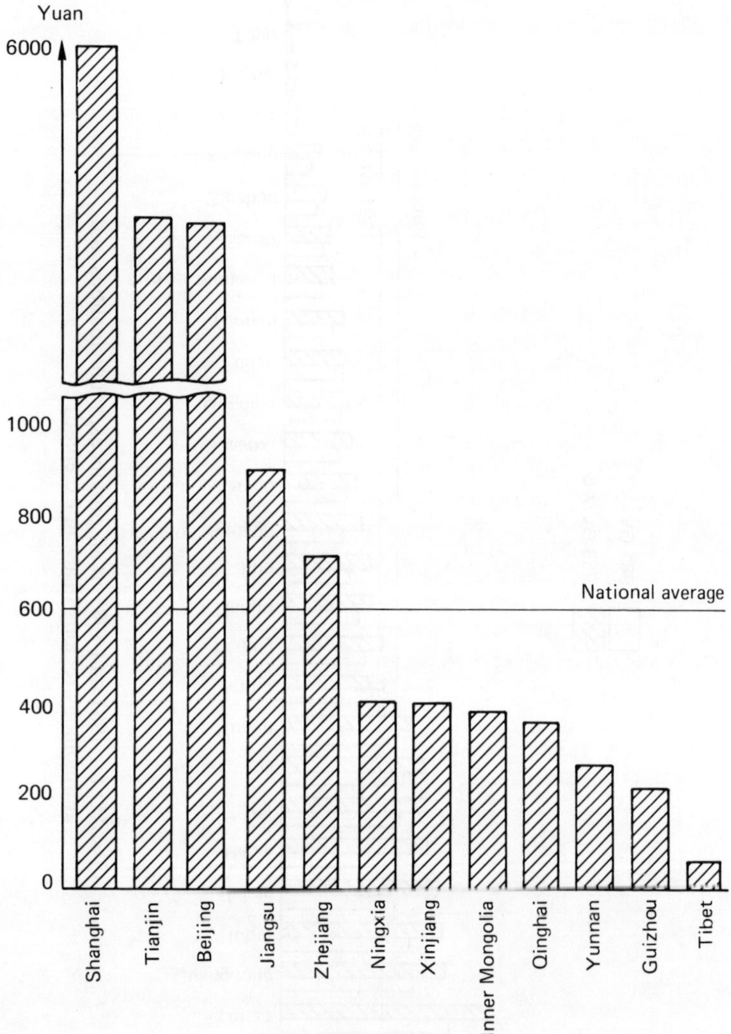

Figure 1.2 Average per capita GVIO in developed and backward regions, 1983

Table 1.1 Average annual rate of increase in GVIAO for selected provinces and regions 1979–1983

Province/Region	*Jiangsu*	*Zhejiang*	*Inner Mongolia*	*Xinjiang*	*Guizhou*	*Tibet*
Av. annual increase %	11.95	15.34	11.80	15.51	11.21	5.31

Note: Figures for Tibet calculated from 1980–1983

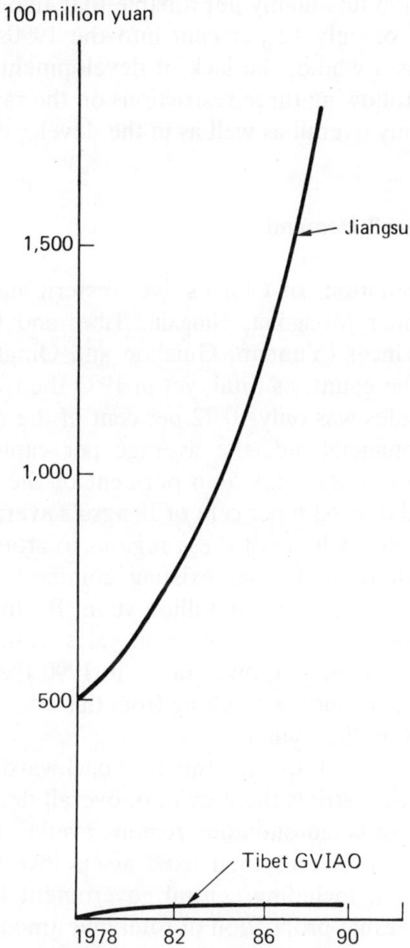

Figure 1.3 Potential growth of GVIAO in Tibet and Jiangsu 1978–1990

and Jiangsu at 1983 levels and prevent it from growing any larger, then it will have to achieve an annual growth rate of 204 per cent starting immediately.

1.2 THE LIMITATIONS OF BACKWARDNESS

There is no way the gap could be maintained at existing levels. There is no chance that Tibet could achieve a 204 per cent rate of development, and in addition it is highly improbable that Jiangsu will maintain a growth rate of only 12 per cent into the 1990s. Looking at China's situation as a whole, the lack of development in backward regions places the following three restrictions on the rapid growth of the national economy overall as well as in the developed coastal and interior provinces.

1 Insufficient Overall Demand

The combined populations of China's five western autonomous regions (Xinjiang, Inner Mongolia, Ningxia, Tibet and Guangxi) and three western provinces (Yunnan, Guizhou and Qinghai) make up 13.86 per cent of the country's total, yet in 1983 the total volume of commodity retail sales was only 10.72 per cent of the national total. Even with state financial aid, the average per capita volume of commodity retail sales was only 74.6 per cent of the average elsewhere in China and only 63.6 per cent of Jiangsu's average. Were the commodity retail sales volume of these regions to attain the level of the average elsewhere in China, existing commodity retail sales would increase by close on 10 000 million yuan. Basing our calculations on the respective commodity retail sales volumes of these regions and on their average growth rates, in 1990 the accumulated losses to the national economy resulting from this one shortfall alone will exceed 100 000 million yuan.

The insufficient demand for investment in backward regions is yet another factor which restricts the growth of overall demand. In 1983 the five ethnic minority autonomous regions availed themselves of only 6.24 per cent of China's total fixed assets investment sum of 136 906 million yuan, including central government funding which makes up a considerable proportion of total investment in backward regions. If we include the three provinces of Yunnan, Guizhou and Qinghai the percentage still does not exceed 9.93 per cent. The per capita investment in all eight regions in 1983 was 95.63 yuan, which is 68.44 per cent of the average for regions elsewhere in China. Even if we exclude direct state investment as far as possible and look only at 'investment in entities under urban and rural collective ownership' and 'private investment in housing in urban and rural areas', nevertheless the eight regions would still only have shares of 3.76 per cent and 7.22 per cent respectively of the national total. Despite the fact that together the eight regions cover an area 56 times the size of Jiangsu and have 2.3 times the population, the combined 'investment in entities under urban and rural collective ownership' of the eight regions is scarcely 588 million yuan or 27 per cent of Jiangsu's investment, while 'private investment in housing in urban and rural areas' is only half that of Jiangsu. In terms of the average level of total fixed assets investment attained in China's other provinces, investment demand within the eight regions is insufficient. This will result in market losses to the country of over 500 000 million yuan in 1990.

This is merely a very rough calculation based upon a comparison of existing levels of demand in backward regions and the national average. By extension, insufficient demand will ultimately lead to the lack of an even greater number of derived demands for a whole range of intermediate products. According to the composition of fixed asset accumulation for 1983, full consumption coefficients calculated from China's investment and output figures require 24 200 yuan in direct or indirect output value for every 10 000 yuan increase in fixed asset accumulation. Turning next to the composition of consumption for 1983, we calculate that every 10 000 yuan increase in consumption will require an extra 20 300 yuan in direct or indirect output value. Ignoring progression and merely adding average values together, the overall insufficiency of demand in backward regions in 1990 in both investment and consumption will therefore mean that China's national economy as a whole will lose close on 400 000 million yuan's worth of development opportunities – a figure equivalent to China's entire GVIO for 1978 or more than half of that for 1984.

China is a vast nation of small farmers which lags behind in technology. In the initial stages it is not realistic for China to rely heavily upon the international market to invigorate the economy in the highly competitive international environment. There can be no controversy over the fundamental strategy of reliance upon and the development of the domestic market. The lack of development in backward regions (and we are not referring solely to the five regions and three provinces mentioned above) increasingly restricts in degree and extent the opening up of the domestic market, and holds back the potential development of the national economy as a whole.

2 An Imbalance in Provision

The poor and backward regions which cover over half of China's total area are precisely where resources of crucial importance for the nation's economic invigoration are to be found. Taking water resources alone as an example, the annual discharge of major northern rivers such as the Yellow River accounts for just 18 per cent of China's total water discharge. Yet this region contains 46 per cent of the total population and 64 per cent of all land under cultivation. The Haihe and Huaihe Rivers are especially important, providing between them 4 per cent of the country's total water supply in areas containing 27 per cent of China's population and land under cultivation. At present 67 per cent of the Haihe River basin's discharge is utilised, while the figures for other rivers are 68 per cent for the Liaohe River, 63 per cent for the Huaihe River, 39 per cent for the Yellow River and 32 per cent for the Neishanhe River. A utilisation rate of 49 per cent has been achieved for shallow groundwater in the Yellow River basin, while in the Haihe River flatlands the rate is as high as 87 per cent, but still the demand generated by economic development cannot be met.

Among China's existing urban areas 154 towns and cities in the north and east experience water shortages of varying degrees of seriousness, and statistics show that daily shortfalls have already reached 8.8 million tons. Assuming an assured water supply rate of P=75 per cent, by the year 2000 21 of China's 40 divisions will be unable to supply enough water, with a total shortfall in the region of 100 000 million cubic metres. Water shortages result in the critical overuse of groundwater resources in many places, so that groundwater is siphoned off from a large area and the water table is lowered in some regions. As a consequence, the groundwater resources in a number of urban industrial zones are already being threatened by imminent exhaustion. Meanwhile, vast water resources are going to waste in western regions with a utilisation rate of just 16 per cent for the Yangtse River discharge, or even lower in the upper reaches. As for the major southwestern rivers, less than 1 per cent of their water discharge is made use of.

The same is true for the exploitation of power and mining resources

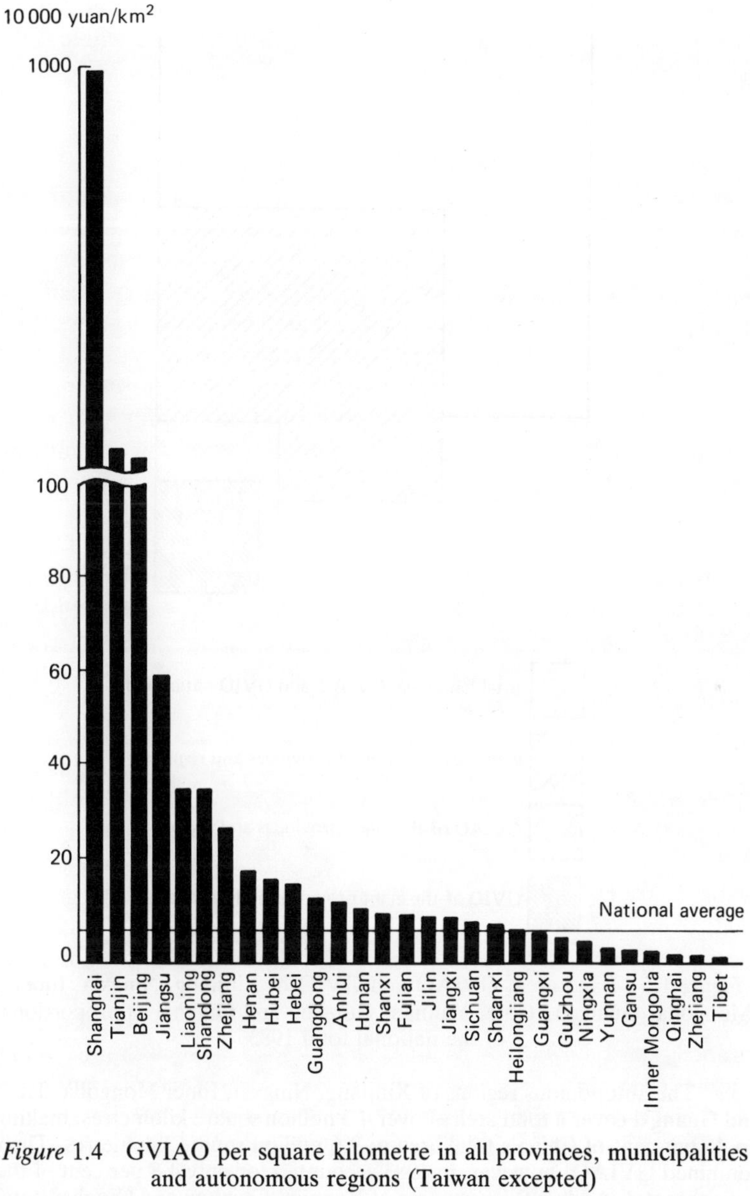

Figure 1.4 GVIAO per square kilometre in all provinces, municipalities and autonomous regions (Taiwan excepted)

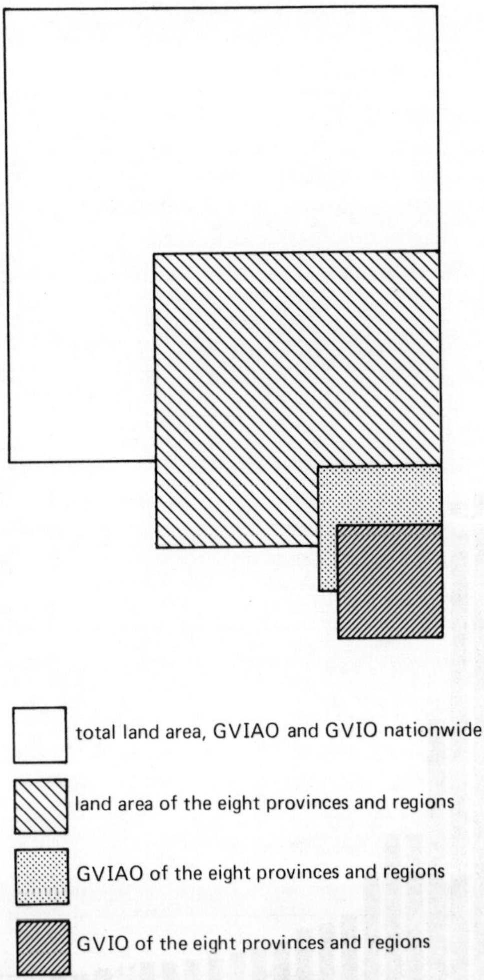

Figure 1.5 Land area, GVIAO and GVIO of Xinjiang, Ningxia, Inner Mongolia, Guangxi, Tibet, Yunnan, Guizhou and Qinghai as proportions of the national total 1983

Note: The autonomous regions of Xinjiang, Ningxia, Inner Mongolia, Tibet and Guangxi cover a total area of over 4.3 million square kilometres, making up 46 per cent of China's total area of 9.6 million square kilometres. Their combined GVIAO, however, in 1983 accounted for only 4.8 per cent of the national total. Adding the provinces of Yunnan, Guizhou and Qinghai, total land area is more than 5.6 million square kilometres, comprising 59 per cent of China's total, but GVIAO still only reaches 8.4 per cent of the overall total. If a high GVIO signifies modern development, the comparison is even more disappointing. In 1983 the GVIO of the five autonomous regions combined was only 3.9 per cent of the national total, rising to no higher than 6.6 per cent if we include the GVIO of the three provinces.

(see Chapter 2). Our success in exploiting as rapidly as possible the rich and extensive resources to be found in the vast backward regions will determine the possible speed of economic growth in more advanced regions with dwindling resources, and also decide the extent to which the steadily worsening structural imbalance of China's national economy can be rectified.

3 Ethnic Unity and Social Stability

Although the populations of backward regions form but a small proportion of China's total population, they make up a large part of the country's overall ethnic minority population. Sixty-four per cent of all ethnic minority peoples live in the five provincial-level national minority autonomous regions and the three provinces where ethnic minority populations are concentrated, which we have discussed above. Sharing borders with eleven different countries – the Soviet Union, Mongolia, Afghanistan, Pakistan, India, Nepal, Sikkim, Bhutan, Burma, Laos and Vietnam – their combined area accounts for 93 per cent of all ethnic minority autonomous areas in China as a whole, while their extensive borders make up 90 per cent of China's total land border length.

China's ethnic unity and social stability is closely tied up with the economic growth and prosperity of these regions. The yawning gulf in the level of economic development which exists between developed regions on the coast and in the interior and the backward border regions populated by ethnic minorities may bring with it a series of delicate social problems – of a nationalist character, for instance. We can say with certainty that even if we manage to solve the economic problems of insufficient overall demand and imbalance in provision by seeking a solution in the international environment, and even if we manage to achieve the precipitous growth needed to reduce the gap between Jiangsu and Tibet as depicted in Figure 1.3, we nevertheless have no means of eliminating the possibility of upset in ethnic unity and social stability.

We have before us a vast array of serious problems which urgently require investigation and policy decisions. Of course, it is not just the lack of development in undeveloped regions which will prove the decisive factor. However, looking into the future, research into solutions to the problems of backwardness in these regions, be it with a view to China's economic growth or social stability, will be of a vital strategic and theoretical importance that is hard to visualise.

2 Contradictory Reality

China's first peasant aircraft owner has appeared. His name is Guo Yuanying and he runs a specialised peasant household in Zhao hamlet on the outskirts of Zhengzhou in Henan Province. Even after his rise to riches he did not forget his fellow villagers, spending 19 500 yuan on a Honeybee 3 aircraft which he has presented to the local village government authorities to be used for fertiliser and pesticide spraying in the whole village.

The house boasts a television set, radio recorder and twintub washing machine, while outside in the courtyard stand a Jialing motorbike and a car. We sat in parlour smoking Peony brand cigarettes, sipping fragrant jasmine tea, and admiring the freshly blooming flowers in the courtyard and the swooping swallows. As we contemplated this scene of flourishing prosperity, we could scarcely imagine that a mere eight or nine years ago Guo Yuanying had been hard pressed to fill his belly![1]

Twenty-seven year old Cheng Xiuzhi of Pingleyuan brigade, Nanmofang commune, in the Chaoyang district of Beijing came back home after last year's end of year bonus share-out with a medium-sized grand piano, an elegant, finely crafted instrument with 88 keys and three pedals, worth 1,680 yuan. She thus became the Beijing Piano Factory's first peasant customer since it started producing Chinese-made Xinghai pianos in 1950 in the city's eastern suburbs.[2]

Yanbei's famed specialised transportation village – Huanshang village in Yanggao county, Shanxi Province – is a small hamlet of only 75 families (300 odd inhabitants) . . . yet this year the village as a whole has purchased 46 television sets and radio recorders. As for the young people, they buy all the latest fashions, while the old and middle-aged commune members who run transportation businesses in and out of Datong each have at least two good sets of clothes worth over 70 yuan apiece. In the slack season, all the inhabitants of Huanshang set off to go sightseeing in such places as Datong and Beijing. The villagers are right: 'Since we're making a lot of money then we ought to see to our home comforts a bit and make life a little better.' This year, at over 200 yuan per person, domestic consumption in the village topped 68,000 yuan.[3]

On 22nd November, a gourmet cookery competition was held amongst the 270 families of Talinpo village in Anliang township, Sha'an county.[4]

Nowadays, the inhabitants of Xingfu (Happiness) village in Xifeng town, Xifeng county really do lead a life of happiness: 'Flour and rice have become everyday fare; wood smoke scarcely ever rises from the kitchens, as every family has electrical household appliances and every home is replete with modern consumer articles' . . . Today, 110 households in the 138-family village have television sets, while over 120 possess electric rice cookers. Over half the families in the village own washing machines. Yet there's still money left over in a number of households. It's being saved for high quality consumer durables, such as colour televisions and motorbikes in particular.[5]

What should we do after we get rich? Shi Zhimin is a keen consumer and has built up a prosperous home. In the last three years he has constructed a six-room mixed brick and timber/steel and concrete type dwelling and has acquired seventeen new pieces of furniture including wardrobes, chests of various sizes, sofas, armchairs and sprung beds, not to mention a large colour television, a six-speaker cabinet hifi system, washing machine, motorbike and other such quality consumer goods. Shi Zhimin dresses smartly and rides a Jialing motorbike when he goes out on business. Monthly living expenses for his family of six never fall below 200 yuan, and many visitors leave his home saying, 'Just like a hotel'.[6]

2.1 STAGGERING POVERTY

The First Scenario

In Gansu Province's Shangzhuang commune, situated in Yuzhong county barely forty-odd kilometres from the provincial capital Lanzhou, the grain ration in every one of the production teams last year was a paltry 40 to 100 catties (20 to 50 kilograms) per person!

State credit alone averaged out at over 102.60 yuan per capita. Shangzhuang's No 4 team, consisting of 174 people in 32 households, is about average for the whole commune. Workpoint value in 1979 stood at 0.19 yuan, and 71.8 per cent of all households were in debt. Average grain rations in the same year were 54 catties (27 kilograms) per person. Altogether the team possessed 65 bed quilts, three of which were new, 35 old, and 27 tattered, threadbare and ingrained with dirt. With an average of two quilts per household, this meant that there could be up to three people sharing one quilt. Blankets numbered thirteen altogether, or one for every three families. Roughly two-thirds of the *kangs* (the earthern platform, heated from below, which serves as a bed-cum-seat in rural north China) had no covering whatsoever, save a worn-out old sheet, and winter and summer the whole family, young and old alike, slept on the bare earth of the *kang*, huddled together under one old quilt. Of the commune's 49 production teams, all but one had a per capita income of under 40 yuan, while the total possessions (excluding houses and livestock) of 188 households (13.4 per cent of the total) were worth less than 30 yuan apiece. Families with less than 15 yuan's worth of possessions numbered 41, or almost one in thirty. At this level, a household might own nothing but a single worn-out quilt, one roll of tattered cotton wadding, and a few cooking pots, bowls and chopsticks. Song Tong'an of Shangzhuang's No. 7 team lives together with his son and daughter. Between them they possess only one tattered old quilt that they have had for nineteen years. Lacking even a cover for the *kang*, they sleep on two opened-out cement bags. In addition they share one battered nineteen-year-old cupboard, a chopping board, one small cooking pot, three bowls and a few pairs of chopsticks. That is the sum total of their possessions. Zhang Lunqing of Matan's No 2 team was once in the volunteers army. There are six people in his family including four children, and they all sleep on the one *kang* without an undersheet and with only one quilt between them. Nineteen years old, it is the very same quilt that was handed out to him in the army. Out of the commune's 758 young men aged between 25 and 30, 288 or 38 per cent have neither wives nor girlfriends. The commune's total population is over 7,000 but 4,371 inhabitants either do not possess padded clothing, or if they do it is so worn out as to be useless. The moment day breaks many children climb up onto haystacks and ridges to bask naked in the sun! Furthermore, these inadequately clothed and undernourished people live in chilly, damp mountainous areas 2,300 to 2,800 metres above sealevel.[7]

The Second Scenario

In 1981 work teams with a per capita income of under 60 yuan numbered altogether 135 in the Qoqek (Tacheng) region and 81 in the Altay region of Xinjiang, comprising 20 per cent of all production teams in the region as a whole. In the western counties, an average of one in three households was in debt. The herdspeople live in rudimentary housing. Out of the 80,000 or so nomad families in northern Xinjiang, over 16,000 live in tents which are beyond repair. Southern Xinjiang has more than 41,000 nomad families of whom 14,000 have no tents, sleeping out under the walnut trees in the summer and sheltering in caves or spending the nights on the warmed desert sands in the winter.[8]

The Third Scenario

1983 saw grain production at its highest level in Guizhou Province. Yet annual grain output per capita of the rural population did not exceed 523 catties (262 kilograms), and grain rations were no higher than 366 catties (183 kilograms) per person. People did not have enough to eat. According to the provincial economic committee's survey of 32,914 households in 87 counties, 43.6 per cent of households had a per capita grain output of over 700 catties (350 kilograms), while at the same time 20 per cent remained at a level of poverty where per capita income was below 100 yuan and the grain ration less than 300 catties (150 kilograms) per person. Even in Anshun, a fairly well-developed region, 15 per cent of rural households still had a per capita income of 80 yuan with grain rationed to under 400 catties (200 kilograms) per person.

Guanling county was the first county in the Anshun region to institute the rural responsibility system. In 1982 the combined industrial and agricultural gross output value doubled in the county as a whole, making it one of the hundred or so counties to double its output throughout China. In 1982 grain production in the county reached an all-time high, but even so per capita production did not exceed 474 catties (237 kilograms). Natural disasters in 1983 brought this figure down to just over 350 catties (175 kilograms), which basically meant that there was not enough to eat.

Today, in 18 per cent of the county's production teams grain is rationed to less than 300 catties (150 kilograms) per person.

A provincial economic committee survey of 215 poor production teams (11.24 per cent of the total number of households and 10.88 per cent of the rural population of the county) revealed that the per capita grain ration was 276 catties (138 kilograms), per capita net income was 39 yuan, and that there were 1.6 sets of clothes per person, 1.4 quilts per household and an average of 3.57 people to each bed. The survey included Baobao commune's six production teams with 499 inhabitants in 91 households. There, grain rations stood at 294 catties (147 kilograms) per person, per capita income at 33 yuan, with one set of clothes per person (ie a jacket and a pair of trousers). There was an average of one quilt per household and 5.48 people to each bed. Linggang and 13 other teams of Jichang commune comprised 272 households of 1,368 inhabitants who owned one set of clothes per person and slept 5.56 people to a bed with less than one quilt per household. Huangnibao production team, part of this commune with 18 households and 73 inhabitants, possessed only 10 quilts in total which, assuming that each household owned a bed, means that half the population did not even have a quilt. For each bed there were altogether seven people. In Shangguan commune, Guanling county, grain rations stood at 385 catties (193 kilograms) per person in 1983, while about 10 per cent of rural households did not possess a quilt and the same percentage either had no accomodation or lived in rickety huts. Seventy to eighty per cent of the commune's rural population had only straw sandals to wear all through the year.

Hospitals and medicines as well as food and clothing are scarce in the vast mountainous regions. Compared to the national average, the percentages of skilled health workers and hospital beds in the entire Anshun district are only 66.7 per cent and 45.5 per cent respectively, while in the Liuma district of Zhenning county, which covers 620 square kilometres with nearly 50,000 inhabitants in nine communes, the twelve-bed district hospital has neither fluoroscopy equipment nor laboratory testing. Each of the nine commune health clinics is staffed by two or three workers who are volunteers from the community and have no specialised training. Leyun commune has 5,473 members, but in 1981 its health clinic possessed only 31.5 yuan's worth of medicine and equipment. Goitre affects 6.35 per cent of the local population of the region as a whole, with percentages reaching as high as 18 per cent in

Zhenning, 20 per cent in Guanling and even 23 per cent in Ziyun.

The authors carried out an investigation in Hujia'ao production team, Tuanyuanhe brigade which is located in Anlong commune by the side of the asphalt road. The poverty of the people there was staggering. The production team is situated 20 km from the county town and 1,400 metres above sealevel, and during our visit it was enveloped in mist and continuous drizzle. On top of our sweaters and woolly longjohns we put on down jackets but we still felt cold, yet the locals were practically all still wearing a single layer of clothing. There were fourteen- and fifteen-year-old girls who didn't even have a pair of trousers to their name, their bare legs mottled red with cold. Every one of the six homes we visited was a leaky, draughty adobe and thatch hut, with people and animals crowded together in one room. Chinese cabbage and maize gruel were cooking in a pot, grain being only available up to March or April of the year following harvest. Shivering with cold, the children huddled up to the open fire.

There are nine people in Yang Kaiming's family, with two tattered quilts amongst them. Yang and one of the children were lying on the single blackened bed. They had been suffering from vomiting and diarrhoea for over two days, but did not have the money to see a doctor. Three years ago, commune member Wang Dehu's wife had set out to buy medicine, taking the eldest daughter along with her. They never came back, and nothing was ever heard of them again. As the family owns neither a bed nor a quilt, the daughter sleeps on a pile of straw in the loft, while Wang himself, dressed in a blue cotton jacket received as state aid three years ago, sleeps on another pile of straw two metres away from the huge draught ox.[9]

2.2 STAGGERING WEALTH

People often associate poverty with desolation, and believe that backwardness is frequently due to excessively severe resource limitations. If this were the case we could rest assured. What does give cause for concern is that in any attempt to look into these complex reasons, the first thing that usually strikes the investigator is the staggering wealth of natural resources in backward regions.

Yunnan

Yunnan is famous as the 'Plant Kingdom'. Xishuangbanna alone, which covers 19 000 square metres, contains over 3500 species of higher order plants of which 1000 can be cultivated as cash crops. As for mineral resources, Yunnan's reserves of tin, lead and zinc are the biggest in China, and it has the third-largest deposits of lead and zinc in the world. Deposits of copper, antimony and nickel rank second in the country as a whole, and there are also considerable reserves of gold, silver, aluminium, tungsten, titanium, zirconium, mercury and 'black gold' such as iron and manganese. Coal deposits stand at 14 000 million tons, second only to Guizhou in the whole of the southwest, while there are nearly 20 000 million tons of phosphate bearing rock, which is scarce in China. Yunnan's rock salt reserves are enough to supply the entire province for centuries to come. The region is also famous for its marble, quarried throughout the extensive Diancang Mountains. In a statement on resources, the Geological Bureau has said that of the 140 or so utilisable minerals found worldwide, over 130 have been discovered in Yunnan and 80 of these in proven deposits which it is possible to exploit. In geothermal resources, Yunnan's natural hot springs alone number well over a hundred, making up 25 per cent of all such springs in China.

Guangxi

Extolled as the 'Land of Non-ferrous Metals', mineral deposits exist in over 70 counties throughout the region, 17 already proven. Guangxi's 'non-ferrous metals' include tin, lead, zinc, antimony and tungsten which stand in first, second, third, fourth and fifth place respectively in the nation's total reserves of these metals. Manganese deposits in the region make up 33.7 per cent of China's total, while there are also sizeable reserves in national terms of mercury, lead tantalum and niobium. Guangxi ranks sixth nationally in hydroelectric power. There are proven deposits of 73 non-metallic mineral reserves and 26 of these rank in the first ten places nationwide. As for raw materials for concrete, Guangxi possesses China's largest reserves of carbolic salts, standing at 1500 million tons.

Qinghai

Qinghai possesses proven reserves of over 60 different minerals including petroleum, salt, potassium, iron, copper, coal, lead, zinc, magnesium, borax, asbestos, rock crystal, mica, sulphur, chromium and gold. These come from over 270 places, more than 50 of which engage in medium- and large-scale mineral production. Geological Bureau appraisals made in 1979 show that ten of Qinghai's minerals rank first nationwide in grade and quantity, four rank second and five rank third. The 50 000 million tons of Qaidam salt alone account for more than half the reserves on the Chinese mainland.

The Inner Mongolia–Xinjiang Region

As well as possessing the two largest areas of natural pastureland in China, Inner Mongolia has coal reserves which rank second nationwide, and the region provides 98 per cent of the country's rare earths, equivalent to 400 per cent of all other reserves worldwide. Xinjiang's white mica, serpentine and 'Khotan jade' also rank foremost nationwide, and the region possesses 117 of the 147 different proven mineral reserves to be found in China. Accumulated oil and gas reserves in the Junggar Basin top 8000 million tons at least. The region's proven coal deposits account for 2.3 per cent of the nation's total, with long-range reserves making up 35.64 per cent.

Tibet

Long viewed as a barren desert, one would never guess that Tibet's waterpower resources rank foremost in China as a whole. There are over 370 lakes on the northern Tibetan plateau, the heaviest concentration in any region throughout the country. The annual average rate of flow in Tibet is four times the national average, while the additional subterranean water flow is over three times the national average. Annual flow per capita is the highest in the world, higher even than in Canada. In addition to its plentiful waterpower resources, Tibet also enjoys long sunshine periods, strong sunlight, a great range of temperatures and high intensity photosynthesis, all of which well equip Tibet for the development of horticulture. Who could have guessed that the world record for a single crop of wheat was achieved on this land, the inhabitants of which rely on grain being sold back to them by the state in order to survive?

This 'barren desert' supports timberland with a forest stock five times the national average, slightly lower than that of Heilongjiang, putting it in second place nationwide. Forest area and stock per capita both rank foremost in China, respectively 4.7 times and 12.3 times greater than in second-place Heilongjiang. Indeed forest stock per capita in Tibet is far and away the highest in the world. Tibet abounds in all kinds of rare medicinal materials such as musk, pilose antler and fritillary bulb.

Tibet is equally rich in mineral resources for the development of industry. At present there exist proven reserves of iron, chromium, copper, lead, cobalt, piezocrystal, veined crystal, sulphur, salt, arsenic, borax, barite, china clay, gypsum, white mica, graphite, corundum, coal and so on. Rich deposits of these minerals are to be found everywhere, with borax and chromium deposits ranking first nationwide and copper in second place. Rare throughout the world are the precious boron concentrate and naturally occurring diamonds.

Guizhou

The region's guaranteed coal reserves are second only to those of Shanxi and Inner Mongolia, ranking third in the nation overall. Also in third place nationwide are phosphorous deposits, the best in China in terms of grade and ease of extraction. Another front-ranking resource is aluminium which makes up one quarter of China's entire aluminium output. Guizhou is the foremost producer of mercury in the country, and its rare earth reserves also rank within the first few places. Rich deposits of lead, zinc, iron, antimony, vanadium, copper, tungsten, tin, gold, silver, ferromanganese, barite, gypsum, limestone for making cement, brick and tile clay and other mineral resources are also to be found.

Guizhou is evenly criss-crossed with a dense network of high volume waterways. Per capita surface water volume is 1.4 times higher than the national average. In theory, the hydroelectric capacity for the entire province is 18.769 million kilowatts with potentially exploitable resources accounting for 13.25 million kilowatts. Hydroelectric resources in the north, south, east, west and centre of the province supply medium- and large-scale power stations, and small-scale power stations are fed by resources all over the province. With investment costs as low as 0.01 yuan per kilowatt/hour on average, hydroelectric power is an ideal resource to be tapped.

The province as a whole supports a wide range of flora. Ideal natural conditions raise annual local timber growth to over twice as much as in the north-east. China firs, oil-tea camellias, tung oil trees, lacquer trees, Chinese tallow trees and Huashan pines are all well established. The cultivation, processing and use of tung oil and lacquer dates from the Tang Dynasty and today the province's tung oil production ranks second nationwide. Over thirty kinds of grain and cash crops (not including vegetables) are grown in Guizhou. Rape yields are the second highest in the country and some varieties have an oil content of as high as 46 per cent. Flue-cured tobacco is Guizhou's most famous product, and is one of the major tobacco leaf exports. Guizhou also has a long history as a major tea-growing area, and famous varieties include the Guiding 'clouds and mist tea', once sent as imperial tribute. Excellent natural conditions mean that the tea comes into leaf four to five times a year, as compared to three to four times a year in Hangzhou. Both tropical and warm temperate zone fruits are grown in Guizhou. Apart from mandarin oranges, apples and pears, the major varieties under cultivation are peaches, plums, apricots, persimmons, grapes, Chinese pear-leaved crabapple, bananas, coffee, walnuts, Chinese chestnuts and gingko.

The warm climate, lush mountains and extensive grasslands of Guizhou provide a wealth of natural resources for industry, agriculture, forestry and animal husbandry, and it can truly be said that whatever is done in these areas will be successful.

3 The Intrinsic Determinant of Backwardness

What is backwardness? This, surprisingly, is one of the elementary questions of developmental economics. Scholars of developmental economics almost without exception devote their first chapter to an academic discussion of how to discern 'backwardness' – gross value of output, per capita value of output, national income, per capita income, rate of growth, quality of life, and so on. All sorts of economic indicators are used in an attempt to prove the precise economic significance of 'backwardness', but all these economic indicators reveal only one thing about the reasons for backwardness: the reason for backwardness is backwardness.

CCP leadership and the need to reform the 'one big pot' economic system (characterised by state control, centralised planning, unified distribution and collectivism in agriculture) are the same everywhere in China. Most importantly, the same reform of the rural responsibility system has been instituted in backward regions. Why then after several years of greatly increased enthusiasm for production among the rural population has such a great and growing gulf appeared between different regions? The reason: under the same policies human behaviour differs. Conclusion: the intrinsic determinant of backwardness is the poor quality of human resources.

3.1 UNTAPPED WEALTH

The poverty of life in the backward regions is staggering, yet even more astonishing is the wealth of natural resources to be found in the same regions. But what really gives pause for thought is what happens when the poverty-stricken inhabitants of backward regions are faced with rich resources. In a situation where gains should be proportional to effort, they get no return on their efforts.

Take Guizhou as an example. Coal is found in over 70 per cent of its counties and clay is also plentiful. Nevertheless, people are obliged to send to Hunan and Sichuan for bricks and tiles. A local comrade said: 'Guizhou transports its coal to Sichuan in exchange for Sichuan's mud'.

Precious forestry resources are under-utilised, with serious wastage. Processed timber finished products utilise less than 20 per cent of the standing timber area. Only 7 per cent of the felled surplus is made use of, while the processing surplus utilisation rate is a mere 5 per cent. Even though coal is found everywhere throughout the province, huge quantities of wood are still burnt every year. Peoples' timber requirements in the province as a whole are more than 1 000 000 cubic metres a year, 70 per cent of which is burnt as firewood. There were 70 timber producing counties in the 1950s, but today 51 counties are no longer self-sufficient in wood. In the 1950s a cubic metre of wood required only two to three trees, now over ten are needed.

Output of traditional products with a long history such as tung oil, raw lacquer, tea-oil and tallow seeds has still not attained past levels. In 1956 procurement of tung oil seeds, long the pride of Guizhou, reached 178 million catties (89 million kilograms), yet over the past ten years purchases have fluctuated round the 100 million catties (50 million kilograms) mark.

Guizhou used to be one of the four big producers of tussah in China, and in 1956 production stood at 1.43 million catties (715 000 kilograms). Twenty-seven years later output had fallen to 557 400 catties (278 700 kilograms), equivalent to 39 per cent of the 1956 output. Guizhou and Sichuan embarked together upon silkworm raising at the same time, and in the 1950s output averaged 1 million catties (500 000 kilograms) or so. By 1982 production had grown to 130 million catties (65 million kilograms) in Sichuan but in Guizhou it had dropped below 1 million catties (500 000 kilograms).

Output of the long-famous Guizhou Yunwu (Cloud and Mist) tea was 2.65 million catties (1.325 million kilograms) in 1949, and had risen to 16.8 million catties (8.4 million kilograms) by 1980. Surprisingly enough, this 5.3-fold increase was achieved through a 43.7-fold expansion of the cultivated area. Yields per mu of tea leaves were 233.5 catties (116.75 kilograms) in 1949 and only 33.9 catties (16.95 kilograms) in 1982, or 14.5 per cent of 1949 yields.

The oranges of Guizhou, which have world market potential, have still not regained the level of output reached in the early years after 1949. Production of Guizhou pears remains at a steady 10 million catties (5 million kilograms) or thereabouts, but only two to three million catties (one to one and a half million kilograms) can be transported out to be sold. Very little is available in the way of fruit processing capacity. Huishui county produces large quantities of many varieties of fruits. While 70 000 catties (35 000 kilograms) of oranges were purchased in 1981, only 5.8 per cent of this amount was processed, and a mere 6.1 per cent of the total 90 000 catties (45 000 kilograms) of plums purchased and 1.5 per cent of the 15 000 catties (7500 kilograms) of bayberries went for processing. The prickly pear has great potential for development in the future. Annual output in the province stands at around 12 million catties (6 million kilograms) – all wild prickly pears – but even after several years of development there are still only 34 households engaged in prickly pear processing, and their purchasing capacity represents only about 1 per cent of this uncultivated output.

Side by side with resources lying idle and being wasted we find resource destruction. On the one hand no use is made of the natural soil resources of the barren mountains and wasteland, and on the other hand in regions with concentrated populations vast numbers of trees and plants are destroyed and hillsides cut away in opening up wasteland, while in less populous areas slash and burn methods of land reclamation are universally employed when the land has become exhausted. On average each year in the province, 400 000 mu (26 640 hectares) of land is ravaged by fire and over 700 000 mu (46 620 hectares) of forest is chopped down. On top of this, year after year vegetated hillsides are dug away for use as fertiliser. The accumulated effect of all this is the depletion of the topsoil in many mountainous areas, exposure of bare rock and serious run-off soil erosion.

Aerial photographs from different years show that the area of exposed rock has increased at a rate of 5000 mu (333 hectares) a year in Qingzhen county over the last fifteen years, and by 8000 mu (532.8 hectares) a year in Puding county. Before 1959 annual soil erosion in the entire province was 553 tons, rising to 657 tons in 1961, 758 tons in 1979 and 910 tons in 1980. By 1981 over half the arid land in the whole province was to be found in hilly areas on slopes over 30°. An area of 35 000 square kilometres or roughly 20 per cent of total land area was affected by soil erosion. Hillsides suffering from water, soil and fertiliser run-off amounted to 13 million mu (865 800 hectares), accounting for 81 per cent of the total arid land area. In the province as a whole, the annual river discharge of silt and sand was close to 58 million tons, equivalent to over 380 000 mu (25 308 hectares) of rich arable land topsoil. Assuming this had an approximate nitrogen content of 116 000 tons and phosphate content of 87 000 tons, it was equivalent to 314 per cent and 83 per cent of the annual average application of nitrous and phosphate fertiliser respectively for the entire province in recent years.

'Burn off a mountainside, plant a slope, harvest a basketful, cook a potful.' The harder people work, the more wasteland they reclaim and the more land is reclaimed, the harder they toil. The consequence is drought when it doesn't rain and flood when it does. Hillsides are washed away and valleys become waterlogged. For generations the people of Leishan county have toiled to build 170 000 mu (11 322 hectares) of terraces, but a single heavy rainfall washed away 20 000 mu (1332 hectares) at one go. Knowing that the damage was irreparable, the people wept as they ran about their fields. One heavy downpour in Puding county in 1983 caused a landslide which totally engulfed a seven-household hamlet, killing all 21 inhabitants. Previously there had been a huge tree on the hillside above the hamlet, and an oriental white oak wood below together with three springs and seven mu (0.5 hectares) of good irrigated land. Later, the tree was felled to reclaim land for planting and it was this which led to the tragedy. Tree felling in the mountains brings disaster even to the plains. Anshun county, a region of flatland and dykes, had no history of tree felling to open up the land, but on 22 June 1983 a sudden rainstorm washed out 523 mu (34.8 hectares) of cropland and left it covered in a layer of silt, causing crop losses of over 3 million catties (1.5 million kilograms). In the last few years the counties of Nayong, Zhijin, Weining and Pan one after another have been struck by landslides and mud and rock flows inundating several thousand mu of fields and killing over a hundred people.

The facts show that possession of rich resource advantages does not automatically mean economic advantages. This truth has been generally accepted. 'Transform resource advantages into production advantages, and transform production advantages into economic advantages' has become the fashionable slogan of the day. In the end, however, we are confronted by a simple question: *who* is to carry out the transformation?

This question is the crux of all the problems. Whoever it is decides not only what is to be considered 'a resource' but also what measures are to be used to tap these 'resources'. In fact what people call 'resources' (including those given in the previous chapter) are pre-existing objective materials. Whatever we choose to call them does not alter the fact of their existence. Separated from subjective judgement and human knowledge of them, their existence is of little or no consequence. If coal, which has existed for tens of thousands of years, suddenly becomes 'a resource', it is because people have discovered that it can be burnt, and moreover possess the means to extract, transport and burn it. Similarly, when today something is not seen as a resource but even viewed as an obstacle, something to be destroyed, then perhaps once we have gained a new understanding of it and discovered new means of exploiting it, it will become a precious 'resource'. If we accept the philosophical concept that people have an unlimited capacity for knowledge, then we can turn this statement round the other way: whenever we do not consider something to be a 'resource', it merely shows that up until now we have not attained the capacity to recognise it as such nor do we yet have the technical means to exploit it. Therefore, as far as the human race is concerned, what are called 'resources' are a function of the socio-economic structure and the quality of human resources.

The significance of resources varies for different business approaches and exploitation measures. In the case of a three-dimensional style of exploitation characterised by diversified undertakings, integrated utilisation, a high degree of processing and specialisation and commercialised production, rich natural resources such as Guizhou possesses can provide an excellent basis for the rapid growth of any modern socio-economic system. Conversely, in the case of turning mountainsides into cropland, a one-dimensional land reclamation approach to production characterised by undiversified self-sufficiency, the forests and grasslands covering the mountains and open country far from being 'resources' are in fact serious obstacles to relieving poverty and attaining wealth. Putting ourselves in this position for a moment, who would not want to grow cereals on flat, fertile land? Sweat pouring as they wildly hack away at the vegetation, the people are after all labouring to fill their bellies.

3.2 TWO-WAY INITIATIVE

The implementation of the household responsibility system in the rural areas has met with undreamt of success, publicised through reams of articles appearing in newspapers and magazines. In our report of our investigations we too include an example:

> In the crowded Wenzhou area where population density reaches 525 per square kilometre, there is only 0.55 mu (367 square metres) of farmland for each farmer. Within the 1.89 million strong

agricultural labour force, surplus labour amounts to between 0.8 and one million. Since the Third Plenum of the Eleventh Party Congress, rural production has experienced massive growth while the rural commodity economy too has achieved rapid development.

Jinxiang town, Cangnan county, has become a small commodity production and marketing base, with its major enterprises producing labels and mouldings made from aluminium and certificate folders bound in red. Arable land in the town is only 0.36 mu per capita, and in 1979 5600 people in the town were unemployed. Following great expansion in production of the three items mentioned above, the town now possesses over 2000 pieces of machinery and equipment of all types with total fixed assets worth two million yuan, and 90.8 per cent of the town's population aged between 15 and 45 is now employed in the production and marketing of these three products. The value of output for 1982 is estimated to be 15 million yuan, five times higher than in 1979 and equivalent to nearly 30 times the town's gross value of agricultural output. This gives an annual per capita income of 380 yuan. More than 60 per cent of the inhabitants have built new houses, and personal savings deposits have increased 25-fold over 1978!

Yishan district in Cangnan county is a production and marketing base for reprocessing acrylic textiles and making plastic woven carrier bags. In the district per capita arable land averages 0.47 mu, and only 20 000 of the 72 576 strong labour force is needed to work the land. The district has a long-established local weaving tradition, and on the basis of this traditional craft a textile industry for reprocessing leftover pieces of acrylic was developed. By 1982 textile machinery and equipment of all types in the district amounted to over 33 000 pieces, with fixed assets totalling 11 million yuan, and 92.6 per cent of the entire labour force was engaged in textile production. Altogether 23 million catties (12.5 million kilograms) of spun acrylic yarn were reprocessed into 150 million acrylic sweaters that year. In the past four years a total of 460 million textile goods have been produced, which means that there are an average of 4.6 Yishan sweaters for every ten Chinese. In 1982, the gross output value of textiles reached 93.15 million yuan, representing a 20-fold increase over 1979. This put the average per capita income at 430 yuan, with 320 yuan of that coming from the textile industry alone.

Shencheng district and Tangxia district in Rui'an county are production and marketing bases for plastic twine, providing the raw materials for plastic woven carrier bags. In Shencheng district cultivated land amounts to 0.46 mu per capita, and commune/brigade enterprises have combined with joint entities to undertake industrial and sideline production. In 1982 the commune/brigade enterprises realised a gross output value of 20.66 million yuan, and employed a workforce of 15 517. The district's 208 combines provided employment for 4727 people, 4526 of whom worked in the 184 combines engaged in the manufacture of plastic twine. In the first half of 1983, the output value of these 184 combines reached 8.93 million yuan. Private savings in Shencheng district increased 7.9 times between 1977 and 1982.

Leqing county's Liushi district is a production and marketing base for hardware and electrical goods and enjoys the highest output value of all the specialised commodity production and marketing bases in the Wenzhou area. In 1982 the gross output value for commune/brigade industries in the district as a whole reached 702.51 million yuan, showing a 1.8-fold increase over 1978. In April 1982 industrial enterprise taxes accounted for over 80 per cent of the total 1.49 million yuan's worth of industrial and commercial taxes in Liushi district. This year industrial and commercial tax revenue for the entire district has reached 10.55 million yuan. Of the district's commune/brigade enterprise 1981 tax revenue of 9 718 100 yuan, collective accumulation worth 7 817 100 yuan was turned over to the higher authorities. Urban and rural savings throughout the region rose 33.8 times between 1977 and 1982.

Over the past few years Qiaotou town in Yongjia county has become a marketplace for small commodity trading, mostly dealing in buttons and watch straps. The town has a per capita average of 0.3 mu of cultivated land. The 606-stall market is attended daily by over 3000 traders, who transact business worth usually between 60 000 and 70 000 yuan, and sometimes as much as 100 000 yuan or more. In the last two years taxes handed over to the higher authorities have amounted to nearly one million yuan. Sales of buttons alone were worth over 20 million yuan in 1982.

Xianxiang commune in Xianxiang district, Rui'an county manufactures shoes with plastic soles and manmade uppers. In 1982 output value was 5 million yuan. At present, all 14 of the commune's brigades are engaged in shoe production, and there are four brigades in which 80 per cent of all households are employed in this way. In 1979 four of the Xianxiang brigades maintained a perilous day-to-day existence by living off yam beans for months on end, but by 1982 481 commune member households possessed over 700 sewing machines, producing 4 million pairs of shoes and earning a profit of 600 000 yuan. Shoe manufacture alone accounted for 64 per cent of the commune members' total income. In the past two years 27 per cent of peasant households have built houses with two or more storeys. Compared to 1978, private savings were 92 times greater in 1981.

Within the space of a very short time, industrial output value in Yishan district, Liushi district and Jinxiang town has grown to make up 81 per cent, 85 per cent and 97 per cent respectively of each area's gross value of industrial and agricultural output. Industry has risen from its position as a sideline to become an important sector, and along with this growth agriculture too has rapidly improved. In 1982 total grain production in several of the bases reached an all-time high. In Jinxiang town total grain output for 1982 was 4.81 million catties (2.405 million kilograms) with a per mu yield of 1596 catties (798 kilograms), which showed a 14 per cent increase over 1973. Yishan district's output for the same year was over double that of 1973, while in Qiaotou town total grain output for three years increased by 27 per cent. The 1982 total grain output of 231.78 million catties (165.89 million kilograms) in Liushi district, representing a per mu yield of 1685 catties (842.5 kilograms), showed respective increases of 3.9 and 4.5 per cent over the previous record in 1980.

In just a few years, buildings have appeared out of nowhere and multiplied in these districts, all built upon 'small goods' worth just a few yuan or even cents. What worked this miracle? It was not state investment or planned design but the responsibility system which has liberated thousands upon thousands of rural households![1]

'Loosing the bonds' thus unleashes the great commodity economy show of success. All we need to do is 'liberate our minds' and undergo reform and then everything will be a good deal easier.

In Guizhou they liberated their minds long ago. The production responsibility system began to be implemented on a wide scale right from the beginning of 1979. 'Loosing the bonds' had a tremendous impact on production enthusiasm among the peasants, and to a great extent alleviated the problems of adequate food and clothing for the masses which under the 'one big pot' system had for thirty years remained unsolved. We should note, however, that it was this same enthusiasm which also brought about the miracle of destroying forests to open up new land. In 1980 320 250 mu (21 329 hectares) of forest were felled for land in the province as a whole. In 1981 an area of 506 000 mu (33 700 hectares) was destroyed, and in 1982 despite controlling measures forest totalling 305 600 mu (20 353 hectares) nevertheless disappeared. The tremendous enthusiasm for production sparked off by 'loosing the bonds' wiped out 1 134 100 mu (75 531 hectares) of forest, making it, so people reckon, the third greatest case of destruction after the campaign to smelt steel in the countryside during the Great Leap Forward of 1958 and the 'take grain as the key link' campaign of the Cultural Revolution.

Are we being sarcastic? It is sarcasm directed at the unthinking view of those who reduce and simplify reform to the nutshell of 'loosing the bonds', at the simplistic understanding of those who ignore the significance of theory based on research into the development of backward regions, but instead believe that by aping Western models of commodity economies they will find solutions to China's developmental problems.

It is well known that China is in the midst of the historical process of transformation from a natural economy to a commodity economy. Since it is a transformation and what is more an ongoing transformation, so it is a process of one business approach superseding in time and space another, different business approach. In this transition from old to new, arousing the enthusiasm of the producers means perhaps arousing simultaneously the potential to move in two opposite directions: towards the development of the natural economy or alternatively towards the development of the commodity economy. Without enthusiasm, neither type of development can take place. But the presence of enthusiasm by no means guarantees successful completion of the reform. The responsibility system has fanned into flame the enthusiasm of the rural population to save themselves from poverty and become wealthy, but at the same time has inevitably engendered different goals being pursued by different people, and equally ineluctably sparked off two kinds of enthusiasm, each with a different social content, one geared towards developing the natural economy and the other geared towards developing the commodity economy. This is to be expected.

In the light of Guizhou's destruction of the forests to open up more land, we must make an addition to the conclusion of the extract from the Wenzhou investigation report: 'It is the responsibility system which has freed the enthusiasm of hundreds and thousands of rural households for the development not of the natural economy but of a commodity economy!'

The success of the household responsibility system reform lies in the fact that it not only in a general sense stimulated production enthusiasm among the rural population, but also in a more specific sense it stimulated the enthusiasm of rural people in the majority of regions to develop a commodity economy. Of course, this hardly amounts to a denial of the need to 'free' the rural inhabitants in backward regions, for however long it is delayed, relaxation will still be better than controls. Neither does it mean that the level of enthusiasm for developing production is any lower amongst the rural population in backward regions than in more advanced regions, or that their labour is half-hearted. Bringing in the academic concept of 'two-way enthusiasm' primarily enables us to see the problems at a deeper level behind the set of economic indicators such as output value, national income, etc.

The actual extent of backwardness in backward regions is even greater than in the sensational picture painted in Chapter 1, which was based on economic indicators such as output value and growth rate. This is because the values for a considerable number of such indicators are arrived at by means of development within the natural economy. Unfortunately matters are in fact worse than they seem. Development within the natural economy is achieved through the wide-scale elimination of obstacles to the natural economy which happen to be precisely the resources needed for the development of a commodity economy. This directly affects the way in which we view the existing output values and growth rates in backward regions. It must be said that the higher the output value or rate of growth achieved in backward regions within the natural economy, the more serious and pronounced is the backwardness of these regions. Due to the complexities of economic dynamics in practice, no method has as yet been found which can make this 'negative' output value and rate of growth show up in the statistics. Nevertheless the truth of the matter is that as long as there is wasteland to open up and forests to burn, output value and rate of growth in backward regions may continue to rise, and the gap between these regions and more advanced areas may possibly appear to be shrinking compared to the situation as it appears today.

There is another question facing scholars. How can the same responsibility system call forth two diametrically opposed forms of production enthusiasm, one for developing the commodity economy and one for developing the natural economy? Thirty years on the rural areas are still poor and backward, and this is because the 'one big pot' system of distribution has tied the hands of the peasants. Loosing these bonds is the fundamental way to stimulate rural production initiative. However, it is not the be all and end all of reform. Let us say that at the very least simply 'loosing the bonds' can in a broad sense directly bring with it commodity economy development for the inhabitants of developed regions who ought to possess the hypothetical attributes of Western economists' 'economic man' in addition to the capacity to produce in accordance with commodity economy principles. In the case of backward regions, however, where there is a clear tendency towards the development of the natural economy in the wake of relaxing controls, it would appear that such thinking is too superficial. The situation in backward regions, and also perhaps in a backward China surrounded by developed countries and regions, has opened our eyes to reality. (Of course, we are not simply talking about developing wasteland.) When we have expressed all due indignation over the ossified 'one big pot' distribution system, we must embark upon research which squarely faces up to reality and is of great theoretical significance.

Two-way initiative poses a fundamental problem which in our research from start to finish we have been unable to avoid. The two impulses are diametrically opposed and so they exert an equally great pull. While the peasants of Guizhou and Yunnan work felling trees in the forests, the village and town enterprises of Jiangsu and Zhejiang are springing up like bamboos after rain; and while the herders of Tibet and Qinghai are braving all weathers as they wander from place to place, over 60 per cent of China's 4 670 000 new economic combines in rural areas are to be found in the coastal regions.[2] Look at Guizhou where controls were relaxed first, and at Wenzhou where they were removed last; look at resource-rich Guizhou and then at Wenzhou which lacks any sort of natural resources – what has happened? Like a genie out of a bottle, the household responsibility system has with one blow shattered the traditional circulation system of the coastal regions and revealed all its inadequacies. Yet in

Guizhou the same policies, introduced some years before, brought about a spate of tree chopping and land clearing. Then all activity came to a halt and melted away without trace amidst the inertia of the natural economy. What is the reason behind this? It is the quality of human resources.

3.3 QUALITY OF HUMAN RESOURCES

Tibet

Even today, as if the past few thousand years were but one day, the major agricultural techniques and implements are still coupled ploughing, wooden ploughs and double oxen yokes. Broadcast sowing is prevalent in many areas, and as the sower casts the seed, the crows follow behind to feed. In almost all cases, people transport things on their own backs. In harvesting, house building and road-making no carts are used but instead people shoulder loads of water, fodder, rocks and mud. Even today the local people maintain long-standing ill feeling against the 'division of labour' and look down on craftsmen such as blacksmiths, carpenters, masons, tanners, butchers and so on as inferior, shifty characters.

Besides such negative religious ideas as withdrawing from the world and fatalism, the superstitious side of religion still exerts an influence. Whenever difficulty or disaster crops up in daily life or work, many people pray to the gods rather than relying on their own efforts. Instead of taking steps to combat pests or drought, they burn incense and bow before the gods asking for help by performing religious rites. Fritillary bulbs (an important item in the Chinese pharmacopoeia) grow in profusion, but it is forbidden to pick them because they are believed to be the heart of the Buddha. Caterpillars are allowed to crawl right into sacks of *tsampa* (roasted barley flour) because the precept of not taking life forbids their destruction. It is considered a sin to build a road because the vehicles that drive along it indiscriminately kill a whole range of small living things. Even when people become wealthy they do not forget the gods. When the first 'ten thousand yuan household' eventually emerged in the Chamdo region the family went and built a temple. Subsequently, the next 'ten thousand yuan household' to appear built another bigger and more beautiful temple. The first 'ten thousand yuan household' took this amiss and resolved to carry on making money so they could build an even bigger, even more beautiful temple.

Yunnan

In many mountainous regions slash-and-burn cultivation is considered appropriate behaviour, and trade and commerce are looked down on as dishonourable and immoral dealings. Pigs and poultry are raised for a family's own consumption and a household will raise cattle to show how wealthy it is. Each household grows between ten and ninety kinds of crops and vegetables in order to remain self-sufficient. One household in Xiding district in Menghai county killed a pig to sell in the district, but after three days had still failed to find a buyer. The brigade leader of a Hani nationality brigade in Yiwu district in Mengla county, ordered the people to attend a local fair as he had been directed by higher authorities. Halfway there even he turned back – he didn't want to lose face.[3]

Guizhou

Most skilled handicraft workers in rural areas come from outside the province. From road and bridge builders, brickmakers and house-builders down to cobblers and cotton teasers, almost all these jobs are undertaken by people from Hunan, Sichuan, Guangdong and so on. Teams of workers from outside the province are hired year after year for a number of essential projects, and even for unskilled jobs contract workteams are brought in from outside. Meanwhile the locals are quite happy to wash their hands of the responsibility and watch others make money. During a field trip to Guizhou, the authors asked why in such simple, unskilled jobs as house building and road working everyone from master worker to labourer was from outside the province.

Q: Why don't the locals do this work?

A: They don't want to.

Are they busy with field work? The flourishing Anshun highway and railway line from the key link between Guizhou and Yunnan. Historically, this area was a meeting place for merchants, and every locality in the region shows a far greater degree of social advancement than commonly found elsewhere. Despite this, even though the area sown to improved varieties of paddy rice rose sharply in 1983 by 23 per cent over the previous year, it nevertheless only accounted for 42 per cent of the total area under paddy rice. Similarly hybrid maize, despite an increase in sown area of 25.8 per cent over the past year, made up only 10 per cent of the total area sown to maize. The mountainous regions did even worse.

Huang Shixiong, accountant of Chengguan commune's Xinfu brigade in Luodian county in Qiannan Prefecture, runs a model scientific and technical household under the technical direction of Li Guilian, researcher from the provincial Agricultural Institute. In 1982 Li tried to get Huang to find 0.2 mu (133 square metres) of land to grow early ripening vegetables using the soil covering technique. Li was to provide all the necessary inputs and technical guidance. Huang would only agree to relinquish about half a square metre and comrades from the county had to work on him repeatedly before he reluctantly gave way. When Huang began planting earlier than usual and covered the bed with plastic sheeting, the rest of the villagers advised him not to carry out the experiment. A member of his own family even laid a bet on the outcome: 'I'll give you a mu of cucumbers if you manage to grow anything under that contraption!'[4]

In Liuma district in Zhenning county, only 20 per cent of households in difficulty applied for state aid. Most peasants simply did not know that there was such a thing as state aid.

Zhongdong production team from Zongdi commune in Ziyun county, consists of 16 households comprising 63 people, all of whom for generations have lived in dark, sunless caves. They wash neither themselves nor their clothes, and their drinking water comes from cave seepage. Crop yields per mu (0.06 hectares) are 242 catties (121 kilograms), while the swift, long-bristled skinny pigs they raise weigh under 90 catties (45 kilograms) at most. When the local people's congress heard about this they spent 30 000 yuan on building houses so that the inhabitants could move out of their caves. Moreover, everybody who could walk was taken on a trip to Guiyang by bus so that they could see a new way of life. As a result, the inhabitants concluded that the reason the government was making all this effort to persuade them to move house must be because their caves were very valuable. So they refused to move.

Faced with this kind of attitude and leaving aside measures to 'relax controls' which are talked about rather mindlessly, what else can be done once Keynes has been brought back to life? The problem is not a lack of resources, nor the value of output, nor yet the pace of growth. The intrinsic determinant of the concept of 'backwardness' is nothing less than the poor quality of human resources.

The quality of human resources is an abstract and indeterminate concept which can be identified and assessed from many different viewpoints. Human quality can also be manifested in many different ways; different requirements call for correspondingly different qualities of all types. The quality we want to stress here is that pertaining to the development of the social economy, particularly the commodity economy. In simple terms this refers in particular to the quality of engaging in commodity production and management.

In October 1982 we carried out a survey of the entrepreneurial spirit amongst the rural community of Ji'an prefecture (formerly Jinggangshan prefecture), an undeveloped area in Jiangxi Province. The survey took the form of a questionnaire which contained eight criteria of entrepreneurial spirit including initiative and drive, risk-taking and so on for comprehensively evaluating the attitude, sense of value and behaviour of the farmers in entrepreneurship. The eight criteria in the questionnaire were as follows:

1. *Willingness to change*: if a farmer is prepared to break away from tradition and customs, and change to new agricultural techniques, product varieties or projects etc in order to raise yields, income or efficiency in production, then this shows a high degree of entrepreneurship, and vice versa.
2. *Openness to new ideas*: whether or not a farmer is ready to seek out and accept new experiences and learn through practice also shows the degree of entrepreneurial spirit.
3. *Participation in community activities*: the extent to which, and the amount of enthusiasm with which, a farmer participates in community affairs such as team or village projects or the discussion and solution of serious production or social problems affecting an individual team or village reflects another aspect of the rural entrepreneurial spirit.
4. *Sense of efficiency*: this can be divided into two criteria: first, independence in production and lifestyle; second, sense of importance of scientific and technical development. The level of these two criteria corresponds to the degree of entrepreneurship.
5. *Knowledge and experience*: this can be measured by, for example, the level of awareness of the problems facing the team or village, which reflects another aspect of the entrepreneurial spirit.
6. *Initiative and drive*: for example, to what extent (if at all) a farmer is prepared to undergo hardship in working to get ahead of the rest.
7. *Risk-taking*: whether or not a farmer is willing to take risks or endure difficulties and setbacks, for example in the course of working to achieve prosperity, the number of worries and doubts encountered; and when a problem crops up whether a farmer

Table 3.1 Entrepreneurial spirit

Occupation/identity	*No. of people*	*Av. overall entrepreneurship evaluation score*
Local farmers	377	54.61
Local workers in commune enterprises	177	63.81
Migrants from outside the province	108	67.42
Total	662	59.16

slackens off or continues to make efforts all reflect the degree of entrepreneurship.

8. *Planning*: the strength of planning in production and way of life is another way to measure the level of entrepreneurial spirit.

The results of the survey showed that a considerable difference existed between the local inhabitants and migrants from outside the province (the majority of whom were farmers from Zhejiang, brought in by the government to work on the reservoir.) This difference in quality between the two groups under the same conditions in the same area serves all the more to show that it is the poor quality of human resources which intrinsically determines backwardness.

In a backward region with few rural enterprises, the majority of workers in commune enterprises tend to be the cream of the rural population in that they are reasonably up-to-date, know something of the outside world and have a broader range of experience, while generally speaking their ambition, culture and knowledge far outstrip those of the ordinary farmer. The interesting thing about Table 3.1 is that in average overall entrepreneurial evaluation, the Zhejiang farmer migrants, who were not specially selected, not only scored higher than the local inhabitants of Ji'an prefecture, but surprisingly did better than the local workers in commune enterprises. The entrepreneurship evaluation scores can be grouped into upper, middle and lower ranges. In the upper range of scores, for example, there are far more migrants than local farmers or workers. The disparity in the quality of human resources is as wide as this.

In comparison with developed regions, the rural inhabitants of backward regions are clearly characterised by a general lack of entrepreneurial spirit and an excessive adherence to old ways. For

Table 3.2 Distribution of entrepreneurship evaluation scores

Occupation/identity	*Score Ranges* *Lower* *(1–53)*	*Middle* *(54–65)*	*Upper* *(66–100)*
Local farmers	46.9%	31.6%	21.5%
Local workers in commune enterprises	21.5%	32.1%	46.4%
Migrants from outside the province	15.8%	26.8%	57.4%
Total	35.0%	31.0%	34.0%

example: when initiative and drive are weak, satisfaction is easily obtained. When there is a low capacity to bear risks, then major difficulties and setbacks cannot be withstood. Without a willingness to take risks, independence and initiative in production and way of life are limited, and there is a greater stress on the dependent mentality and fatalistic view. If it is difficult to break with tradition and old customs and accept new production techniques and lifestyles, as well as the great majority of new things and phenomena, then there will be a lack of enthusiasm for new experiences and people will be content with things as they are. This is a well-known fact. The worst of it is that this fact is constantly being renewed.

Just like developed regions, backward regions are in transition from the traditional to the modern, from the conservative to the innovative mentality. The lack of motivation for this transition in mentality amongst the population of backward regions means that the process is naturally rather slow. In this revolutionary age of rapid change it is inevitable that this will result in backward regions lagging further and further behind developed areas, so that the existing gap in the quality of human resources will continue to grow. Among the respondents in the Jiangxi Province survey of Ji'an prefecture, 19.6 per cent of local farmers expressed dissatisfaction with their present standards of living, while amongst migrants from outside the province the figure reached 32.4 per cent. Conversely, a mere 25.9 per cent of migrants from outside the province expressed satisfaction compared to as many as 41.4 per cent of the local farmers, even though *the migrants actually had a slightly higher standard of living than the local farmers*. As to possible anxieties in the course of getting rich – such as 'when you're in the limelight, other people get jealous', 'techniques that have not been tried and tested can lead to losses', 'when you're unclear about the policies, you're frightened of going against them', 'policies might change' and so on – 32.2 per cent of local farmers expressed no concern about these sorts of problems, while for migrants from outside the province the figure was as high as 66.7 per cent.

The difference in quality of human resources reveals an obvious difference in attitudes towards the present and future. In practical economic activity this disparity in entrepreneurial spirit is the prime motive force behind the 'Matthew effect' described in Chapter 1. Once left behind at the first step then you will never catch up in subsequent steps. The poorer the quality of human resources the less eagerness there is to make progress, so naturally there is a greater lack of entrepreneurial spirit. Conversely, the better the quality of human resources the greater the urge to get on, and of course this entails entrepreneurial potential. The poor quality of human resources not only results in the present backwardness of backward regions but may well also be the reason for even greater backwardness in the future. The clear disparity in entrepreneurship amongst the inhabitants of backward regions on the one hand and developed regions on the other, or more to the point the trend towards growth in this disparity, presages gloomy prospects for the future of growing inequalities in such economic indicators as output value and national income.

3.4 SOCIAL DEVELOPMENT

The complete contrast in behaviour of the inhabitants of backward regions and developed areas following the implementation of the household responsibility system forces us to abandon the notion that economic and social indicators are equivalent, and even discard the traditional thinking that economic indicators are a substitute for social indicators. Instead we must begin to consider the problem in the light of the degree of development of the social system as a whole.

If we view human activity as a unified natural historical process, economic and social development then become virtually synonymous. Without economic development clearly there can be no social development, and vice versa. They are two sides of the same coin. In the long run this provides an adequate interpretation of history. In modern society, however, there are enormous disparities and even head-on collisions between economic and social development in different countries and regions. In such a situation the issue raised is not chiefly one of the inevitable end-result for mankind as a whole, but that of how the economy of a certain nationality, or a certain region, can develop at some specified stage. In raising this issue time and time again one inevitably comes up against the reality of the level of economic development as expressed in terms of purely economic indicators such as output value etc, in addition to the degree of social development. To some extent these can be separated from one another.

The economic development of Japan and China in the 1950s was much the same in terms of a range of economic indicators. In natural resources China was far superior to Japan. Yet the consequence was that Japan forged ahead while China fell behind. Clearly nobody could explain this in terms of the physical stature of the Chinese or their commercial abilities. It was most commonly blamed on the 'one big pot' system. If we look into the matter this seems rather far-fetched. It was not the Japanese but the Chinese themselves who planned the 'one big pot' system.

The problems addressed in this book show similar difficulties to the one described above. Looking at the statistics from before the Third Plenum in 1978, the gap between the economies of Guizhou and Wenzhou was not nearly as alarming. But in a very short time following the opening of the valve of reform a rapid change suddenly took place in the development of the two regions. An explanation of this change will contribute to our understanding of the backwardness of backward regions. Whether we like it or not, the truth is that the level of economic development as expressed by economic indicators is not duplicated by the degree of social development. In other words, the degree of social development cannot be directly explained by the level of economic development as expressed by economic indicators. In the absence of specific indicators we can only assert that prior to the Third Plenum there was no significant disparity in the level of economic development as expressed by economic indicators between Guizhou and Wenzhou, but in terms of the degree of social development there was a clear difference.

In the case of Wenzhou, the 'historical impulse' towards the development of a commodity economy built up. In fact, the economic indicators stagnated at a low level but the degree of social development satisfied the demands for the development of a commodity economy. But in the case of Guizhou, the natural economy was preserved – or in other words, the degree of social development did not meet the requirements for the stage commodity economy development. Thus, it could only be in the wake of the rural reforms that the locus of movement and levels of development of the two regions' economic systems increasingly diverged.

Using the quality of human resources as our starting point, we will attempt to describe the state of social development in backward regions. In our survey of entrepreneurship amongst the rural inhabitants of the Ji'an prefecture we analysed the two-way correlation between the composite entrepreneurial spirit score and individuals' basic situation, and from this extrapolated factors which affect the level of entrepreneurial spirit. The non-relevant factors having been eliminated, the result is shown in Table 3.3 below.

Socioeconomic Structure

Table 3.3 shows that projects undertaken rank first among all the factors, with a correlation coefficient of 0.242. This means that the variety and complexity of projects undertaken is closely related to the degree of entrepreneurial spirit among the farmers; the greater the variety and complexity of projects, the higher the degree of entrepreneurial spirit among those running enterprises. Compared to the other factors, projects undertaken have the greatest effect on entrepreneurial spirit.

Table 3.3 Factors affecting entrepreneurial spirit

Factor	*Correlation coefficient*	*Ranking*
Projects undertaken	0.242	1
State aid	–0.198	2
Educational level	0.162	3
Mass media	0.128	4
Mobility	0.107	5

Notes: 1) These correlation coefficients represent the degree of correlation between a single factor and entrepreneurial spirit after all other affecting factors have been removed. Above a certain level of significance the greater the coefficient the more influence the said factor has on entrepreneurial spirit, and the greater its importance amongst the factors as a group.
2) Significance is set at 0.01. Those factors which do not reach this level of significance have been excluded from the table as insignificant.

Table 3.4 Structure of GVAO in the eight backward regions and other regions

			1983
Region	*Agriculture (arable, livestock, forestry, fisheries) (%)*	*Sidelines (%)*	*Village-run industry as part of sidelines (%)*
Backward regions	87.0	13.0	5.3
Other regions	82.0	18.0	14.3
Total	82.6	17.4	12.9

Table 3.5 Structure of GVAO in Guizhou, Qinghai, Jiangsu and Zhejiang

			1983
Region	*Agriculture (arable, livestock, forestry, fisheries) (%)*	*Sidelines (%)*	*Village-run industry as part of sidelines (%)*
Qinghai	92.6	7.4	5.5
Guizhou	83.0	17.0	5.4
Jiangsu	74.0	26.0	24.1
Zhejiang	70.9	29.1	24.1

Economic Structure

The general picture in the rural areas of backward regions is one of no diversification in undertakings.

In the eight backward provinces and regions, the output value of sidelines and in particular village-run industry clearly lags behind that of other areas. A comparison of the structure of the value of output in individual provinces shows an even greater disparity, as seen in Table 3.5.

For every 100 yuan of agricultural output value, the amount derived from sidelines is 29 yuan in Zhejiang, 26 yuan in Jiangsu and a mere 7 yuan or so in Qinghai. The amount derived from village-run industry is 24 yuan in both Zhejiang and Jiangsu, and only a little over 5 yuan in both Qinghai and Guizhou.

Backward regions are also characterised by an unsophisticated economy. The great majority of the rural inhabitants of backward regions restrict their activities to the home and its surroundings and

Table 3.6 Village and town enterprises in Guizhou and Jiangsu

					1983
Region	*No. of enterprises*	*Employees (10,000)*	*Output value (100m yuan)*	*Taxes (100m yuan)*	*Net profit (100m yuan)*
Guizhou	13549	20.89	3.47	0.24	0.47
Jiangsu	70580	454.08	168.70	12.18	16.73
Guizhou/Jiangsu %	19.2	4.6	2.1	1.97	2.8

engage in traditional undertakings. Apart from a few loose mutual aid ties, very few community-type economic groupings within the village or township (previously commune) actually cut across the family, while professional-type economic associations based on purely economic ties which cut across the community (township and above) are even rarer. We will just take village and town enterprises as an example in Table 3.6.

Leaving aside regions in an even worse position such as Tibet and Qinghai (for example, in Qinghai in 1983 there were only 2000 enterprises, or 2.8 per cent of Jiangsu's total), despite the fact that Guizhou is relatively developed its village and town enterprises amount to only 19.2 per cent of Jiangsu's, employee numbers are only 4.6 per cent of Jiangsu's and output value is a mere 2.1 per cent of the figure for Jiangsu (or less than a third of what the latter pays in tax).

Village and town enterprises in Jiangsu include plant growing, aquatic breeding, industry, construction, transportation, commerce and service industries. The fifteen types of industry produce metallurgical products, coal, chemicals, machinery, electrical goods, building materials, foodstuffs, textiles, clothes, shoes and paper, providing a complete range and variety of products. In recent years the province's village and town enterprises have embarked upon a new period of growth, developing a variety of different forms of combination and moving in the direction of greater specialisation of production. There has been a massive growth in urban-rural co-ordination, alliances that cut across community boundaries, combinations within the village and town enterprise system, co-operative-style production of parts for large-scale industry and in partnership with specialised companies, and so on. In 1983 Wuxi county's 733 village and town enterprises linked up with universities, colleges and scientific research institutes in the cities of Shanghai, Fushun and Wuxi, and brought in 949 items of technology. The city of Changzhou emphasises town and country industrial links and plans to organise batches of town and township industries into various production system 'chains'. The first batch to be so transformed comprises 256 village and town enterprises. The township-run industries of Wujin county manufacture electrical components for Shanghai 'Feiyue' and 'Kaige' brand televisions. Wuxi county's 200 or so village and town industries separately participate in the joint production of parts and components with the county's four complexes – iron and steel, printing, electric fans and boiler manufacturing – and a specialist services company.

The vigorous expansion of village and town enterprises in the Jiangsu-Zhejiang region together with the large numbers of specialised households, all kinds of new joint economic entities, household and joint-household enterprises, plus many types of specialised villages and townships engaged mainly in single or diversified sideline operations, have all stimulated the rural economy, created a diversity of forms of undertakings, expanded and made economic ties more complex and linked town and country to a high degree. This has a great effect on improving the quality of human resources. Furthermore, in Jiangsu Province 925.6 out of every 10 000 village and township inhabitants work in village and town enterprises. For Guizhou the figure is only 89.5, or just 9.7 per cent of the number in Jiangsu. To a great extent, this delays the improvement of the quality of human resources in backward regions.

The Function of the Community

In rural areas in backward regions the serious functional failure of the grassroots community is as apparent as that of the economic structure. As in every other region of China, the majority of grassroots rural communities in backward regions are centred on a market town with a surrounding service area.

The functional nexus of the market town area – the market town or small city – becomes the centre of the community through its cohesive force over and polarisation of social and economic life. Its basic function is to provide services, co-ordination and control over economic, social and political aspects pertaining to the market town area as a whole. Cohesion in social and economic life is created through the movement of population, information, funds and materials. The higher the rate and volume of flow of these basic social necessities, the greater the internal organic unity of the community, the closer the various links between individual units, and thus the greater the degree of polarisation or differentiation of the market town or small city, and the better it fulfils its function. A properly functioning market town or small city can provide services and co-ordination for the market town area as a whole in economic aspects such as commerce, finance, production services, technical services, industrial and commercial supervision and taxation, in social aspects such as information flow, education, cultural life, healthcare and welfare, and in political aspects such as administration, public security and judicial affairs. In this way, the size of the service area of a market town (that is, the density of market towns), and whether or not a market town possesses the functional system and organisation described above provide objective criteria for deciding whether or not the grassroots community is functioning well and effectively.

In backward regions, the restrictive natural environment, backward social infrastructure and low level of economic development result in the poor flow of population, information, funds and materials, insufficient internal cohesion within the community and, consequently, a lack of polarisation. Therefore, backward regions cannot compare with advanced regions be it in numbers of market towns and small cities or in their functional efficiency.

If we look at the density of market towns, Jiangsu Province has 135 county towns (that is, those officially set up on a municipal system) in 62 counties, giving an average of 2.2 towns per county. For Zhejiang the figures are 158 towns in 62 counties, averaging 2.5 towns per county. Compare this with Guizhou which has only 115 towns in 82 counties, or 1.4 towns per county, and most of these are small towns which lack the appropriate official municipal structure. Small towns of this type in Jiangsu number 1765 which, combined with towns proper, give an overall average of 30.6 market towns and small cities per county. Also in Jiangsu, there are an average of 1.83 towns per 100 square kilometres, way above the national average of 0.6. The market town service area in Jiangsu Province averages 54 square kilometres, or only 32 per cent of the national average of 169 square kilometres. The scarcity of market towns in backward regions means that there are places within the market town service area which because of their distance from the market town do not receive services, communications or administration worthy of the name, and those that they do receive fall far below the level of efficient functioning of the community. In mountainous Guizhou, for example, in many cases the district seat is just a market town, while the township is located in an ordinary natural village. If we take the township as the grassroots community, the lack of even the most basic organisational infrastructure means that the community is far from a functional unit. And if we set the grassroots community at the level of the district, the much greater size of the area and its inhospitable terrain greatly limit the contact between farmers and the centre of the community or members of other communities, so that it is difficult to see this as a grassroots community in any real sense.

Turning now to the organisational aspect, the market towns and small cities of Jiangsu Province have a network of altogether 8095 commercial and service units, and 3042 country fairs. In Guizhou however, economic activity in the commercial sector of market towns is severely limited, and volume of business is only 36.2 per cent that of Jiangsu. With the growth of the rural commodity economy and the expansion of village and town enterprises, economic activity in Jiangsu's market town commercial sector has progressively diversified in type, level of undertaking and circulation channels. The province's market town commercial sector generally comprises more than ten different types and channels including state-run companies, supply and marketing co-operatives, collective commercial enterprises, village and town factory retail sales departments, many kinds of labour and management service companies, individual households and country fair trade.

In the areas of production services and the dissemination of technology, Jiangsu Province has a relatively complete structure and organisation due to the fact that the township seat is almost always a market town. In Guizhou, however, most townships are located in natural villages and so all there is usually is a branch of the supply and marketing co-operative and a credit co-operative and, if it is also a district seat, the subordinate organisations such as an agricultural techniques popularisation station, forestry station, water control station, clinic, supply and marketing co-operative, rural bank branch, grain station, industrial and commercial office and tax office. With such a wide service area and a large number of clients there is a severe shortage of specialist and technical personnel, plus production and technical services are rendered almost non-existent in a difficult natural environment with inconvenient postal and telephone services and communications.

Generally speaking, technicians are unable to visit farmers throughout the year and in some areas farmers go from one year to the next without a visit. Daxiqiao commune, in Anshun county, is situated on the Anshun–Guiyang highway, a mere dozen kilometres from the city of Anshun. Yet even the commune secretary rarely gets to see anyone from the district agrotechnical popularisation station. At the commune and brigade level there is usually no way of getting information about even popular scientific materials. By contrast, in Jiangsu nearly one-third of all townships have set up popular scientific organisations, and newspapers on popular science are published in 54 counties (on average one in ten households subscribes). Moreover, courses by radio on popular science are broadcast at regular intervals in 50 counties, and over 500 towns and townships have set up agrotechnical colleges. At the same time 119 rural vocational middle schools have been built or renovated and agricultural vocational classses have been started in 561 ordinary high schools in market towns and small towns.

In the cultural sphere, 886 rural and market town cultural centres and 2223 cultural stations had been set up in Jiangsu by the end of 1983, roughly one per township (town). There were 364 cinemas in market towns and over 80 per cent of small towns possessed permanent projection spaces. There were over 5330 book distributors below county level (including towns and small towns under county jurisdiction), an average of 2.8 distribution points for every market town service area. In Guizhou, however, there were only 190 cinemas in the province as a whole, including the cities. Anshun prefecture had just 47 district and commune cultural stations, comprising 11.19 per cent of all district town and commune numbers. Practically no commune possessed a cultural station. In the entire province there was a total of 400 or so book distribution retailers and special book counters, which amounted to less than one-seventh of the number in Jiangsu.

Interpersonal Relations

In comparison with developed regions, interpersonal relations in backward regions are clearly characterised by a weak commodity sense in economic relations and a strong traditionalism in social relations (see Table 3.7).

In 1983 the commodity rate (that is, the proportion of produce traded) for agricultural and sideline produce reached 70 per cent in Jiangsu Province, while in Guizhou it did not exceed 40 per cent and in Qinghai it was just 30 per cent or so. Calculating from the rural

Table 3.7 Commodity relations among rural inhabitants of Guizhou and Jiangsu

		1983
Region	*Av. income from agric. and sideline produce per head of rural population (yuan)*	*Av. per capita social commodity retail sales (yuan)*
Guizhou	57.54	146.69
Jiangsu	205.50	338.19
Nationwide	161.42	278.00
Guizhou/Jiangsu %	28.0	43.4

Note: Due to the differences in rural and urban proportions, the average per capita social commodity retail sales cannot show the actual commodity consumption of the vast rural population. In Guizhou, for instance, calculations based on the population of the entire province show that social commodity retail sales are equivalent to 52.8 per cent of the national average, whereas in actual fact social commodity retail sales for the urban population are 403.41 yuan per person, not far off the national figure of 488.8 yuan per person. Among the rural population, however, social commodity retail sales are only 86.51 yuan per person, just 40.6 per cent of the comparable national figure of 213.09 yuan per person. On these figures, every farmer in Guizhou is fully 126.58 yuan short!

population, the per capita income from social agricultural and sideline produce in Guizhou was equivalent to 28.0 per cent of Jiangsu's, while per capita social commodity retail sales were only 43.4 per cent that of Jiangsu.

Due to sluggish economic growth, labour and sectoral distribution is undeveloped and economic relations are oversimplified. This means that social relations are simple and therefore uniform, and there is a strongly homogeneous social structure. Looking at the individual and the family – the basic social units – without the opportunity for much choice there is little difference in people's values and way of life (including production methods). If a community is a mechanical combination of numerous similar individuals it is, as Marx says, just like simple addition of identical elements. The economic activities of the vast majority of the rural population are limited to the home and there are few community-based economic ties and organisations, while professional economic organisations which extend beyond the community are extremely rare.

As for social organisations and relations, blood ties still frequently play the major role in the countryside in backward regions. There are very few organisations based on locality, and absolutely none based on a trade or profession. Basically, in the form of social life, these regions are still at the stage where the 'group dependent on a leader' (primary group) predominates. Compared with developed regions, social experience is limited and less sophisticated in backward regions, covering a much narrower range of activity, restricted as it is mainly to the family, neighbourhood, group of friends, village and neighbouring villages. The state of transport, communications and information together with the serious dysfunctioning of the community mean that even within the market town service area there is very little social activity. Social organisations and interpersonal relations are uniform, and in the rare case of joint activities face-to-face interaction predominates. Association of individuals remains mainly based on emotional bonds, and rationally-based notions of mutual exploitation, co-operation and competition do not play a big role.

The three aspects which make up the socioeconomic structure – the economic structure, function of the community and interpersonal relations – are ultimately manifested in the numbers of projects undertaken and potential scope for choice, and as such have an effect of primary importance on the quality of human resources.

Social Infrastructure

Education

In the survey of entrepreneurship, educational level came third in the list of relevant factors, with a significant correlation (0.162) between educational level and entrepreneurship. This shows that the educational level of the peasants has a considerable effect on entrepreneurial spirit, so that the higher the educational level the greater the degree of entrepreneurship. Educational level is ranked according to the following scale: illiterate, elementary primary school, higher primary school, junior middle school, and senior middle school and above (see Table 3.8).

This table shows the wide disparity in educational level amongst the population as a whole, a disparity which is directly and closely linked to the fact that educational institutions in backward regions are undeveloped, as Table 3.9 indicates.

Table 3.8 Educational levels

								1983
Region	*Av. level of education received*	*Av. no of years schooling*	*Educational levels (per 10 000)*					*Rate of illiteracy in pop. over 12 (%)*
			Univ	*Sen Mid*	*Jun Mid*	*Prim*	*Illit/ semi-lit*	
Tibet	0.39	2.5	42	121	361	1647	5719	70.5
Guizhou	0.82	4.0	39	296	1142	2878	3210	47.6
Nationwide	1.11	5.0	55	660	1780	3540	2350	31.9
Tibet/Nat (%)	35.1	50.0	76.4	18.3	20.3	46.5	220	220
Guizhou/Nat (%)	73.9	80.0	70.9	44.8	64.2	81.3	140	150

Note: The average level of education received is calculated according to a system of weighting in which University = 4, Senior Middle = 3, Junior Middle = 2, Primary = 1, and Illiterate/Semiliterate = 0. The average number of years schooling is based on the following norms: University = 14, Senior Middle = 10, Junior Middle = 8, Primary = 5, Illiterate/Semiliterate = 1.

Backwardness in education has resulted in low cultural and educational standards among the inhabitants of backward regions, while it has also affected the growth of the commodity economy and the quality of human resources. Backward cultural levels mean that the great majority of the population is content with or restricted to the familiarity of tradition and things which can be grasped through direct experience. They have no desire to seek out and try out new things and ideas, and this has a direct effect on entrepreneurial spirit, the ability to manage an undertaking and the capacity to grasp up-to-date knowledge and techniques, as well as affecting cadres' capabilities in work and administration.

Information Flow

In our survey of entrepreneurial spirit, the use made by the farmers of the mass media came fourth in the list of factors affecting entrepreneurship with a correlation coefficient of 0.128. The scale for determining use of the mass media was based on the number of days the

Table 3.9 Student numbers at all levels

					1983
	Av. no. of students per 10 000 population				
Region	*Colleges and universities*	*Polytechnic secondary schools*	*General middle schools*	*Agric. and vocational middle schools*	*Primary schools*
Eight backward regions	7.7	12.5	357.1	8.3	1383.8
Other regions	12.4	10.9	440.8	12.5	1315.6
Total nationwide	11.8	11.2	429.1	11.9	1324.7

Note: With the exception of primary schools and polytechnic secondary schools, the numbers of enrolled students per 10 000 population in backward regions are lower than in other regions and in China as a whole. The high numbers in polytechnic secondary schools are related to the low proportion of students in backward regions going on to higher education. A large number of junior middle school students do not go on to senior middle school, and then to university, but choose to go on to polytechnic secondary schools. Because university places are limited this is the only way rural students can leave the countryside and urban students escape unemployment. The high numbers of primary school students are related to the relaxed population control policies instituted among the national minorities. The primary school-age population in backward regions is bigger than in the other regions.

Table 3.10 Students at all levels by province

					1983
	Av. no. of students per 10 000 population				
Region	*Colleges and universities*	*Polytechnic secondary schools*	*General middle schools*	*Agric. and vocational middle schools*	*Primary schools*
Tibet	5.2	5.2	93.3	0.0	647.7
Guizhou	5.9	12.8	284.0	6.5	1433.3
Hubei	15.5	9.3	505.7	16.1	1405.2
Liaoning	18.5	14.1	500.7	21.8	1181.0
Tibet/Liaoning (%)	28.1	36.9	18.6	0.0	54.8
Guizhou/ Liaoning (%)	31.9	90.8	56.7	29.8	121.3

Table 3.11 Student enrolment at lower levels and proportion of students entering schools of higher grade

			1983
Region	*Enrolled percentage of starting school-age population*	*Percentage of primary students continuing education*	*Percentage of junior middle school students continuing education*
Guizhou	81.2	51.5	27.4
Nationwide	94.0	67.3	35.5

Table 3.12 Teacher–student ratio

				1983
	Average number of students per teacher			
Region	*Colleges and universities*	*Polytechnic secondary schools*	*General middle schools*	*Primary schools*
Guizhou	4.0	9.1	18.8	27.3
Nationwide	4.0	7.3	16.9	25.0

Table 3.13 School buildings and accommodation for teachers, administrative staff and workers in Guizhou

	Required area (1000 m^2)	*Actual area (1000 m^2)*	*Actual/ required (%)*	*Remarks*
Primary school buildings	7190	4284	59.6	Required area = 3.5 m^2 per person
Middle school buildings	3451	2031	58.9	Required area = 4.5 m^2 per person
Accomodation for teachers, admin staff and workers	3200			Required area = 42 m^2 per household for 70 per cent of staff
Total	13 841	6315	45.6	

farmers read newspapers or listened to broadcasts, using the following categories: never, rarely, once or twice a week, daily.

This correlation shows that there is a correspondence between entrepreneurial spirit and exposure to the mass media. Those who read newspapers and listen to broadcasts more frequently exhibit a correspondingly higher degree of entrepreneurship. Similarly, the

Table 3.14 Basic school furniture (desks and chairs) in Guizhou

Jan-Jun 1983

	Required no. of sets	*Actual no. of sets*	*Actual/ required (%)*	*Remarks*
Primary school	2 056 800	1 452 300	70.6	Required sets = one per student
Middle school	787 400	726 400	92.3	
Total	2 844 200	2 178 700	76.6	

Note: That is, 23.4 per cent of students (665 500) have no desk or chair, and must stand when they attend class unless they sit squeezed several to a seat.

Table 3.15 Educational equipment in Guizhou

	Required amount (million yuan)	*Actual amount (million yuan)*	*Actual/ required (%)*	*Remarks*
Primary and middle schools	19.941	2.5	12.5	Required amount based on 2nd category standard equipment stipulated by Ministry
Institutes of higher education	65.9	20.9	31.7	Required amount based on standards stipulated by Ministry
Total	85.841	23.4	27.3	

Note: From a survey of 2368 primary schools, 199 junior middle schools, 30 comprehensive middle schools and 7 polytechnic secondary schools and teacher training colleges in 10 counties in various parts of the province.

development of facilities for the flow of relevant information is of vital importance in its effect on the quality of human resources in backward regions.

The eight backward regions and provinces cover 58.85 per cent of China's total land area, while their populations account for 13.86 per cent of the nation's total population. In 1983 these regions accounted for a total of only 11.41 per cent of the posts and telecommunications business in the country as a whole, as shown in Tables 3.18 to 3.20.

Such a huge gap coupled with inconvenient communications has

Table 3.16 Availability of practical lab sessions in Guizhou

				1983
Availability	*Nat. hist. practicals in primary schools*	*Physics & chemistry practical lab sessions*		
		Junior middle schools	*Comprehensive middle schools*	*Polytechnics and TTCs*
100%	0	0.5	13.3	0
80%	0.30	2.5	20.0	0
60%	2.10	3.0	6.7	28.6
40%	1.18	6.0	16.7	0
20%	0.26	9.0	10.0	14.3
10%	1.52	8.0	20.0	14.3
Not available	94.64	71.0	13.3	42.8

Note: The majority of schools are unable to offer practical laboratory sessions, so teachers are forced to explain experiments on paper without recourse to any kind of practical demonstration. Things are not much better in higher education. The Guizhou Education Office stated that at universities on average 60 per cent of elementary and 20 to 30 per cent of specialised practical laboratory work can be carried out, while 56 per cent of basic courses and 50 per cent of teacher training and specialised classes are available. The situation in new schools is even worse. Students in the higher level and technical classes at Liupanshui, for example, have to make a special journey of several dozen miles to the Bijie Specialised School for Teacher Training in order to carry out ordinary scientific experiments. If this is the situation in schools coming under the Ministry of Education, then conditions in the majority of farmer-run schools can well be imagined.

undoubtedly resulted in serious difficulties for the postal and telecommunications service in backward regions. In Tibet, for example, each post office serves an area averaging a massive 10 169 square kilometres. Moreover, for every square kilometre mail routes cover a mere 61 metres while there are just 8.7 metres of overhead telegraph lines. In Guizhou, which has the most extensive posts and telecommunications network among the backward regions, up to the end of 1983 there were still 32 districts (6 per cent) without through circuits, while 75 per cent of communes (nearly 2900) had no P & T office compared with the national figure of 35.3 per cent. In 14 counties in the province (17 per cent) it took three days to deliver the provincial newspaper, and in 70 per cent of communes (about 2700) postal

Table 3.17 Adult education

			1983
	Av. no. of adults in education per 10 000 population		
Region	*Adult higher education*	*Adult intermed. education*	*Adult elementary education*
Guizhou	3.4	4.3	157.6
Nationwide	11.0	95.1	79.7
Guizhou/Nat (%)	30.9	4.5	197.7

Notes: 1) Adult higher education encompasses the television university, workers' university, sparetime university, peasants' university, correspondence university, evening university, administrative cadres' training schools, institutes of education and middle school teachers' continuing education institutes. Adult intermediate education comprises adult intermediate technical colleges, adult middle schools and primary school teachers' continuing education institutes. Primary-level and literacy classes come under adult elementary education.

2) The table shows that Guizhou falls far below national levels in adult higher and intermediate education. Moreover, the high level of adult elementary education is quite simply due to the high incidence of illiteracy and semiliteracy in the province. According to the statistical breakdown, for every 10 000 population in Guizhou there are 5.2 adults attending primary-level classes (or only 18.5 per cent of the national figure of 28.1 adults), and as many as 154.2 adults attending literacy classes, three times as many as the national figure of 51.6 adults.

deliveries took two to four days. Even looking at communications in Anshun prefecture where conditions are excellent, the postal service is shocking.

There, 41.8 per cent of brigades and 79.7 per cent of production teams subscribe to no major periodical, while 36.5 per cent of brigades and 54.3 per cent of teams rely on passing deliveries for their mail, newspapers and magazines. These last are equivalent to 66.8 per cent and 65.9 per cent respectively of the national average. These are the officially reported figures, but according to figures provided by responsible officials in the Anshun post office, the percentage is even lower, as shown in Table 3.22 below.

According to these figures, there is one commune that does not subscribe to a major periodical, while about 80 per cent of brigades and around 83 per cent of production teams are dependent on passing

Table 3.18 Posts and telecommunications business in the eight backward regions and other regions

1983

Region	*Total P&T business per cap. (yuan)*	*No. of letters/ parcels per cap.*	*No. of newspapers/ magazines per cap.*	*No. of telegrams per cap.*	*Long-distance telephone calls per cap.*
Backward regions	1.79	2.74	0.19	0.20	0.18
Other regions	2.23	3.55	0.23	0.17	0.27
Nationwide	2.17	3.44	0.22	0.18	0.26

Note: In all categories with the exception of telegrams, the figures for backward regions are lower than those for other regions and the country as a whole. The high figure for telegrams can be ascribed to the fact that far less use is made of long-distance telephone calls than in other areas and in China as a whole.

Table 3.19 Posts and telecommunications business in Guizhou and Jiangsu

1983

Region	*Total P&T business per cap. (yuan)*	*No. of letters/ parcels per cap.*	*No. of newspapers/ magazines per cap.*	*No. of telegrams per cap.*	*Long-distance telephone calls per cap.*
Guizhou	1.10	1.72	0.12	0.10	0.11
Jiangsu	3.15	5.85	0.22	0.23	0.40
Guizhou/ Jiangsu %	34.9	29.4	54.5	43.5	27.5

deliveries for their mail. The delivery figures also include a group of brigades and teams wich are situated on the road and concentrated around commune and district seats. If this is the state of affairs in Anshun prefecture, one of the province's frontrunners in terms of natural conditions and socioeconomic level, then the situation in other regions and the average for the whole province can well be imagined. But even within Anshun prefecture itself there are counties with even worse conditions. One example is Zhenning county, which the authors visited (see Table 3.23).

Here 83.5 per cent of brigades and 95.8 of teams subscribed to no major periodical, while 85 per cent of brigades and 97 per cent of

Table 3.20 Posts and telecommunications network in the eight backward regions and other regions

			1983
Region	*Av. service area per post office (sq. km)*	*Density of postal routes (km per sq. km)*	*Density of overhead telegraph wires (km per sq. km)*
Backward regions	720.0	0.168	0.110
Other regions	89.8	0.958	0.645
Nationwide	191.4	0.477	0.319
Backward/Other regions %	800	17.5	17.1

Table 3.21 Posts and telecommunications services in Anshun Prefecture, Guizhou (1)

					4th quarter 1983
	Newspaper and periodical subscription (%)	*Frequency of deliveries*			
		Total	*Breakdown of frequency*		
			Daily	*Every 2 days*	*Every 3 days*
Commune	100.0	100.0	44.1	44.4	11.5
Brigade	58.2	63.5	27.3	28.8	7.4
Team	20.3	45.7	16.5	22.6	6.6

Note: Newspaper and periodical subscriptions refer to any of the major publications, namely *Red Flag*, *People's Daily* and *Guizhou Daily*.

Table 3.22 Posts and telecommunications services in Anshun Prefecture, Guizhou (2)

	No.	*No. with periodical subscriptions*	*% subscribing to periodicals*	*Delivery rate (%)*
Communes	329	328	99.7	over 95
Brigades	2755	1332	48.3	c20
Teams	22299	4434	19.9	c17

Table 3.23 Posts and telecommunications services in Zhenning county, Guizhou

4th quarter 1983

	Newspaper and periodical subscription (%)	*Frequency of deliveries*			
		Total	*Breakdown of frequency*		
			Daily	*Every 2 days*	*Every 3 days*
Communes	100.0	100.0	28.1	71.9	–
Brigades	16.5	15.0	7.4	7.6	–
Teams	4.2	3.0	1.0	1.8	0.7

teams received no deliveries! In 1981 not a single one of Zhenning county's 1732 production teams subscribed to *Guizhou Daily*. As the district head of the county's Liuma district said: 'The post only gets delivered as far as the commune, after that you have to wait for someone passing to deliver it the rest of the way. The daily becomes a weekly, fornightly or even monthly paper.'

By 1982 there were 0.23 telephones per 100 population in Guizhou Province as a whole, half as many as the national figure of 0.46 telephones per 100 population. In the countryside, there were 0.06 subscribers per 100 population, 60 per cent of the average 0.10 subscribers per 100 population nationwide. These, however, are figures on paper, and it is still uncertain how many of these telephones are in a usable condition. According to the statistics 98.9 per cent of communes, 18.6 per cent of brigades and 4.8 per cent of production teams are on the telephone, but in actual fact the real figures are far below these. Why?

1. The figures given above include district and commune seats and their surrounding brigades and production teams, as well as teams of the brigade seat. These brigades and teams are considered to be on the telephone if the line is connected as far as the relevant district, commune or brigade seat. Shared lines which a number of units have access to are counted separately and therefore should not have been reduplicated in the statistics given above. In Anshun prefecture 329 communes (100 per cent), 474 brigades (17.4 per cent) and 1930 production teams (9 per cent) are connected by

telephone. From these figures there would seem to be a total of 2733 subscribers. In fact, with only 1213 rural subscribers in all, there are less than half this number.

2. 85 per cent of the province's existing rural telephone wiring was laid down in the co-operativisation movement and Great Leap Forward between 1956 and 1958, and has never been overhauled. Most are subscriber lines, that is 2.5 to 3mm thick flexible steel cables, which in the course of a decade have been eaten away by rust, rot and insects and are no longer serviceable. According to the authors' practical survey, of the total 4213 km of telephone wiring, 45 per cent was in disrepair and 40 per cent had rusted away. What is more, all the wiring dated from twenty years before. Even just looking at the 2596 kilometres of wiring from county to district, 50 per cent of this was in poor condition. Guanling county in this prefecture has 32 communes, eight of which are not connected to the telephone. Two of the nine communes in Zhenning's Liuma district are partially connected, while one has been off the telephone for over two years. Whenever there is a meeting in the district someone has to be paid 5 yuan a day to go on the four-day trip to notify the four outlying communes. Dalang commune in Ziyun county has only eight brigades, but it takes six days for someone to go round and notify all eight of any meeting.
3. Telephones in newly set up communes come under the control of the P&T departments at county rather than above prefectural level. This means that a smaller proportion of communes are in fact connected than given in the figures of provincial and prefectural P&T departments. Twenty new communes have been set up in Anshun prefecture but only six are connected to the telephone. But according to the figures given above by the P&T office, there is 100 per cent connection at the commune level.

The situation in TV and radio broadcasting is infinitely worse, as Table 3.24 below shows. Broadcasting and TV coverage in Guizhou is only one-third of the national level, while wired broadcasting coverage is less than a seventh of that nationwide. As many as 93.9 per cent of households receive no wired broadcasts.

In 1982 the whole of Guizhou produced only 41 hours of TV programmes, 0.73 per cent of the national figure of 5622 hours of regional programmes. Together with Qinghai, Guizhou ranked second last nationwide, higher only than Tibet. By 1983 TV programmes had further fallen to 17.9 hours comprising 335 programmes of just 3.2 minutes each, putting Guizhou second last nationally.

Transportation

In the survey of entrepreneurial spirit there was a correlation coefficient of 0.107 between entrepreneurship and mobility, making this the fifth most important factor. This shows that the more extensive the area of farmer activity, and the further and more frequently they travel, the greater their knowledge of the world and the greater their entrepreneurship.

Mobility is ranked into four categories based on the distance from their own locality travelled by the respondents. The four categories are: within own county, other counties within own province, neighbouring provinces and other provinces. The first and foremost requirement of mobility, and especially business mobility, is means of transportation. We have therefore provided some comparative tables.

The average density of haulage routes in the eight backward regions is equivalent to 19.0 per cent of that in other regions, and 37.5 per cent of the national average. Expressed as a percentage in comparison with the density in non-backward regions, the density of haulage routes is 6.7 per cent in Xinjiang, 8.1 per cent in Tibet, 10.6 per cent in Qinghai and 17.4 per cent in Inner Mongolia. But compared with a developed region such as Jiangsu, the percentages are 3.2, 3.9, 5.1 and 8.4 respectively.

Guizhou's haulage route density is not particularly low: at 17.45 kilometres per square kilometre it is higher than the national average. But because of its mountainous terrain, 17.6 per cent of

Table 3.24 TV and radio broadcasting in Guizhou

1982

Region	*Broadcast coverage of population (%)*	*Television coverage of population (%)*	*Wired broadcast coverage of population (%)*
Guizhou	22.5	20.6	6.1
Nationwide	64.1	57.3	44.0
Guizhou/National	35.1	36.0	13.9
National ranking	29th	25th	26th

Table 3.25 Density of haulage routes in the eight backward regions and other regions

1983

Region	Density of haulage routes (km/sq. km)	Region	Density of haulage routes (km/sq. km)
Backward regions:	4.20	Other regions:	22.05
Xinjiang	1.47	Jiangsu	45.55
Tibet	1.79	Guangdong	34.23
Qinghai	2.33	Zhejiang	32.85
Inner Mongolia	3.83	Fujian	32.79

communes and 47.9 per cent of brigades in the province as a whole still cannot be reached by road. And a considerable number of those that are on the road are cut off some of the time. There are nine communes in Liuma district in Zhenning county, only three of which can in fact be reached by road, and they are all in the vicinity of the district seat. The road is closed some of the time for three others, while the remaining three are totally cut off without even a trace of a road. These are all dozens of kilometres from the district office. Just 13 of the 70 brigades are on the road. The district office lies 64 kilometres from the county town and is sometimes reachable by road. In 1982 the road and telephone line to the county were cut off for an entire month. So it is not enough simply to look at the extent of the road network. In backward regions highways are generally built to a low standard, are of poor quality and are not always passable.

Highways are the most important means of transport and communications in Guizhou Province, accounting for over 90 per cent

Table 3.26 Road haulage in Guizhou

1982

	Highways in haulage routes (%)	Substandard highways in haulage routes (%)	Cost of road haulage (yuan/1000 ton-km)	Fuel consumption in road haulage (lit/100 ton-km)
Guizhou	90.1	77.5	192	11.1
Nationwide	85.1	39.0	163	8.1

(which is higher than the national average). But only 22.5 per cent of these roads are standard highways (4th grade or above), with sub-standard highways accounting for as much as 77.5 per cent, the highest percentage in China and twice the national average. Due to the appalling condition of road surfaces, the ton-kilometre cost of haulage and fuel consumption are both higher than the national average.

Socioeconomic development is closely bound up with the growth of transport and communications, and particularly highway transportation. On the one hand, without the growth of transport and communications the commodity economy cannot flourish. According to a survey conducted by the China Motor Vehicle Industry Company at the end of 1983, for every average 10 000 yuan increase in output value in China's countryside there needs to be a corresponding increase of 1.5 to 1.8 million ton-kilometres in road haulage freight turnover. Poor communications greatly restrict the flow and turnover of freight, and inevitably pose a serious obstacle to the growth of the commodity economy. This is abundantly clear in backward regions.

Per capita freight turnover in backward regions is a mere 63.9 per cent of the national average, and 44.1 per cent of the figure for other regions. As a percentage of the figure for non-backward regions, per capita freight turnover is 15.0 per cent in Tibet, 16.1 per cent in Yunnan, 20.9 per cent in Qinghai and 28.7 per cent in Guizhou.

Of course the size of a region's freight turnover is determined not only by supply (transport and communications conditions) but also by demand (the state of economic growth). In backward regions restrictions on supply no doubt have a great impact. Guizhou's

Table 3.27 Per capita freight in the eight backward regions and other regions

	1983
Region	*Per capita freight turnover (ton-km per person)*
Nationwide	930.9
Non-backward regions	1349.2
Backward regions:	594.9
Tibet	202.1
Yunnan	216.9
Qinghai	281.7
Guizhou	387.7

famous tung oil is largely transported out of the region on horseback. It takes two to three days with each horse carrying a load of several dozen to a few hundred catties. In Bacao commune in Liuma district, over one million catties (500 000 kilograms) of sugarcane rotted because it could not be transported out. Similarly, vast amounts of oriental white oak fruits and boughs rot away in the mountains. Nobody wants pears or olives. If they cannot be transported out, bananas sell for just over one yuan for a 100 catties (50 kilograms). Jianao village of Shazi commune in Zhenning county produces 3 million catties (1.5 million kilograms) of fruit. One million catties (500 000 kilograms) are left to rot because horses are the only means of transportation and the journey takes two days. At Dalang commune in Ziyun county selling a pig entails finding four people to carry it to market over hill and dale, a two day journey there and back. Transportation costs alone can come to 30 to 40 yuan, or 40 per cent of the selling price of the pig.

Turning now to the second aspect, the backward state of transport and communications also has a substantial effect on the quality of human resources. Taken together with the backward information flow, intellectual development and technical services (not to mention its effect as a brake on the development of these aspects), in acting as obstacles to the commodity economy these elements prevent people from overcoming isolation, backwardness, ignorance, conservatism, lack of initiative and contentment with past achievements (see Table 3.28).

A low traveller turnover implies low mobility and limited activity, and as a consequence this limits to a great extent the amount of and capacity for extensive knowledge, new experiences, tendency towards change, as well as acceptance of new things and ideas. In this

Table 3.28 Turnover of travellers in Guizhou and Qinghai compared with the national average

1983

Region	*Per capita turnover of travellers (person-km/person)*	*% of national average*
Nationwide	302.0	–
Guizhou	75.0	24.8
Qinghai	109.1	36.1

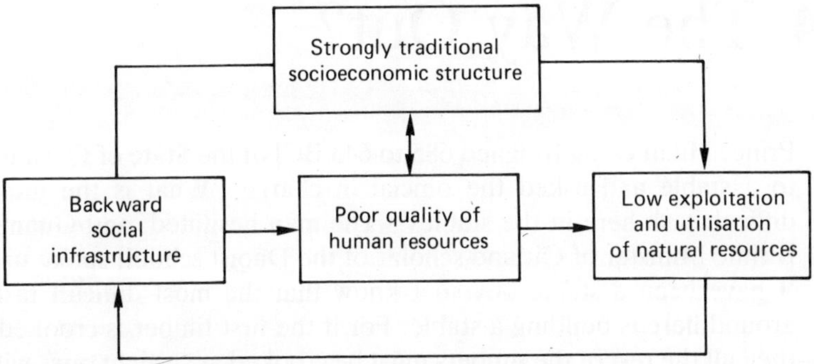

Figure 3.1 The immature social system

way it delays the change in the quality of human resources from traditional to modern, from conservative to innovative, from acceptance of the status quo to development.

Up to this point we have completed a preliminary outline of the extent of development of the social system in backward regions, which includes the quality of human resources, the socioeconomic structure and social infrastructure. It is apparent that compared with developed regions this is very much a social system in its infancy.

We have now been able to conclude this chapter's analytical process. The backward social infrastructure holds back the course of modernisation within the socioeconomic structure and among the population; a traditional socioeconomic structure and a population engaged in a low level of commodity production means that there is no effective way of exploiting the various resources and creating greater social wealth; the level of resource exploitation and the poor quality of human resources fetter the halting steps of the social infrastructure. This is the immature social system and its vicious circle of poverty. It tells us that in researching the developmental problems of the economies of backward regions, we should expand our vision to include the non-economic problems which fall outside the compass of the hypothetical 'economic man'.

4 The Way Out?

> Prince Huan Gong [reigned 685 to 643 BC] of the State of Qi came to a stable and asked the official in charge, 'What is the most difficult task here in the stables?' The man hesitated, and Guanzi [Prime Minister of Qi, and scholar of the Daoist school] spoke up: 'I have been a stable boy so I know that the most difficult task around here is building a stable. For if the first timber is crooked, then all the rest of the timbers must be crooked as straight ones will not fit. Conversely, if the first timber used is straight, then the following timbers must be straight, as there will be no use for crooked timbers.'[1]

4.1 THE GREATER THE BLOOD TRANSFUSION, THE WORSE THE ANAEMIA

Aid is imperative in helping a backward area to shake off its poverty. This was the general view in development economics of the 1960s as regards the economic development of those countries lagging behind.

> In the thirty years between 1950 and 1980, state capital investment in the minority nationality autonomous regions amounted to 69 112 million yuan. As for financial resources pumped into these areas every year in the form of loans, relief aid, production subsidies and so on, spending on such special items as subsidies for national minority areas, border region development and capital construction, and funds to aid undeveloped areas alone came to roughly 1,000 million yuan per annum.[2]

In terms of territory, these regions make up 60 per cent of China's total area so, taking the country as a whole, the annual expenditure of 70 000 million yuan out of the total national capital construction budget of hundreds of thousands of millions of yuan far from being excessive is rather too little. But from the perspective of development economics and viewing these regions as a relatively independent economic system, if we focus on the relations between central government aid and the local economic system and ignore for the time being economic benefit or the contributions these regions make

Table 4.1 Financial revenue and central government subsidies in Guizhou, Qinghai, Tibet and Inner Mongolia (million yuan 1983)

	Guizhou	*Qinghai*	*Inner Mongolia*	*Tibet*
Local financial revenue	872.33	156.37	690.00	–59.88
Central govt subsidy	682.24	542.26	1 800.00	686.55
Subsidy as % of total revenue	43.89	77.62	72.29	100.00
Subsidy as % of local financial revenue	78.21	346.78	260.87	–

to the country as a whole, then pumping money in without return poses a serious problem.

Deficits are common to backward regions. This is in sharp contrast to the more developed provinces such as Jiangsu which turn over approximately 10 000 million yuan annually to the national treasury. But what is well worth our attention is the fact that despite years of heavily subsidised economic construction, to this day financial expenditure in these regions still relies to a large extent, or even totally, on central government subsidies.

Savings surplus

Shortage of funds seems to be an integral feature of backward regions, hence loans or grants from external sources are a must. In this respect Chenery and Strout (1966) have put forward a two-gap model of the economies of developing countries based on Harrod *et al*'s objective economic analysis. The two-gap model is as follows:

Viewed from total expenditure: $Y' = C + I + E$
(Expenditure = consumption + investment + exports)
Viewed from total supply: $Y' = C + S + M$
(Supply = supply for consumption + savings + imports)

Combining the two equations gives $I - S = M - E$, or the difference between investment and savings is equal to the difference between imports and exports. For developing countries this last equation does not balance because there are two gaps: $I - S$ showing a savings gap, and $M - E$ an external trade gap. This is because in developing countries per capita incomes are so low that local savings are insignificant, so that foreign savings are required in order to raise the rate of investment. On the other hand, accelerating the rate of investment inevitably leads to the import of machinery and equipment on a large scale which creates an imbalance of payments. Thus in the course of development a developing country must cope with the two problems of foreign exchange shortage and inadequate local savings at the same time. These gaps may be filled by external funds and so there needs to be a stress on external aid in government policies. This theory had a tremendous impact both in theory and in practice on developed and developing countries alike in the 1950s and 1960s.

During this period, there was a dramatic increase in foreign aid payments by the capital exporting countries such as Britain and the United States, while countries such as India became prominent recipients. In absolute terms, external funds do make a difference to a developing economy. Measured by the yardsticks of shaking off poverty and backwardness, however, the results are disappointing. From the perspective of the development process in backward regions in China, this theory of relying on external assistance is quite simply sheer absurdity. Ordinarily, if a country provides vast amounts of aid with no strings attached, and does not demand the kind of negotiations on terms of repayment required by external funds, then the problems of recipient backward regions should have long since been solved. But what have the consequences actually been? Two examples can be cited, the case of Qinghai and, in greater detail, the case of Tibet.

Between 1951 and 1983 total financial revenue in Qinghai Province stood at 4065.07 million yuan, while central government subsidies totalled 7371.45 million yuan, or 181 per cent of the former. More perplexing is what seems to be an irreversible trend towards an increase in the proportion of subsidy. In 1962 subsidies were equivalent to 62 per cent of local financial revenue, but by the 1980s the proportion had risen to 83 per cent.

The grimmest picture is seen in the case of Tibet. In 1983 the region's local revenue was 500.8 million yuan, but disposable revenue came to 1000.5 million yuan, or 180.79 per cent of the former. The discrepancy was entirely due to central government subsidies (see Figure 4.3).

Since 1955 central government subsidies have consistently comprised the predominant share in the regional government's total revenue, as can be seen in Figure 4.3. In 1967 annual local financial revenue dropped below zero, and since then has remained in the red

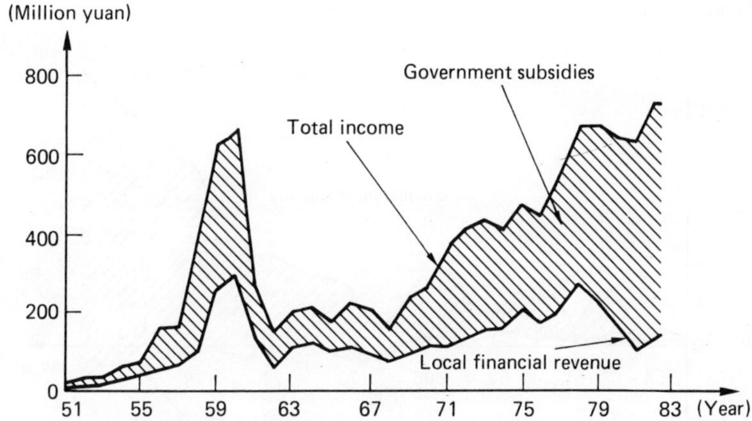

Figure 4.1 Trends of local financial revenue and central government subsidies, Qinghai 1951–83

Note: The ratio of local financial revenue to central government subsidies reached its peak at 60.10 per cent in 1965, and then fell steadily to 17.84 per cent in 1982.

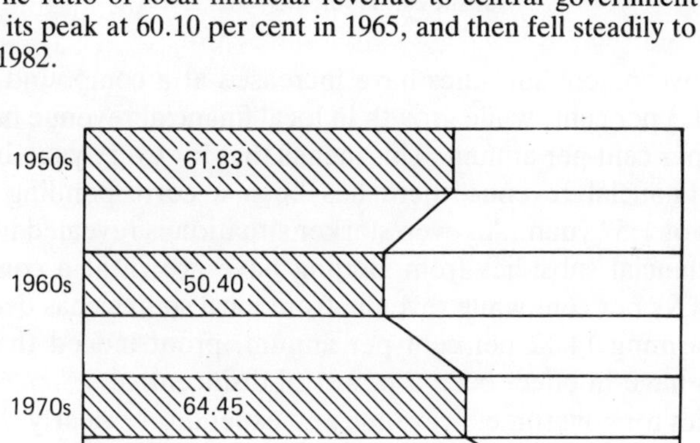

Figure 4.2 Percentage of central government subsidies in local financial revenue, Qinghai 1950s–1980s

so that regional government expenditure in Tibet is 100 per cent funded by central government subsidies. From 1952 to 1983 these amounted to 7088.15 million yuan in total, while in the same period local financial revenue actually showed a deficit of 162.94 million yuan. The trend in the past three decades has been that in Qinghai

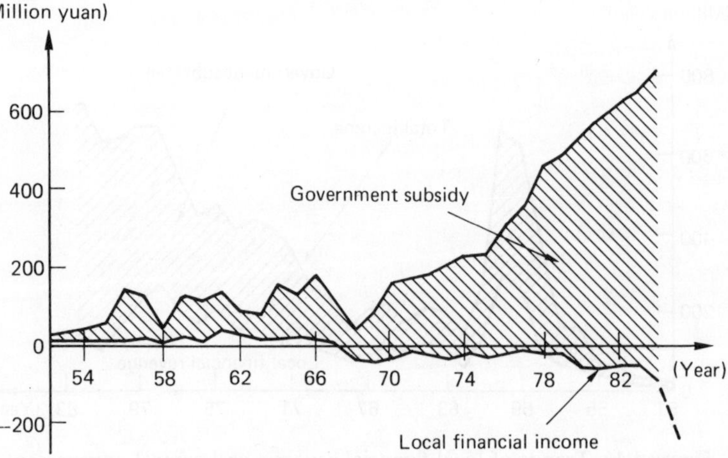

Figure 4.3 Trends of local financial revenue and central government subsidies, Tibet 1954–82

central government subsidies have increased at a compound annual rate of 14.3 per cent, while growth in local financial revenue has been only 9.4 per cent per annum. This means that for every yuan increase in local financial revenue there has been a corresponding rise in subsidies of 1.52 yuan. An even starker situation is revealed in Tibet, where financial subsidies from Beijing have grown at a compound rate of 14.97 per cent while revenue from local sources has decreased by an alarming 14.12 per cent per annum, proof indeed that these subsidies have in effect been a powerful disincentive.

Statistics for government revenue and expenditure clearly show the deficit difficulties of backward regions, but this does not mean that there is a shortage of funds for investment in the wider social sphere. In fact quite the contrary is the case if we examine banking figures. Even with the proviso that the year-end loan and deposit balance figures do not necessarily reflect the actual money supply and demand conditions of the regions, nevertheless when compared with the rest of China the money supply in backward regions does not seem to pose a serious problem. Almost all these regions show a surplus of funds for lending and the poorer the community the larger the proportion of deposits as against loans.

While elsewhere a situation prevails in which loans exceed deposits, creating a critical shortage of funds, the banks in Xinjiang taken together had a surplus equivalent to 43 per cent of the balance of deposits lying idle at the end of 1982. The banking system in Qinghai showed a deposit balance of 1000 million yuan at the end of 1982, which had grown by 15 per cent by the end of 1983. In the same period total lending showed an increase of only 10 per cent. In fact, outstanding loans amounted to only 50 per cent of the balance of deposits. In comparison, Guizhou's banking system is more advanced. As of the end of 1983 its loan balance was greater than the balance of deposits, albeit by an almost negligible 0.79 per cent. With the 1984 lending deregulation banks all over China rushed to offer loans on a competitive basis. Hard put to find qualified borrowers locally, the Bank of Guizhou directed 700 million yuan out of the province in loans, an amount equivalent to 80 per cent of that year's total financial revenue of the province. The bank's action was *tantamount to allowing the entire sum of central government subsidies to flow out of the region*.

Rural areas in Tibet are among the poorest in China, and as such the two-gap model would have us believe that there must be a serious money supply shortage or 'inadequate savings', and that external sources of funding must be sought. The fact is, at the end of 1983 private deposits in the Agricultural Bank in Tibet stood at 44.24 million yuan, while lending totalled a mere 11.6 million yuan. In two categories of rural loans, one for farm implements and the other for production costs, nothing happened throughout the entire year. By the end of 1983 the balance of deposits in credit co-ops amounted to 130.82 million yuan, as against outstanding loans of 14.69 million yuan. Idle deposits comprised a staggering 89 per cent of the total. Total lending for the whole year was only 18.77 million yuan, indicating that 86 per cent of the money deposited had not been disturbed at all for the entire period.

One cannot help but wonder whether the problems in these regions are due to the 'savings gap' or to 'surplus savings'; inadequate funds or inadequate demand for investment; no money to spend or nowhere to spend the money. This question is perplexing indeed. Judging by the banking figures we have examined there is no evidence of a 'savings gap' as conceptualised in Western development economics, in spite of the fact that backward regions hanker after subsidies. Because bank rates are not permitted to fluctuate, and because the year-end balance of loans against deposits does not reflect the real magnitude of the flow of funds, we have been unable to establish the link between these data and financial deficits and examine the theoretical implications. Nevertheless, at least on the evidence of the large outflow of funds from Guizhou and the fact that 86 per cent of rural deposits in Tibet lay idle for a whole year, and even more importantly based on our own feelings while doing field work in these regions, it may not be too bold or risky to make the following assumption: central government subsidies *are not intended as an answer to investment needs arising from inadequate local savings*. On this account, the flow of subsidies and the movement of local funds are dichotomised to such an extent that they never mix.

The theory of the two-gap model rests upon two premises. First, the pressure for investment is too strong to be accomodated by local financial resources. This disparity is the very cause of the savings gap, resulting from low income engendered low savings on the one hand and high investment aspirations on the other. Second, in the long run the short-term inflow of external funds will enable developing regions to absorb advanced technologies, expand exports and eventually balance their external trade gap. The second premise can be true only when the first is valid. That is, only when there is a strong urge to invest and acquire wealth, and enough funds in circulation to that end, can a development strategy aimed at balancing external trade accounts through export expansion or import substitution be a possibility.

Poverty and the shortage of funds are not always the same thing. In areas such as Jiangsu and Zhejiang Provinces where the quality of human resources is higher, the demand for funds engendered by the high rate of investment may create a visible gap which cannot be filled by local savings. Total bank lending in these regions has often been greater than the sum of deposits, leaving much of the demand for investment funds unsatisfied – and usury has flourished. In an environment where the money market is already active, funds invested by or borrowed from external sources for purchasing advanced equipment soon mix with local funds, accelerate the flow of money, expand the scale of investment and strengthen the economy. In regions where the quality of human resources is lower, however, 'economic man' in a natural economy seeks means of acquiring wealth without using money as the medium of exchange. In this kind of situation, where there is no rapid change in the natural economy mode of production, even if investment is on a massive scale local and external funds remain completely separate. This is the fundamental reason why the 'savings gap' concept in the two-gap model has been transformed into a 'savings surplus', in which finances are inadequate while the banks are overloaded with idle money.

Of course, it would be absurd to say that the backward regions have no need of central government subsidies. Our purpose in focusing on the 'surplus savings' in these regions is to try to show that the hypothetical 'economic man' of modern economics, cornerstone of the two-gap theory, is a mythical figure. All we have is 'natural man' who has little motivation to make financial investments, and thus the 'economic development' created by the injection of external funds quite separate from the local monetary flow is but a mirage in the desert of the natural economy.

External Funds for External Goods

The per capita value of industrial and agricultural output in Tibet in 1983 was 364 yuan, while the per capita subsidies from Beijing in the same year amounted to 357 yuan or 98 per cent of the value generated locally. Such huge subsidies are indeed extraordinary anywhere in the world. Because of the complex method of calculation, it would be wrong to conclude that the seven yuan remaining when subsidies are subtracted from the total value is all that a local inhabitant has created. But it is correct to say that in Tibet the realisation of this output figure is largely the result of central government subsidies. Table 4.2 shows the breakdown over the past decades.

Table 4.2 Central government subsidies as a percentage of GVIAO in Tibet 1950s–1980s

1950s	30.55
1960s	45.49
1970s	80.46
1980s	97.07

(GVIAO = 100 per cent)

The authors performed a correlation and regression analysis on data from 1957 to 1983 to show the coefficient between the total value of output and financial subsidies. The indicator was found to be 0.9728 and the rate of inclination 1.2368. That is, for every yuan increase in the value of output, the corresponding increase in subsidies was 1.24 yuan.

The lion's share of the money provided by the central government has been used to pay for goods purchased from the rest of the country (see Figures 4.4 and 4.5).

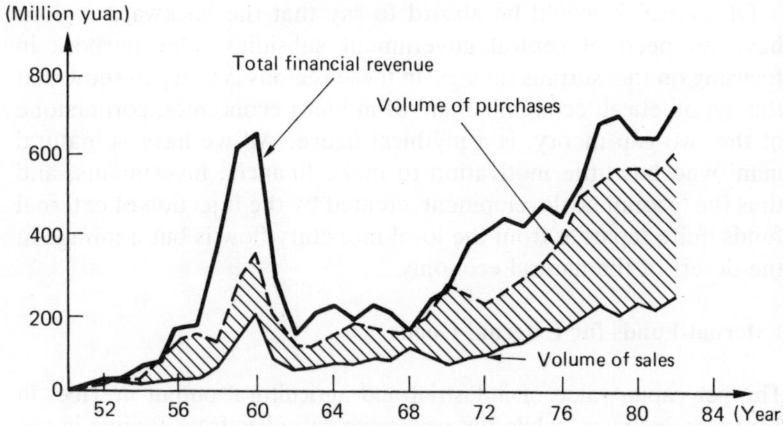

Figure 4.4 Total volume of purchases from and sales to other regions by Qinghai commercial department and the province's total financial revenue 1952–84

The shaded part in the graph represents Qinghai's trade deficit with the rest of China. Since 80 per cent of the province's financial revenue consists of subsidies from Beijing, there is no alternative but to offset the recurrent yearly deficit against these subsidies. In the three year period 1980 to 1982 the trade deficit grew to a sizeable 65.29 per cent of the total income including subsidies. As subsidies made up 82.73 per cent of the total budget, this means that more than half was going towards balancing the 'external trade gap'.

Tibet's financial revenue from local sources has long shown a deficit, and as Figure 4.5 clearly shows expenditure has been virtually dependent on central government subsidies. The graph tells us at least two things. First, in backward regions where the economy is more developed in terms of GVIAO the trade deficit tends to be greater. In other words, this so-called development is largely achieved at the expense of the trade balance. The coefficient of the trade deficit and Tibet's total output value for 1959 to 1983 is as high as 0.9157. In fact, this trade deficit has become a major feature of the development of China's backward regions. Far from losing momentum, this trend is actually growing. Between 1959 and 1983 the annual rate of increase in GVIAO in Qinghai was 6.68 per cent, while the trade deficit grew at an average 14.58 per cent per annum. The corresponding figures for Tibet were 5.45 per cent and 10.60 per cent respectively. This means that for every percentage point in-

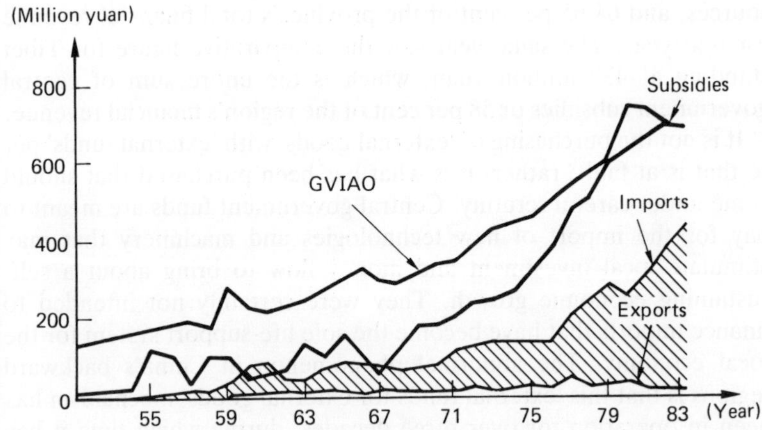

Figure 4.5 Tibet's regional trade deficit and central government subsidies and total value of output 1955–83

Table 4.3 Trade deficit in Tibet as a percentage of GVIAO 1950s–1980s

1950s	19.00
1960s	26.00
1970s	33.00
1980s	56.00

(GVIAO = 100 per cent)

crease in the value of output the trade deficit grew by 1.94 per cent.

Second, given the situation that financial revenues of backward regions are almost entirely composed of central government subsidies, any trade imbalance resulting from economic development would perforce be compensated for by these subsidies. And vice versa, it is the availability of increasing subsidies that has enabled such trade deficits to flourish, which in turn has made development possible in backward regions. As our analysis shows, there is a positive correlation of 0.9424 between central government subsidies and the trade deficit. Between 1959 and 1982 subsidies disbursed to fill the gap in 'national revenue and expenditure' created by Tibet's 'external trade gap' amounted to 340 million yuan, the entire sum of subsidies for this period or half of the region's total financial revenue. In 1983 the trade gap in Qinghai Province stood at 451.68 million yuan, equivalent to 288.85 per cent of financial revenue from local sources, and 64.65 per cent of the province's total financial revenue for that year. The same year saw the comparative figure for Tibet standing at 430 million yuan, which is the entire sum of central government subsidies or 58 per cent of the region's financial revenue.

It is not the purchasing of 'external goods' with 'external funds' per se that is at fault; rather, it is what has been purchased that should come under careful scrutiny. Central government funds are meant to pay for the import of new technologies and machinery that may stimulate local investment and money flow to bring about a self-sustaining economic growth. They were certainly not intended to finance imports that have become the sole life-support system for the local economy. The abnormal phenomenon in China's backward regions is that this 'external funds for external goods' mechanism has been in operation for over three decades, during which time it has become all but indispensable.

In the 28 years between 1955 and 1983, 82 per cent of the merchandise sold in Tibet was imported. In 1983 alone the figure was 94.12 per cent. As imports are financed by subsidies, the local economy obviously supplies almost nothing for exchange with the rest of China or for local markets. The unhappy situation, then, is that any cut in subsidies would mean fewer imports and a reduction in total volume of sales in Tibet, resulting in a slowdown in growth and market vitality. Total suspension of these subsidies would mean no imports and no merchandise to sell in the markets, and the whole economy would collapse.

The 'external funds for external goods' mechanism has resulted in the loss of the ability to sustain itself on the part of the backward economy. Reliant on external funds and merchandise, it has become an economy that survives on blood transfusions.

The Profit Feedback Loop

In China's backward regions there is an obvious asymmetry between the 'savings surplus' and 'external trade gap', yet there is a high correspondence between financial deficits and the trade imbalance. While local authorities are hard pressed for funds, local banks are awash with deposits and no-one to lend them to. Why is this?

Spending external funds on goods from outside has brought in cars, sealed roads, big machinery, thermos flasks, etc, which have been eye-openers to the local inhabitants. The positive impact of these novel items on the historical development of local society cannot be

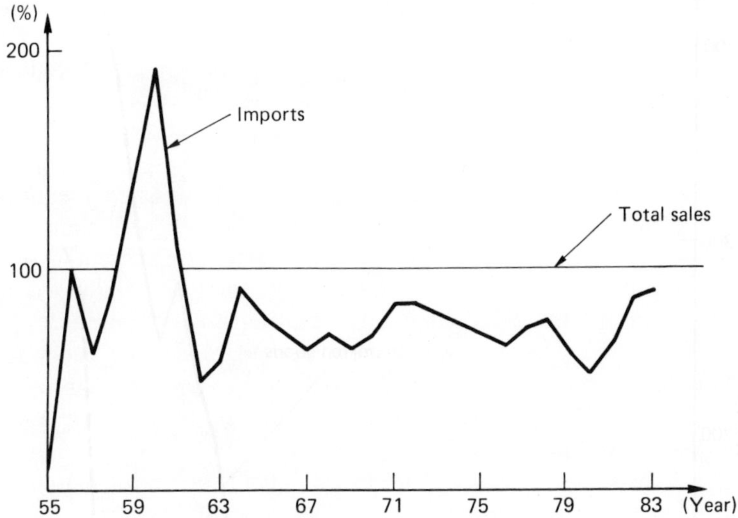

Figure 4.6 State commercial sector 'imports' as a percentage of total sales in the region 1955–83

assessed in monetary terms, but it is precisely because of these imports that such huge unprecedented deficits have occurred, for they have been introduced before the social foundation is ready to absorb them and, worse still, while the egalitarian ideal of the 'one big pot' system still pervades economic life in these regions. In the face of deficit expansion in line with the increase in subsidies from the central government, if the local 'savings surplus' is used to make up the deficits, whether it be directed towards investment or towards balancing the 'trade gap', it will disappear without trace into the 'black hole' of business losses.

Data for the 32 years between 1952 and 1985 show a correlation coefficient of 0.6010 between business losses and capital construction financed by central government subsidies. Every extra yuan put into such construction resulted in increased business losses of 0.45 yuan.

Elsewhere in China investors generally make a profit; investors in Tibet suffer losses. It is little wonder, then, that local funds provide no help for local public finance, but compete for more lucrative investments outside the region.

In analysing the structure of exports in underdeveloped countries, the Western development economist Singer follows Prebisch in applying the concept of 'terms of trade' to explain the outflow of profits

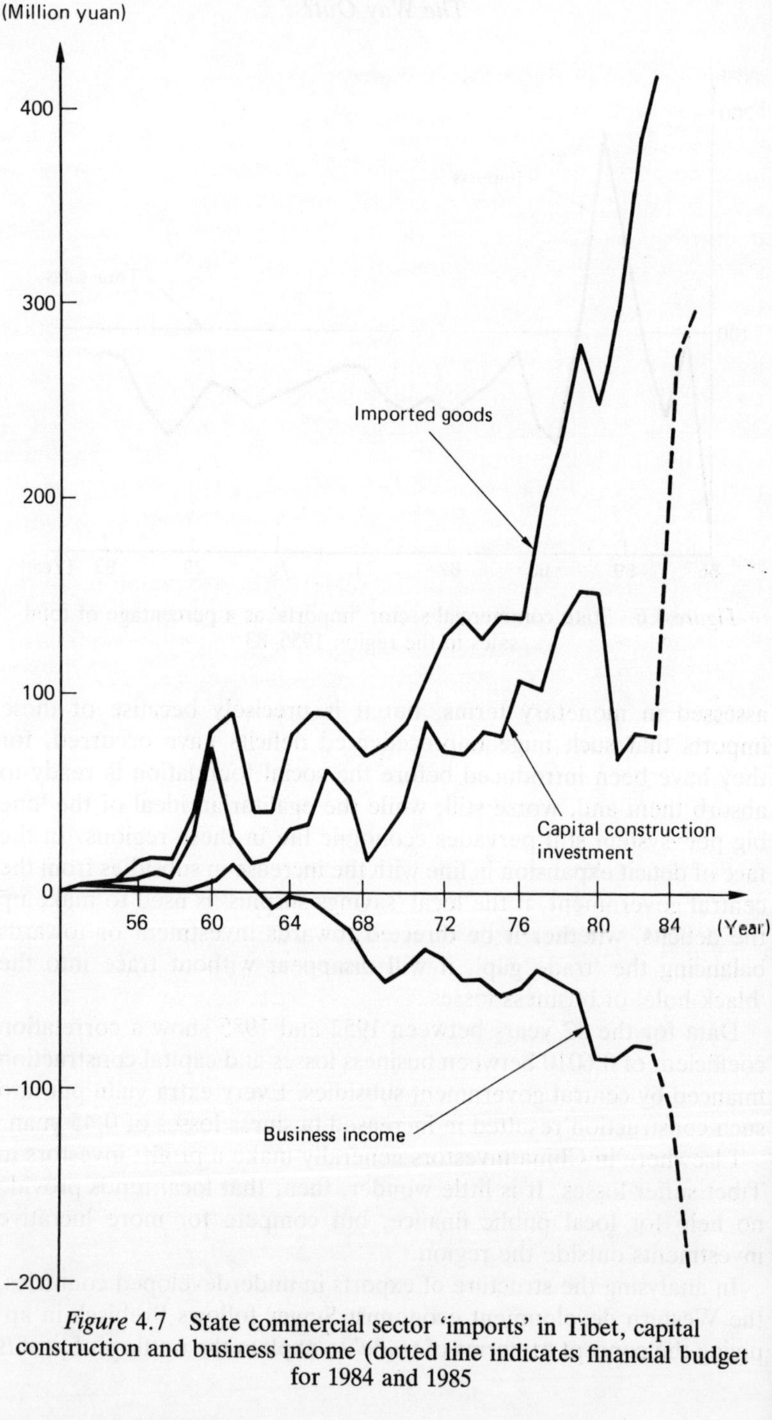

Figure 4.7 State commercial sector 'imports' in Tibet, capital construction and business income (dotted line indicates financial budget for 1984 and 1985

and purchasing power through the export of primary products, whose long-term price movements are downward, and the import of manufactures that display stable or rising price trends. While cheap raw materials help the developed countries to maintain a slowly rising level of wages and living standards, the developing countries are doomed to backwardness characterised by a fixed low level of income, especially when foreign investments in these countries are directed towards producing cheap raw materials or developing markets for goods from developed countries. Such investments contribute little to the local economy, and in fact work to its detriment by causing the outflow of profits and purchasing power.

The relations between the developing and developed areas within China are not as complicated since they are subject to the jurisdiction of the financial authorities' unified command. However, using the above analysis and tracing the flow of funds, we can detect a covert compensation mechanism, a 'profit feedback loop' from the developing to the developed areas, at the same time as the central government is taking from the rich regions to assist the poorer areas.

To simplify the issue we may assume that all financial aid given to backward regions is sourced from the developed areas' contribution to the national treasury. Again, we assume that all goods imported into backward regions originate in the developed areas. Then we can clearly see this 'profit feedback loop' that serves to offset the effect of central government subsidies.

There are four stages in the flow of funds:

1. Central government subsidies flow into backward regions where demand for investment, rather than supply of funds, is lacking.
2. These subsidies assist in capital construction or in setting up

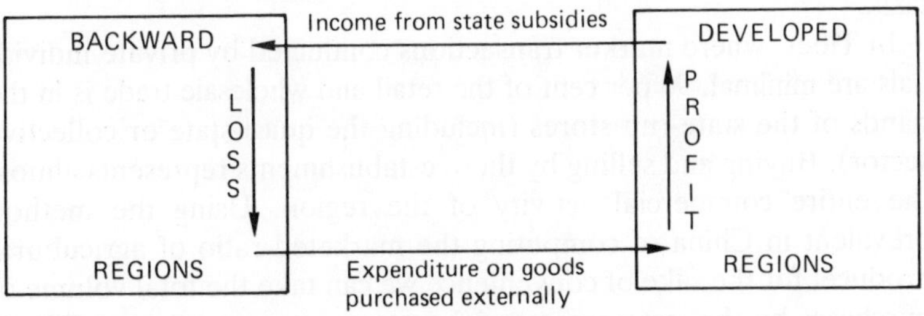

Figure 4.8 The profit feedback loop

industries that produce no 'exports' but instead sustain business losses.
3. In the process, the subsidies are used to pay for goods purchased from the developed areas, hence the backflow.
4. Part of the profits thus generated in the developed areas is remitted to the national treasury, from which money is appropriated as subsidies for the backward areas to form a new cycle in the flow of funds.

The wish to take from the rich to give to the poor has resulted in the 'profit feedback loop' mechanism through which the rich get richer and the poor get poorer, just as it says in St Matthew's gospel. The more the national treasury takes from the developed areas, the more it can give to the backward areas; the stronger the purchasing power of the backward areas, the greater the profits for the developed areas, and the more the national treasury can take from them to give away again. In this way, external funds serve as the original driving force behind the backwardness of backward areas. In the parlance of development economics on international trade, this would be the more funds that are transferred to underdeveloped countries, whether as loans or grants-in-aid, the greater the purchasing power generated and the greater the market share for the developed countries.

Is it feasible for a backward area to simply rely heavily on external funds? More external aid is not the answer to breaking the cycle of profit feedback and turning aid into genuine aid. The proper alternative is to try every method possible to eliminate the business losses caused not by local investments but by the inflow of external funds, make the inflow of funds correspond with local investment demand, and incorporate financial aid from the national treasury with the local savings surplus. To achieve these three objectives will be no easy task.

In Tibet, where market transactions conducted by private individuals are minimal, 90 per cent of the retail and wholesale trade is in the hands of the state-run stores (including the quasi-state or collective sector). Buying and selling by these establishments represents almost the entire commercial activity of the region. Using the method prevalent in China of computing the marketed ratio of agricultural produce, for the sake of convenience we can take the total volume of purchases by the state commercial sector as a proportion of Tibet's GVIAO and call this the composite commodity rate in the region's

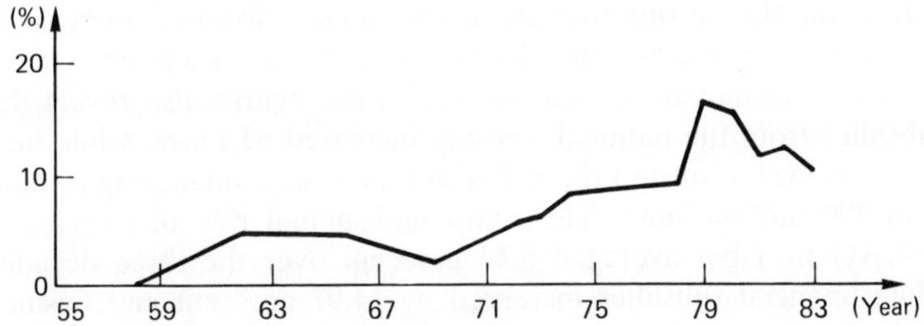

Figure 4.9 Total volume of purchases by the state commercial sector as a percentage of Tibet's GVIAO

economy as a whole. This indicator, which includes compulsory government purchases, averaged only 6.32 per cent over the 26 years from 1958 to 1983 (see Figure 4.9). The highest record for a single year was around 16 per cent. With the lifting of compulsory purchases in 1983, such was the strength of the natural economy initiative that the ratio of marketed produce fell to 9.97 per cent of GVIAO.

All in all, Tibet's GVIAO has increased fourfold in the past 31 years while the composite commodity rate has grown by less than 8 per cent. The lion's share of Tibetan products still do not enter the market, and the goods that do make it are exchanged only at the cost of vastly disproportionate investment. The rationale for the inflow of funds from the national treasury and goods from outside is that these have a favourable impact on the development of the Tibetan economy. But in terms of returns for input the figures are startling. For every yuan's worth of goods procured by the central government agency for the state commercial sector in Tibet, the average subsidies have been in the order of 8.34 yuan since 1959.

Funds and goods provided by the central government for backward regions in the course of more than three decades have not resulted in local productive capacity with which to develop the local economy. Of course no-one can deny that central government investment has brought tangible achievements such as the sealed roads, high rises, motor vehicles, factory chimneys and so on that have changed the face of backward regions. What needs to be stressed is that behind this picture of prosperity lie business losses which have been growing with each passing year, massive investment in the form of ever-increasing subsidies from the national treasury and a situation in which one-third of the inhabitants of backward regions still live in dire poverty.

It is on the record that there has been a fourfold increase in GVIAO in Tibet in the last 31 years. In itself this is a great achievement that cannot be erased. However, the figures also reveal that subsidies from the national treasury increased 65 times, while business earnings went into the red with total losses amounting to more than 700 million yuan. The compound annual rate of increase of GVIAO in Tibet averaged 5.45 per cent over the three decades, while financial subsidies increased by 14.97 per cent and business losses grew by 12.77 per cent. Put under correlation and regression analysis, these facts are even more startling. Taking 1980 as the base year, the rise in business losses and financial subsidies corresponding to the increase in GVIAO in subsequent years are as follows. When GVIAO has doubled, business losses will reach 178.99 million yuan and subsidies will climb to 1262.13 million yuan. When GVIAO has risen by 200 per cent to 2416 million yuan, business losses will increase to 371.38 million yuan and subsidies will, at 2756.16 million yuan, be 14 per cent greater than GVIAO! Thus subsidies are growing faster than total value of output in monetary terms. This is the situation in just one region, Tibet, which is of course the most representative. But what if Xinjiang, Qinghai, Inner Mongolia and Yunnan all join in 'doubling' their total value of output in the same manner?

This kind of simple extrapolation is not unjustified. If present practice continues and subsidies allocated to Tibet remain as high as those indicated above, it will nevertheless still be difficult to attain the target of doubling Tibet's GVIAO, and it is also quite likely that there will be diminishing marginal returns on subsidies. With more subsidies people will be less enterprising. In rural areas of China this phenomenon is most obvious and it has been corroborated by surveys. In one we conducted on entrepreneurial spirit among the rural inhabitants of Ji'an, Jiangxi Province, we found that *among the factors having a major impact on the entrepreneurial spirit, state aid was the next only to the line of trade*, with a negative correlation of 0.198. In terms of distribution, in areas receiving more state aid the rural population displays less entrepreneurial spirit. Precisely in this respect, by giving money the central authorities do an actual disservice to economic development in backward regions.

Unfortunately, comprehensive surveys of this type are still not available for backward regions, but if the data already collected from elsewhere is generally pertinent to the rural population which makes up the great majority of the inhabitants of backward regions, then the increasing adverse effect of subsidies on them will eventually be reflected in the region's GVIAO as the rate of increase in agricultural output falls. That apart, such subsidies affect the quality of human resources among the rural population, and it is not hard to infer what sort of industrial workers they will make when they move into the cities to work. Even if we disregard business losses, it is doubtful whether total output can be doubled by subsidies alone.

Modernisation takes money, but money alone cannot do the job. So long as the natural economy stays as it is, no amount of transferred funds can achieve the intended purpose. Any attempt to 'buy' modernisation can only have the opposite result, as the resulting 'development' would only be a mirage. The truth of the matter is that subsidies from the national treasury bring about business losses in backward regions. Bigger subsidies mean greater business losses, and as the share of the market open to goods from developed parts of China increases, more and more profits are fed back to the richer areas. It is a vicious circle: the greater the blood transfusion, the worse the anaemia.

4.2 INFRASTRUCTURE FIRST?

One intrinsic determinant of backward regions is the poor quality of human resources. The weak social infrastructure acts as a limiting factor in this respect. In order for the backward regions to shake off poverty and raise the quality of human resources, the greatest efforts must be directed towards the development of transport and communications, science, education, culture and public healthcare.

This view, arrived at so easily and yet absolutely correct, informs Western development economists' basic understanding of economic development in backward regions, and is also reflected in the general opinion of outsiders who have made one or two trips to see what life is like in these regions.

But over the last three decades or so, despite interference from leftist policies, the biggest items of local governmental expenditure in these regions have always been precisely the development of science, education, culture and public healthcare. In fact, impressive progress has been made in this respect. Yet in comparison with the rest of China, far from closing, the gap is actually widening. One obvious and serious problem is inadequate funding.

Let us take Guizhou Province as an example. Between 1949 and

1983 the provincial government spent 167 million yuan on road construction, and built or repaired 26 000 km of highway. The average cost per kilometre was less than 6500 yuan, which implies that these are low-grade roads. The entire financial appropriation for capital construction in the transportation sector between 1950 and 1983 was a mere 500 million yuan, a sum equivalent to the investment for one large factory or mining project under the jurisdiction of the central authorities. In one year (1982) the province had only 3 million yuan to spend on capital construction for transportation, when a Grade 2 highway would cost over 1 million yuan per kilometre. This amount was insufficient for a single prefecture in the province. Anshun prefecture, considered to have a fairly good transportation system, needed 10 million yuan for new highways, plus a few extra million yuan to improve existing roads – and this was for highways alone.

Over 20 000 kilometres of highway in the province as a whole are in need of rebuilding, and even if annual highway improvement allocations were pooled and directed strictly towards this item alone, it would take 100 years' worth of funds to complete the job. On top of this, road maintenance adds to the burden. Of Anshun's 1700 kilometres of highway, 400 kilometres fall outside the maintenance plan, whether washed out or deeply rutted, because they are of such a low standard. Over half of the 800 000 yuan subsidy provided by the province for the maintenance of the remaining 1316 kilometres of highway goes on wages for the 600-strong workforce alone. With the maintenance allocation remaining so low, vast amounts of manpower, funds and materials are wasted in eventually rebuilding roads. It also leads to the shortening of their serviceable lives and severely affects road use.

The same story of inadequate funding applies to communications. In 1983 1896 kilometres of county, district and commune telephone lines were down in Anshun prefecture. The prefectural post office had funds of only 100 000 yuan a year for relaying cables, and 70 000 yuan for major repairs. This entire fixed assets depreciation fund was scarcely adequate to relay 50 kilometres of telephone cable – that is, an average of only 5 kilometres per county or town. At this rate it would take 38 years to finish the job, and who is to say how many more lines would need to be replaced over this period.

For radio and television facilities the appropriation in the province for 1982 was 15.19 million yuan, or 1.7 per cent of the national total, and the smallest budget of all the provinces but one. Of this sum, 2.09 million yuan was allocated to capital construction (1 per cent of the national total), of which the provincial broadcasting authorities had only 700 000 yuan a year at their disposal. One television relay station covering a dozen or so counties is costed at 3 million yuan, but due to topographical factors, relay stations in Guizhou have to be sited at greater altitudes than normal in order to achieve the national standard broadcast coverage rate of 95 per cent, and so costs are doubled. The critical shortage of funds also cancels out any attempts to build new relay stations as there are no funds for their upkeep. A 1000 kilowatt relay station costs 70 000 to 80 000 yuan a year to run, and the provincial broadcasting authorities can only afford to run a dozen or so of the province's 270 relay stations, thus providing less power, a restricted broadcast coverage, reduced quality and inadequate maintenance. Some of the smaller relay stations have been closed down. Wired broadcasting is in even greater difficulties. Of the province's previous total of over 200 000 kilometres of wired broadcast cables, only 4.5 per cent was left in 1982. In 1973 to 1974 there were over 2.2 million loudspeaker systems; now only 14.1 per cent remain. The reason, naturally enough, is the lack of cash for maintenance, as funds in county-level broadcasting units only suffice to pay wages.

The same financial problems prevail in other departments such as education, science and technology and culture. The capital construction outlay for the education sector has come close to the national average, but the long years of past neglect have allowed debts to accrue, so that the money now available is not nearly enough to meet the demand. Funds for running schools are also massively inadequate with a per capita figure of 8.07 yuan for the province as a whole in 1982, equivalent to 70.1 per cent of the national average. In the same year per capita expenditure on cultural undertakings was 0.05 yuan, enough just to buy an ice lolly or a copy of the newspaper.

In actual fact, however, the problem of funding is only a minor surface obstacle in the development of the infrastructure. At a deeper level the real problem, as in any development programme, is *who* is going to do the developing? Viewing the matter from this angle, the biggest inhibiting factor in accelerating the rate of development of the infrastructure is still the low quality of human resources.

Education is at the top of the priority list for all advocates of the 'infrastructure first' strategy. Education is indispensible to human development, and as a priority development sector well deserving of having money spent on it. But can we see it as the panacea for the problems confronting these backward regions? In other words, can our understanding of backward regions stop here? We still need to exercise discretion.

In Guizhou Province the intellectual standard of school teachers as a whole is stunningly inadequate. Measured in terms of formal educational level, in comparison with the national average primary school teachers comprise 19 per cent fewer graduates of polytechnic secondary or senior middle schools. Middle school teachers, on the other hand, surpass the national levels of 84 per cent of junior middle school teachers having a college or polytechnic institute education and 34 per cent of senior middle school teachers having a university degree. The teaching body presents a rosy picture until these qualifications are found to be at odds with ability. This has been borne out by examinations in subject material held by the provincial authorities in October 1978 for 55.1 per cent of junior middle school and 78.9 per cent of primary school teachers.[3] All the examination questions were based on the textbooks in use and each teacher took one test in his or her subject. In the case of those teaching two subjects, the teacher could choose which to be examined in . The pass mark was set at 80.

Despite the low pass mark and even after three months of retraining, a shockingly small percentage of teachers passed. Table 4.4 gives a sample of the results of these examinations.

Anshun prefecture consists of 11 counties and towns, and altogether more than 200 000 yuan was spent in three months retraining in order to achieve better results in the examinations. Over 30 000 yuan was spent in Guanling county alone, where teachers were sent to the county town for a refresher course. Despite this, only 2.7 per cent of primary school teachers passed. Education and culture are quite advanced in Qingzhen county, but when it came to the test just 7 per cent of primary school teachers and 12.6 per cent of

Table 4.4 Results of subject material examinations held for teachers in Guizhou

		1983
Subjects	*Pass rate (%)*	
	Province	*Anshun*
Chinese (primary)	15.0	16.8
Mathematics (primary)	7.0	9.2
Chinese (junior middle)	22.9	31.7
Mathematics (junior middle)	14.2	23.9
Physics (junior middle)	29.0	31.7
Chemistry (junior middle)	38.4	31.7

junior middle school teachers made the grade. Only after retraining did the figures rise to 38.7 and 33.6 per cent respectively.

The results in individual counties were even more disastrous. The percentage of primary school teachers who passed was 4.3 per cent in Ziyun county, 2.7 per cent in Guanling county and only 0.3 per cent in Zhenning county, indicating that out of a thousand teachers only three had an adequate understanding of what they were teaching.

A look at the examination results makes it clear just what 'the poor quality of human resources' means. Not a single university graduate teaching primary level arithmetic passed, while among those teaching junior middle school mathematics someone scored just 6 per cent. Nearly 90 per cent failed among teachers of primary level Chinese and mathematics with a college or polytechnic institute education, and the lowest mark was only 9 per cent. The same failure rate applied to primary school teachers with a polytechnic secondary or senior middle school background, and in the mathematics exam several candidates from different counties actually scored zero. Even in the Chinese test there were scores of 4 per cent: just how many Chinese characters could such a candidate know? If this is the general level of the teaching body, then the 10 to 20 per cent graduation rate for school students is understandable.

Aside from junior middle school chemistry, higher marks were achieved in Anshun prefecture when compared with the province as a whole. Table 4.5 shows the results for Anshun prefecture; from it the results for Guizhou as a whole can be well imagined.

If qualified people were available and the problem was merely one of funds, infrastructural development would be a thousand times easier. But if money could in fact compensate for the poor quality of human resources, how much would it take to build up an adequate infrastructure?

Other sectors have not fared any better in comparison with education. Take, for instance, industrial development in Tibet. According to data made available by the Tibet Construction Bank, between 1965 and 1968 the hinterland crash programme focusing on the defence industry invested 72.37 million yuan, and ended up with a total loss in three years of 23 million yuan on account of inferior products that had to be written off. In the 1970s ill-conceived projects in Lhasa and Chamdo all fell flat. Fifteen million yuan of investment in glass, fertiliser, etc manufacturing went to waste. The Xiangyang Colliery, built at a cost of 4.78 million yuan, yielded no coal at all and the miners there had to rely on cow dung for fuel. The three million

Table 4.5 Results of subject material examinations in Anshun prefecture

Subjects \ Teachers	*University graduates*			*College and polytechnic institute graduates*			*Polytechnic secondary and senior middle school graduates*		
	No. of Candidates	*Fail Rate*	*Lowest Mark*	*No. of Candidates*	*Fail Rate*	*Lowest Mark*	*No. of Candidates*	*Fail Rate*	*Lowest Mark*
Chinese (primary)		66.7	42		86.0	17.5		90.2	4
Mathematics (primary)	4	100.0	20		89.7	9	2040	90.2	0
Chinese (junior middle)	43	44.2	51	177	44.1	28.5	608	76.2	17
Mathematics (junior middle)	57	40.4	6	210	48.1	16	664	87.2	1
Physics (junior middle)	31	45.2	32	142	44.4	14	216	86.6	12
Chemistry (junior middle)	22	27.8	51.3	89	24.7	46.5	211	81.5	12.75

yuan invested in the construction of the Jinhe Power Station in the Chamdo area was a total waste, as was the 23.48 million yuan spent on building the Medog road, abandoned in 1983. As for the projects in Tibet which were completed, the cost of each was so high as to be inconceivable in the more developed areas of China. For example the Tanghe Power Station, with a generating capacity of 6400 kilowatts, was completed over a span of nine years and seven months at a cost per kilowatt of 4646 yuan. The tiny 2600 kilowatt Xiandou Power Station was built at a cost of 10 761 yuan per kilowatt, four to five times higher than the national average. It shared the record as the most expensive project with the Lhasa Refrigeration Company which has unit costs of 4163 yuan.

The above are all cases of tangible loss. Much waste is not. In 1982 the highway authorities in Tibet exaggerated their engineering costs and obtained 1.01 million yuan from the national treasury at one stroke. In 1981 the Shigatse education office appropriated a sum of half a million yuan for the repair of school furniture. Two years later government auditors discovered by chance from the 37.16 yuan balance that the original half a million had not even been entered in the books but had disappeared. How all that money was spent, and by whom, still remains a mystery. And how much of the central government subsidies has been squandered in this manner is anybody's guess. Official statistics are unable to shed light on this.

Standing back from the situation this seems a waste of money. High costs make it difficult to complete anything and even once things have been set up they are just as problematic. In the past thirty-odd years 816 small hydroelectric power stations have been built in Tibet. Today 23.3 per cent have been scrapped and 15.7 per cent are malfunctioning – 39 per cent altogether. In the Shigatse area 175 small power stations were set up and already 40 per cent of them are out of commission.

As a principle, the idea of 'infrastructure first' is and always will be a truism. But as implemented in Tibet, what has gone awry? Is it the lack of subsidies or the misdirection of funds? There is no denying that the policy shifts of the central government have at various times and to varying degrees affected the sustained efforts to develop the region's infrastructure. Assuming that things had been different, and assuming too that funds had been concentrated on infrastructure projects at the expense of urban development, manufacturing industries, etc, or that more funds had been obtained from outside, would then the problems of backwardness in these regions have been eliminated once and for all? Things are obviously not that simple. We are faced with a set of interconnected cause and effect factors, namely that underdeveloped infrastructure constrains the upgrading of human quality, which in turn is the root cause of the inability to speed up the slow development of the infrastructure.

What, then, is the answer? Throughout the past thirty years or so the authorities have been cudgelling their brains on how much money to give and in which sectors to invest. On the latter question almost all the possibilities have been tried. The process of gaining experience has been a costly one. In spite of all the money and all the trying, all these 'hardware' experiments have ended in failure on account of the 'software' barrier of the quality of human resources. Given the 'blood transfusion' situation, it makes no difference whether we set up industry, aid agriculture and animal husbandry, or develop the infrastructure first. This dead-end reality has forced us to rise above the two-dimensional plane of giving and spending money, and ascend to a new dimension to look for a way out in the realm of 'software' – reshaping social relations by readjusting the socioeconomic structure.[4]

4.3 STRUCTURE OF TARGETS

The failure of both strategies of 'blood transfusion' and 'infrastructure first' has given rise to the need to reassess the structure of targets for systematic economic growth in China's backward regions.

Economic growth means the growth of social wealth, especially social material wealth. Expressed in statistical form, this is the most readily accepted economic growth target. People work to improve their living conditions, to attain a higher standard of living and to get rich. There is no room for argument on this point. Yet in the same way that entrepreneurial spirit can take two different directions, in social terms there is a difference between personal wealth that is market oriented and wealth in the natural economy where self-sufficiency prevails.

A case in point is Madoi country in Qinghai Province, which was one of the richest counties in the whole of China with a per capita income of 475 yuan in 1981. The county has virtually no industry and its economy is dominated by animal husbandry. In 1981 livestock (mainly sheep and cattle) totalled 670 000 head, an average of 110 per person. Public accumulation came to 11.44 million yuan. However, education remained so neglected in the county that there were only two primary schools and one junior middle school. The way of life and mode of production among the people showed little change from the remote past.[5]

Another example is provided by a bona fide wealthy man from Gangca county, also in Qinghai Province, who owned some 30 horses, more than 100 head of cattle and flocks of over 300 sheep worth around 40 000 yuan altogether. This made him considerably better off than the average peasant farmer elsewhere in China, even rivalling the newly rich 'super ten thousand yuan householders' in rural areas. Yet the man never traded his livestock and could not even afford a new pair of shoes, while all he lived on was gruel.[6]

On our field trip in Tibet we were told of a shepherd in the northern part of the region whose household butter consumption was 250 to 300 kilograms a year. This alone indicated a consumption level of 500 to 600 yuan per person in his family. Also, as we have mentioned elsewhere in this book, there were two wealthy families in the Chamdo area who spent their fortunes in competing with each other to build splendid Buddhist temples. Prosperity of this kind certainly cannot be the objective of any development programme.

In societies where the commodity economy is well established and economic growth is a self-generating process (the more developed regions in China do not fall into this category), objectives of socio-economic development may be expressed in statistical terms, such as Japan's *A Plan for the Doubling of National Income, 1960–1970*. In societies where the social fabric is far from ready to meet the conditions required for the growth of the commodity economy, indicators such as value of output, national income, profit, rate of growth, etc, carry ambiguous connotations. In backward regions impressive figures can be achieved for such indicators at the expense of ruining resources through traditional means of exploitation. From these indicators it is impossible to tell if the economy is being transformed from a natural economy to a commodity economy, or what the social implications of individual prosperity in backward regions might be.

It is understandable that the hardships of life in backward regions might lead any sympathetic and concerned person to believe that raising livestock to keep and not to sell is, after all, better than having absolutely nothing. But from the point of view of the operation of the economic mechanism, output value attained by slash-and-burn farming practices, or wealthy livestock owners consuming nothing but gruel cannot be objectives that a nation would strive for. It is not social wealth per se that constitutes the real problem in China's backward regions, but reversing the attitude of the local inhabitants towards social wealth and changing their traditional ways of exploiting natural resources.

The failure of the 'infrastructure first' strategy reveals that socioeconomic structure and the quality of human resources are more decisive as driving forces in the growth of social systems. In other words, progress in a socioeconomic system is determined by the success of its restructuring and the upgrading of human resources, and the essence of this socioeconomic restructuring is the promotion of an all-embracing commodity economy. Given that factors already exist (including the human factor) that are potentially ready to develop a commodity economy, backward regions should thoroughly reform their economic institutions to enable these latent factors and combinations of them to engage in commodity exchange of equal value. This fundamental measure is also a prerequisite for improving the quality of human resources. Therefore, working through reforms to establish *relations* of commodity exchange extending as far as possible through society is the primary task today.

Stability and order in society are of course important factors which must be taken into consideration, especially in the ethnic minority areas and border regions. Order is indispensible to social life and normal production activity, and even more so to the reform of economic institutions which touches on the vital interests of all.

Summing up the above discussion, the priority list of strategic objectives in the development of backward regions should be as follows, in order of importance:

1. Transformation of socioeconomic relations;
2. Improving the quality of human resources;
3. Growth of social prosperity;
4. Order in society.

'Building a stable is the most difficult task' if the timbers vary in standard. Our catchphrase is: rather a 300 yuan standard of living in a commodity economy than a 500 yuan standard of living in a natural economy. We must be determined not to acquire wealth through 'blood transfusions' or subsidies from central government in the futile attempt to fill up the bottomless egalitarian 'big pot'.

5 Reform

Following the Third Plenum China embarked upon a nationwide reform of the economic administrative system. In the space of a few short years China's economic life has undergone a series of fundamental transformations. In the course of this great reform backward regions have a more pressing need than other regions to carry out a fundamental reorganisation of their socioeconomic structure. Whether they will be able to grasp this historic opportunity and create advantageous conditions for the invigoration of their economies depends crucially on whether or not they grasp the opportunity to make specific choices which accord with the realities of their regions.

5.1 ENCIRCLING THE CITIES FROM THE COUNTRYSIDE?

It is well known that the revolution in China achieved victory by encircling the cities from the countryside. And it is well known that at a time when China was facing economic collapse it was the remote and backward countryside which first raised the curtain on the reform of the economic structure. The initial readjustment of socioeconomic relations in the countryside was more effective than simple investment in productive factors, more effective than the 'learn from Dazhai' movement and more effective than all the panaceas of theoretical deduction and modelling that have been tried over the last thirty years. It has released massive forces of production beyond all expectation. Experience in the rural areas has taught the Chinese people: once the problem of food and clothing is solved, rural specialised households, key households, and village and town enterprises organised in various ways advance along the commodity economy path. In all aspects of social and economic life such as systems of circulation, pricing, personnel mobility and residency administration, the cadre system etc, these elements are infiltrating and assailing the rigid traditional economic administrative structure in the cities. It appears that in China reform is following the particular path of reform in the countryside promoting reform in the cities.

Can reform in backward regions take the same road as the rest of China, through commodity stimulation provided by rural areas?

Logically it should be possible. But in practice progress will be much slower than in developed regions.

The growth of GVIO in village and town enterprises in Figure 5.1 demonstrates to some extent the potential impetus for urban reform supplied by the growth of the commodity economy following implementation of the initial reforms. Apart from Tibet, for which there are no statistics, the remaining seven backward regions in 1984 achieved the following levels of GVIO in village and town enterprises, expressed as a percentage of the figure for Jiangsu Province: Qinghai 0.38 per cent, Ningxia 1.21 per cent, Xinjiang 1.24 per cent, Inner Mongolia 2.21 per cent, Guizhou 3.16 per cent, Yunnan 3.91 per cent, and Guangxi 3.99 per cent. Given that growth of the commodity economy in rural areas in Jiangsu has had a massive impact in promoting urban reform, then what is of most concern to backward regions is how to engage the vitality of commodity economic development in the countryside. Let us take Tibet as an example in analysing the cases where there is a lack of stimulus for rural commodity economy development. When discussing the practical possibility of the rural reform promoting urban reform, we ought at least give full consideration to the following four points concerning the rural economic situation in backward regions.

1. Low commodity rate In 1983 state procurement together with non-governmental exchange among the people was optimistically estimated to be under 10 per cent (the commodity rate for animal products too was only 9 per cent or less). Given that adequate food and clothing still remain a problem, even if the entire rural economy was revitalised the best that could be expected would be for this figure of less than 10 per cent of output to respond to the market mechanism.

Moreover, in backward regions there is greater elasticity between the amount of local produce for own consumption and the amount marketed. In Tibet the herdspeople themselves consume over 90 per cent of all the butter produced in the region, and one can find countless examples of production which never reaches the market. Not only is rural sideline production sensitive to price signals, but it is also tied to 'cost of sale' and whether or not the product can be bartered for useful manufactured commodities.

Also in Tibet there are on average only 1.02 stores and 0.48 shop workers in the commercial network per 1000 population, in both cases only one-third of the national average. Every store serves an

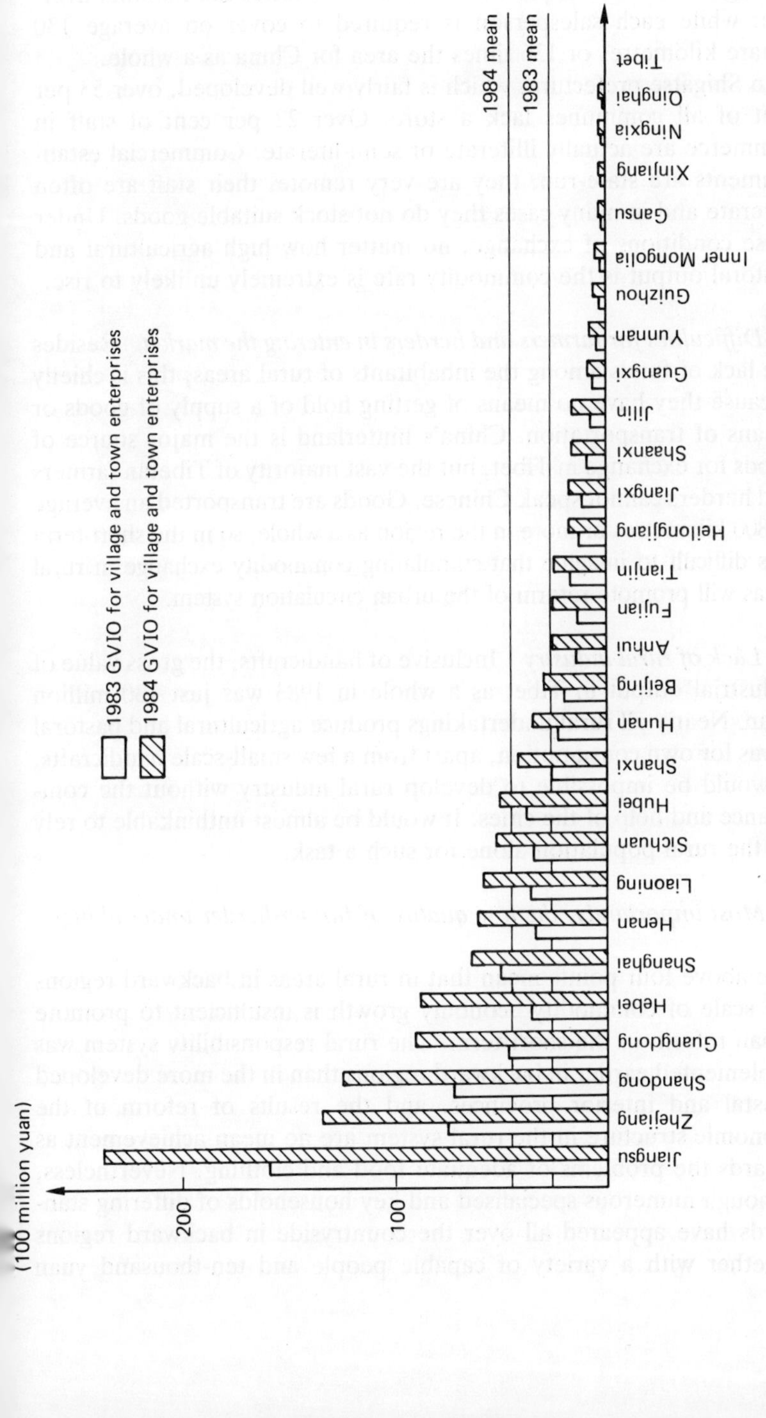

Figure 5.1 GVIO in village and town enterprises for 1983 and 1984 in all provinces, municipalities and autonomous regions

average area of 610 square kilometres, 194 times the national average, while each salesperson is required to cover on average 130 square kilometres or 136 times the area for China as a whole.

In Shigatse prefecture, which is fairly well developed, over 53 per cent of all communes lack a store. Over 22 per cent of staff in commerce are actually illiterate or semi-literate. Commercial establishments are state-run, they are very remote, their staff are often illiterate and in many cases they do not stock suitable goods. Under these conditions of exchange, no matter how high agricultural and pastoral output is the commodity rate is extremely unlikely to rise.

2. Difficulties for farmers and herders in entering the market Besides the lack of funds among the inhabitants of rural areas, this is chiefly because they have no means of getting hold of a supply of goods or means of transportation. China's hinterland is the major source of goods for exchange in Tibet, but the vast majority of Tibetan farmers and herders cannot speak Chinese. Goods are transported an average of 800 kilometres or more in the region as a whole, so in the short-term it is difficult to imagine that stimulating commodity exchange in rural areas will promote reform of the urban circulation system.

3. Lack of rural industry Inclusive of handicrafts, the gross value of industrial output in Tibet as a whole in 1983 was just 130 million yuan. Nearly all rural undertakings produce agricultural and pastoral items for own consumption, apart from a few small-scale handicrafts. It would be impossible to develop rural industry without the compliance and help of the cities. It would be almost unthinkable to rely on the rural population alone for such a task.

4. Most importantly, the low quality of farmer/herder undertakings

The above four points mean that in rural areas in backward regions the scale of commodity economy growth is insufficient to promote urban reform in the short term. The rural responsibility system was implemented earlier in backward regions than in the more developed coastal and interior provinces, and the results of reform of the economic structure in the rural system are no mean achievement as regards the problems of adequate food and clothing. Nevertheless, although numerous specialised and key households of differing standards have appeared all over the countryside in backward regions together with a variety of capable people and ten-thousand yuan households, because of the poor quality of human resources and the greater tendency towards a natural economy in their initiative to develop production on the part of rural inhabitants of backward regions in contrast with the developed areas of the interior, the situation cannot really be compared with what has been happening in Jiangsu and Zhejiang. There, rural economic reform might have started later, but solely through the policy of the household responsibility system all kinds of capable people have come to the fore throughout society, and moreover the entire macroeconomic prospect has been speedily transformed.

Logically speaking, once people in rural areas have enough to eat and wear they will want to sell their surplus production and sooner or later a commodity economy spontaneously emerges. Unfortunately, countless facts have shown that in a situation where no great change has yet occurred in the four aspects mentioned above, this is mere logical inference and wishful thinking. Just like in ancient China where at one time the natural economy developed to a high degree but did not shift to a commodity economy, without the intervention of the modern system we cannot exclude the real possibility of rural areas in backward regions remaining sunk in long-term stagnation (perhaps even prosperous stagnation) within the natural economy, even after the implementation of the household responsibility system.

The key point of transfer for intervention of the modern system is the city. The existence of a key point does not automatically lead to intervention, however, and the existence of a city does not appear to entail transfer. In Western developmental economics urban/rural relations in backward regions also present a stumbling block, a problem without solution. The 'dual structure theory' of developmental economics has been formulated precisely to deal with the sharp antithesis between the modern cities and primitive countryside. Urban/rural relations in backward regions in China are more complex than the 'dual structure' applied in a general sense to developing countries. Here, however, we cannot embark upon a comprehensive analysis of community functions in cities. Two facts have a bearing on the discussion of whether or not reform in backward regions can follow the 'countryside encircling the cities' strategy. Firstly, the existence of the 'one big pot' system of 'everybody eating out of the same big pot' in the cities not only means that cities are unable to act as the point of transfer for the import of a modern system, but also creates an 'insulating effect', thus reducing the likelihood of that modern system which has already been introduced spreading throughout society. Secondly, the 'one big pot' urban system simultaneously creates a 'plunder effect' by creaming off scarce capable personnel from rural areas, thereby forcing the countryside ever further into natural economy stagnation.

The Insulating Effect

Encircling the cities from the countryside presupposes that the interpenetration and interrelatedness of rural and urban economic development must act as a mutual stimulus. Looking at the country as a whole, it may well be natural, even if not intentional, for a large agricultural nation with a weak economic infrastructure to choose to forcibly impose measures for short-term accumulation to achieve industrialisation. Yet even in backward regions where the central authorities did not expect to obtain much accumulation for industrialisation, the 'one big pot' system from the interior was unthinkingly adopted. Because of this, any economic relations which may have existed between city and countryside have been cut for no reason.

The relative difference between rural and urban incomes in backward regions is 128 per cent of the national figure, while the relative difference in consumption between the two is equivalent to 135 per cent of the figure for China as a whole. In Tibet the relative difference in rural and urban incomes is 196 per cent of the national figure. In keeping with the hypothesis that non-agricultural inhabitants spend their entire cash wage on commodity consumption then this

Table 5.1 Income and consumption levels of urban and rural residents in backward regions

1982
yuan per person

	Incomes		*Consumption*	
Region	*Urban staff and workers*	*Rural households*	*Non-agric inhabitants*	*Agricultural inhabitants*
Qinghai	507	219	570	192
Xinjiang	968	138	461	230
Tibet			968	209
Nationwide	796	270	501	212

group, which makes up only 15 per cent of the total population, consumed roughly 65 per cent of that year's total social commodity retail sales. After deducting 'agricultural means of production for rural production teams and commune members' from the social commodity retail sales volume, the 15 per cent non-agricultural population accounted for 70 per cent of all commodity consumption.

Moreover, the overwhelming majority of commodities marketed in the region are brought in from outside. Much of the huge disparity in income distribution and commodity sales in urban and rural Tibet is due not to urban residents' earnings but to state financial imports. In saying this, we are not claiming that urban residents do not work, but rather that the work they do is of no 'benefit'. In the section on 'blood transfusion leading to anaemia' where we described enterprises going from bad to worse with massive growing deficits, the statistical data was drawn from the numerous state-run and collective enterprises staffed by the non-agricultural population. The direct deficits of the rural population frequently appear in the social relief funds: in Tibet in 1983 this was 18.53 million yuan; while the deficit of the non-agricultural population has to be paid out the state treasury: in Tibet in 1983 this came to 76.78 million yuan. In terms of this alone, 320 yuan was spent on every member of the non-agricultural population, which is 29 times the figure of 11 yuan per person among the rural population. From the account books we are aware only of that large portion of investment projects located in the non-agricultural population sector. In addition to this there is the slice taken from the state by the rural inhabitants, the actual size of which is obscured by complex factors such as price and taxation. Figure 5.2, a redrawn version of Figure 4.8, shows the result of our field investigations.

This kind of set-up is the result of the vast deficits which appear in the wake of the import of the modern system, while the reason behind the deficits is the 'one big pot' urban economic system.

Referring back to Figure 4.7, we can see that income of Tibetan enterprises between 1951 and 1961 was consistently in the black and moreover showed a massive annual average growth of 96 per cent. In 1960 it reached 15.56 million yuan. After 1961, however, enterprise income went into the red, with the deficit growing sharply at 12.77 per cent per annum with no recovery. The turning point that marked the plunge into deficit was precisely the year 1960, when Tibetan enterprises which had been primarily regulated by the market were reformed and fully integrated into the 'one big pot' system. At present GVIO in the whole of Tibet is equivalent to that of a single

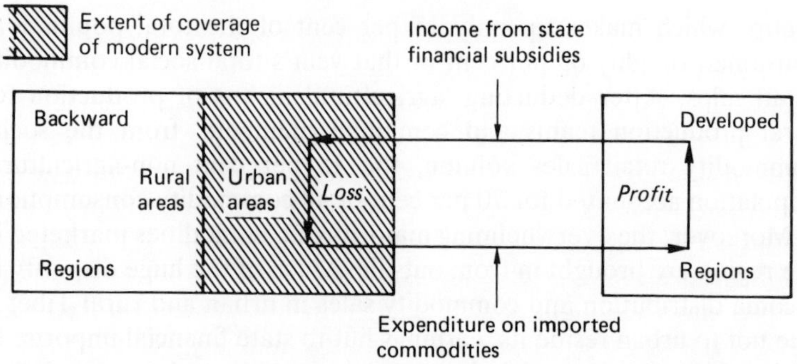

Figure 5.2 Extent of import of the modern system as shown by circulation of funds

commune in developed regions. Yet on this abnormally weak economic base has been erected a massive needlessly redundant superstructure along the lines of those in developed regions. Within this superstructure are all the institutions one expects to find in developed regions. To administer 130 million yuan's worth of GVIO and 80 million yuan's worth of construction investment there are all the appropriate departments such as the Economic Committee, the Planning Committee, the Department of Industry, the Department of Commerce, and the Construction Bank, bringing the total number of departments, offices, committees and bureaux to 62 at the level of the autonomous region alone. In contrast with the extremely weak economic base, the 'one big pot' system has brought with it a 'top-heavy' superstructure.

GVIAO in Tibet has quadrupled in the last thirty years, whereas the expenditure of this dense superstructure on administration and management costs has increased tenfold. All things considered, for every one yuan's worth of commodities bought in, there is a direct outlay of 1.33 yuan in administrative costs; every one yuan of GVIO costs 0.54 yuan in administration expenses, and for every one yuan of construction investment, the highly articulated superstructure is required to pay out 0.63 yuan in administration costs. This does not include cadre allowances and the costs of banquets and gifts paid by enterprises, communes and teams. But how effective is this administration? If we take administrative and management expenses as the input, and enterprise income as the final output of management and executive systems, we obtain a precise assessment of the economic effect of the management and executive systems in this dense superstructure. In the 1950s the final outcome of every one yuan in management and administrative costs was 0.45 yuan in enterprise profits. In the 1960s the final outcome was 0.55 yuan of enterprise loss, and from then on it steadily deteriorated. In the 1970s every one yuan of administrative outlay corresponded to enterprise losses of 1.01 yuan, while in the 1980s the 'negative effect' of administration amounted to 1.26 yuan.

Financial and material help from the central authorities is transformed into a loss in the course of administration and spending by the dense organisational structure within the superstructure. This is a classic example of the action of the 'one big pot' system in the cities of backward regions. Two short examples will suffice to illustrate this point.

Every year the petroleum company in the Tibet Autonomous Region distributes petrol vouchers, and any left over from the previous year become invalid. Once each relevant unit has paid for its petrol vouchers and taken its share, no check is made on how many are actually used. On expiry unused coupons are never returned to the company for exchange or refund. Only in 1983 was it discovered during a financial check that the petroleum company had made an extra 9.37 million yuan on this one item alone. The company had no way of turning over this sum to the higher authorities. Ever since it had been set up in 1963 the company had been lining its own pockets. This incident involved just about all units employing the non-agricultural population. Petrol is the lifeline, the bloodstream. It is first brought in by truck and then sent along a pipeline, so the distances and costs involved can be well imagined. This gives idea of how generous all units were with state funds.

With such generosity in some quarters there is bound to be stinginess in others. In 1981 Yadong imported 834 thermos flasks. When the case was opened for inspection 120 flasks were found to be in pieces. Only after investigations were made at all levels was it discovered that the thermos flasks had been damaged by the time they arrived in Lhasa. Even though they were broken, even though transportation was in such demand, nevertheless no effort was spared in sending these flasks on an additional 485 kilometres. All people cared about was that the 1142 yuan loss should not end up on their own balance sheet. The Yadong commercial bureau was not surprised. Apparently overstocked goods are frequently returned and then irrationally shipped back again. Ask the transportation departments: exactly how many instances are there of this sort of wasted effort? The answer is they are not sure, all they are concerned about is carrying more goods faster. Ask the commercial bureaux with regionally unified accounting: what precisely are their aims? The answer is they are not sure, their biggest immediate worry is the pressure on transportation.

Where and how should this 'modern system' be introduced? On the material side it was originally believed to be eminently possible that advanced equipment, technology and commodities, including information, 'imported' from developed regions could, in accordance with economic laws, penetrate the daily life and production of the people in the vast backward regions, and even promote and assist the prosperity of the rural commodity economy and the rise of rural industry. Unthought of then was the massive deficit created by the urban 'one big pot' system which cut short this possibility. The towns and cities themselves are a case of 'the greater the blood transfusion, the worse the anaemia', and are hardly able to look after themselves let alone the rural areas. All they can do is chalk themselves into circles such as the household registration system, and naturally cannot manage to introduce elsewhere the massive deficit which comes along with the 'modern system'.

The Plunder Effect

The 'one big pot' urban system in China's backward regions, which depends on 'blood tranfusions' from the state, seems to be quite unlike the 'dual structure' of the Third World model which relies primarily on directly plundering the wealth of the inhabitants of rural areas. Worse still than plundering wealth is that the highly articulated superstructure within the 'one big pot' system in urban areas has an extraordinary capacity for self-propagation, in accordance with Parkinson's Law. It is a fact that administration and management costs in Tibet have over the last thirty years risen rapidly by 8.56 per cent per annum. The expansion of this highly articulated structure has drawn to it the vast majority of capable people in backward regions. Supported by state 'transfusions' of financial aid, the brains of both rural areas and the cities to this very day are all drawn inexorably into the voracious 'black hole' of the 'one big pot' urban system.

Educational levels in Gyantse county are among the highest in Tibet. If within the population as a whole, personnel of different educational levels are thus distributed (see Table 5.2), then the

Table 5.2 Distribution of personnel of all educational levels in Gyantse County, Tibet (1983)

Educational Level	*Government departments*	*Towns and cities*	*Villages*	*Ratio of personnel in govt depts and towns/villages*
Junior middle school and above	1013	45	206	4:1
Senior middle school and above	393	3	9	33:1
College and above	92	1	1	46:1
Illiterate and semiliterate (aged 12 and over)	656	968	31 474	1:49

situation in regions where the level of education is lower can be imagined.

The gravity of the problem lies in the fact that despite the serious inequality in the distribution of talented people as shown in the table above, the needs of the highly articulated structure are still far from being met. There is a severe shortage of personnel for government departments at all levels in Tibet at present; at the county level alone over 50 per cent of positions are vacant. People with some degree of literacy and slightly above the average are being recruited into institutions within the 'one big pot' system, but even this is far from adequate. The situation displayed in the table above is such because almost anyone with any degree of literacy is employed in one of these institutions.

The possibility of intervention by the 'modern system' has been curtailed by the insulating effect of the 'one big pot' urban system, while the highly articulated superstructure continues inexhaustibly to swallow up that most scarce resource for the development of the rural commodity economy – educated people. Urban and rural areas within one socioeconomic system cannot maintain an existence isolated from one another. The salient characteristic of the 'dual structure' in China's backward regions is that the existence of the 'one big pot' urban system not only fails to foster and assist the development of the rural commodity economy, but in swallowing up what skills exist in the rural areas in backward regions it completely wipes out the last remaining possibility for rural areas in backward regions to develop a commodity economy. Despite the implementation of the rural responsibility system, despite more relaxed policies, the vast rural areas are as restricted as ever to the real possibility of natural economy stagnation. If this reality is not altered, any hope that under these conditions a rural commodity economy will be stimulated of its own accord and become the motive force for promoting urban reform in the short term is ill-founded.

5.2 URBAN REFORM AS THE INITIAL BREAKTHROUGH POINT

Economic reform in backward regions cannot take the approach of 'encircling the cities from the countryside'. On the contrary, if we do not speedily implement a thorough-going reform of the entire urban state-run system (including collectives: quasi state-run undertakings), then the continuing decline of the economy will not only become irreversible but the situation may actually deteriorate even further.

The Main Strength of a Commodity Economy

Dependent on 'transfusions' for its maintenance, the urban system in backward regions has no close ties with the local rural economy. This economic system which is incapable of running independently is much weaker than that in cities in the interior with their own productive capabilities and commodity exchange. Once the unified system of purchase and marketing in rural Tibet is deregulated, the state-run system of 'one big pot' is faced with two immediate prospects:

1. Collapse The renowned Nyingchi Textile Mill, for example, proudly realised a profit of 2.73 million yuan in 1983. But this in actual fact disguised a serious weakness. The mill now makes 20 different products only 7 of which make a profit and 4 of these are already losing popularity. If the unified purchase and marketing system for wool were to be abolished, and raw materials were bought at market prices, the mill would straightaway make a loss of close on 3 million yuan. If price controls on wood were removed and forestry was put onto the responsibility system, then this mill which burns 26 cubic metres of wood every day, this mill which has featured prominently in films and magazines presenting the new face of Tibet, would simply close down.

2. Complete dependence on external aid If grain requisition and compulsory purchases in Tibet were to be abolished, the state would have to send in grain supplies immediately and provide funds to make up the growing deficit of grain enterprises.

Neither of these two prospects looks particularly promising. But right now the urban system is intensifying its special role, which is similarly unpromising. In the sphere of rural relations the towns continue, through the highly articulated superstructure, to draw off all human resources capable of developing a commodity economy, thereby condemning the countryside to the grip of the natural economy. Thus production initiative aroused by the rural reforms has been slanted towards the natural economy, which has meant that ecological destruction resulting from primitive slash-and-burn methods of cultivation has become more and more acute, which in turn has meant that natural disasters have become more frequent and consequently the welfare relief funds channelled primarily into rural areas have shot up alarmingly at a rate of 30 per cent per annum. In the sphere of state aid relations the towns continue, through the 'one big pot' system, to transform any material conditions for the development of the commodity economy into a huge deficit. In this way, by absorbing more and more of the state's labour power, materials and finance in aid, the 'one big pot' system has increased rather than decreased the financial and material burden of state aid to backward region since the Third Plenum of the Eleventh Central Committee. What is more, with the slight relaxation of rural policies, 'transfusions' have become even more vital so that a complete withdrawal of funds would lead to the total collapse of backward regions and result in acute social repercussions.

What is most absurd is that more rather than less of the finance and materials provided by the state in aid goes not to the old, sick, weak and disabled, not to widows and orphans, not to the less able, nor yet to the poverty-stricken who have lost the ability to increase production. The most part goes to none other than the pick of the population in backward regions, the latent force for developing the commodity economy. Speaking of Tibet, there are at least four clear strengths in the commodity economy growth of the urban system which correspond to the four weaknesses of commodity economy growth in the countryside.

1. High quality of human resources Urban residents in Gyantse county may have a lower average educational level than for China as a whole, but it is 6.4 times higher than in rural parts of the county. In the towns there are 2658 people with a junior middle school education or above, which is 12.9 times higher than the figure for rural areas. Urban dwellers have a higher level of education, and are also better at absorbing new information. Influenced by their government jobs, urban residents are far more practical in their approach to religion than farmers or herders, and very rarely perform prostrations, turn prayer wheels or donate large sums of money in alms. They have some knowledge of the outside world and have a strong sense of national awareness.

2. Responsive to commodity information and price signals The average level of consumption among urban dwellers in 36 times that of the rural population. There is barely any self-sufficiency production and food, clothing, housing and transportation expenses are all met through cash exchange. Unlike the rural areas where purchases and sales are made only a few times a year, purchasing and exchange are frequent daily activities for urban residents, and so when doing business they are visibly more responsive to commodity information and price signals than their rural counterparts.

3. Modern equipment The only equipment, technology and capital capable of modern commodity production is concentrated in the urban state-run sector. The rural areas with their handful of village and town enterprises have practically none of these prerequisites.

4. Easy access to the market Generally speaking, urban dwellers speak both Tibetan and Chinese and so their possibilities for establishing contacts with other regions are incomparably better than those of the farmers and herders. This is particularly so in the case of the majority who work in state-run industrial, transportation and commercial departments for whom doing business is an easy and familiar task. Their poor performance in the 'one big pot' system does not mean that they lack the ability to make money for themselves.

This group of people and materials concentrated within the urban system are the representatives of the advanced productive forces and the major latent force for the development of the commodity economy. Yet they are trapped within sluggish 'relations of production'.

The massive investment by the state should provide a material and social basis for the development of the commodity economy in backward regions, but the 'one big pot' system has transformed this objective basis into a prime force for draining state financial and material resources. *After over thirty years of state aid, the problem in backward regions is not that there is no ability but rather that there is no mechanism for developing a commodity economy, no relations of equal value exchange between individuals, enterprises and producers-consumers.*

In the short term it is not enough to rely on relaxing rural policies alone to engender relations of commodity exchange by means of reform of the economic structure and reorganisation throughout society. The towns and cities have become the focus of all the contradictions in the economic development of backward regions. Whatever the nature of the input, it is useless to expect to skirt round that great transformer, the city. In the light of the reality that the major potential forces for developing the commodity economy are concentrated in the cities, launching a comprehensive and thorough reform of the urban state-run system and completely overhauling the internal mechanisms of this great transformer, is the master switch that will change the situation of 'the greater the blood transfusion, the worse the anaemia' and mobilise all the possibilities for developing the commodity economy throughout the backward regions. At the same time it will be a powerful lever for getting the economic systems in backward regions to make their own 'blood' (that is, develop a commodity economy).

5.3 ADVANTAGEOUS CONDITIONS FOR REFORM

Because of backwardness reform of the urban system in backward regions possesses a number of advantageous conditions by comparison with the interior or with China as a whole in the form of 'disadvantage turned to advantage'.

1. Loose connection between prices and financial administration

One obvious difficulty in overall reform of the urban system in the interior and in China as a whole is that the price system is irrational. Looking at the commodity market alone, there is no fair competition among enterprises producing different goods. What lies behind this irrational pricing is financial administration. Profits and taxes from sales of the so-called 'high price, high profit' commodities all go to the state financial administration. Of course, this is also the major source of state financial subsidies to backward regions. So the intricate links between the prices of tens of thousands of products on the one hand and state revenue and the various areas of income distribution corresponding to wages and benefits on the other pose a serious obstacle on the road to reform of the economic structure and enterprise invigoration.

In backward regions this problem is by no means prominent. Taking Tibet again as an example, the prices of rural produce have been basically freed. The relationship between the prices of agricultural produce and reform of the urban system has not become a conspicuous problem. GVIO in the entire region is just 18 per cent of GVAIO. Apart from a small number of enterprises such as the Nyingchi Textile Mill, there are no high price, high profit tobacco, alcoholic beverages, tea, textiles or light industries. Commercial departments purchase industrial goods worth only 9.5 per cent of the total value of industrial output. Most enterprises run at a loss; not only do they not turn over any profits, quite the reverse, they need to be subsidised by the state. Industrial and commercial taxes and other sundry levies alone are the main source of revenue for local finance departments.

In this situation there is a much weaker connection between the prices of industrial goods and local revenues, wages and benefits than in the developed interior or China as a whole. Admittedly, without a detailed analysis it is hard to give an accurate description of the precise impact price reform might have. Nevertheless, it is true to say that owing to weak industry and a simple industrial and product structure, it will be far easier to carry out the preliminary reform in invigorating enterprises – price reform – in backward regions than in the developed provinces of the interior or in the country as a whole, and there will be far fewer possible related adverse effects.

2. 'Unlimited supply' of manufactured goods

In applying Lewis's concept of an 'unlimited supply' of labour in backward regions to manufactured goods, our intention is merely to explain that the industrial goods market in backward regions is very limited and they have access to preferential supplies from the interior. Local market prices are determined by the prices of supplies from the interior, and this is a great advantage in that price reform can be carried out by making use of state support. Tibet relies almost completely on imports from the interior for supplies of consumer goods for daily use and construction materials. At present the central authorities give special consideration to Tibet's requirements and basically provide the region with whatever it wants. From our own observations and from information provided by trade departments, there is no shortage of commodities just about anywhere in the Tibetan market, and goods which are very scarce on the domestic market elsewhere, such as good quality bicycles and colour TVs, are basically available in Tibet. Therefore once price reform is launched, the extent and cycles of price fluctuations will be basically decided by the inventory structure of trade departments and the speed of purchasing response.

If at the same time reform of the commercial system is initiated, theoretically there should be no sustained great rise in the price of particular commodities. Furthermore, purchases are made on the basis of the prices in the interior which have been more or less stable in recent years. If transportation departments are also reformed, more goods could be brought in faster and the overall price level may well exhibit a tendency to fall. The present pricing system, by way of contrast, seriously hampers management initiative in trade and transportation departments, and the irrational structure and sluggish rate of imports instead results in fluctuating price panics.

3. *Loose planning controls*

Commodity prices are loosely supervised, with only 66 price administrators in the entire region with a population of 1.93 million. There are no departments responsible for price supervision apart from the Commodity Prices Office of the autonomous region. Out of the 74 county-level units in the region only seven have one officer each to supervise commodity prices. Financial departments in Shigatse prefecture are authorised to employ just five price supervisors, and in 19 county-level units there is not one member of staff with responsibility for prices. None of the price supervisors we met were able to give us even basic figures.

Judging by the state of affairs revealed by price checks in the autonomous region and in Shigatse prefecture, all enterprises and institutions are free to fix their own prices to some extent. The

Materials Bureau of Shigatse prefecture was selling cement at 883 yuan a ton, 182 per cent above the list price set by the state. In 1983 the supply and marketing co-operative in Gyirong county put rubber shoes on sale. The moment a queue of eager buyers began to form the co-operative raised the price by 0.5 yuan a pair. In Tingri county six out of the nine state-run enterprises (including collectives, which are quasi state enterprises) were without a bookkeeper. The county's truck team had not even kept accounts for the past few years. Exorbitant prices are commonly demanded by some processing and manufacturing enterprises, and when prices of cotton cloth and chemical fibres were readjusted throughout the country at the beginning of 1983, trade departments in Nagqu prefecture delayed the readjustment right through the middle of 1984 because they had lost their merchandise catalogue. In Shigatse prefecture as many as 22 per cent of the 1399 commercial employees were semi-literate or illiterate.

Many of the grassroots supply and marketing co-operatives have neither bookkeepers or cashiers and do not keep a running account of goods in and out, but just sell what they have. Unfamiliar items have to be sold at an 'average price', arrived at by adding the prices of the most expensive and cheapest items of the same type and dividing the result by two. There are amusing tales of beer being sold off at the price of fermented liqour, quite simply because no-one knew what it was. In fact there is uncontrolled free fluctuation in the prices of a considerable number of commodities.

There are very few grassroots units in Tibet. Many local government departments are only half staffed, and following the implementation of the responsibility system they perform almost no economic management functions other than the distribution of state funds and aid. The structure of enterprises and institutions is not strictly defined (for example, the bureau chief and deputy of the Tingri county bureau of trade are also salaried accountants at the supply and marketing co-operative and grain station respectively). Each enterprise goes about its day-to-day business without much interference from above and economic ties are loose, a far cry from the tight-knit network in the interior. The interdependent effects which would logically be produced when setting the entire structure in motion are in reality often delayed for a considerable length of time.

4. Financial and material assistance from the state

According to statistical forecasts for 1984, the central authorities subsidise enterprise losses to the tune of 230 million yuan and provide funds worth 300 million yuan for capital construction. The 'temporary altitude allowance' alone amounts to 44.04 million yuan. By slightly diverting this money there will be enough and to spare to cope with the effects of reform on the urban population which, at most, is under 280 000 strong.

Superiority in Reform

'The newest and most beautiful pictures can be drawn on a blank sheet of paper'. Reform of the economic system in backward regions not only possesses advantageous conditions which make it easy to achieve a breakthrough, but moreover in the reform of the model of the economic system there is a wider range of choices than within the developed provinces of the interior. The traditional system which exists in these developed provinces has developed a highly complex and tenacious internal mechanism in the course of over thirty years' intensive operation and has penetrated into every aspect of life to a much greater degree than the roughly regulated 'one big pot' system has done in backward regions. If we say that the operation of the 'one big pot' system in the interior has already become merged with everyday life, then in many respects the 'one big pot' system and everyday life in backward regions have no close connection. This enables reform in backward regions to largely escape interference arising from the influence of tradition on many aspects of everyday life. There is greater freedom in the choice of and experimentation with economic models than in developed regions, and also the possibility of taking them further.

5.4 THE DIRECTION OF THE BREAKTHROUGH IN REFORM: CIRCULATION

The aim of reform, first and foremost, is not prosperity, is not an increase in the value of output or a rise in national income, but is a change in the economic relations between individuals, enterprises, consumers and producers towards the relations of a commodity economy, characterised by planned distribution and equal value exchange which makes no distinction between the two parties involved. Thus, the keypoint of the reform is not primarily the immediate producer but the domain of circulation which is directly able to promote exchange. Basically, producer vitality ought to be the take-off point and foothold for reform. However, starting from present realities, imbuing production initiative in enterprises with the qualities of a natural economy or of a commodity economy is primarily determined by the presence or absence of external surroundings in which exchange of equal value can always take place. Circulation is far quicker and more wide-ranging in transmitting reform information (relations of commodity exchange) than anything an enterprise can do through material production. This is particularly so in backward regions where the great majority of goods exchanged are not produced locally. In this way, if we want to achieve as rapidly as possible the most extensive readjustment of society-wide relations of commodity exchange, we ought to give first consideration, in our opinion, to the reform of circulation departments which can link up commerce, transport and banking in the cities and the countryside.

Grain

In backward regions where agriculture and animal husbandry are most important, the problem of adequate food and clothing has still not been entirely solved. A stable supply of daily necessities, most of all grain, remains the guarantor of safe progress in the thoroughgoing reform of the urban system. One great difference with rural areas in the developed provinces of the interior is that following the implementation of the household responsibility system, although the supply of agricultural produce improved dramatically, it by no means matched the interior in creating extensive overall surpluses. Thus, formulating correct policies for managing grain is not only a prerequisite for the overall launch of the economic reforms, but at the same time is an indespensible guarantor of social stability.

There are 1.93 million people in Tibet. Ignoring the 32.57 million catties (16.285 million kilograms) of grain resold back into agricultural areas in the 1980s, for the 480 000 people in pastoral regions and 280 000 in urban areas (39.4 per cent of the total population), commodity grain requirements are stabilised at around 200 million catties (100 million kilograms), equivalent to 23 per cent of the average gross value of output over the past four years. There is not the slightest doubt that grain departments play a crucial managerial role in maintaining socioeconomic stability in Tibet.

Between 1959 and 1983 grain departments sold altogether 3500 million catties (1750 million kilograms) of commodity grain at a loss of over 300 million yuan. As more grain is sold, so more money is lost. In the 1960s grain was sold at a loss of 0.045 yuan per catty (0.09 yuan per kilogram), in the 1970s this loss rose to 0.069 yuan per catty (0.138 yuan per kilogram) and by the 1980s had reached 0.173 per catty (0.346 yuan per kilogram). So not only do the losses of the grain departments increase with the volume of business, but unit losses are also growing.

What is the solution for the grain problem? It is not so simple as opposing the slogan of 'grain self-sufficiency'. The problem Tibet faces is that if its people do not provide for themselves, then who will? There are three possibilities.

1. The central authorities provide all grain. If they provide grain then they must also provide funds. The growing losses suffered by grain reselling organs are directly related to the increased shipment of grain from the interior. Between 1959 and 1983 the amount of grain shipped into the region increased by 12 per cent every year, while enterprise deficits grew at 16 per cent. In 1983 grain was shipped from the interior at a loss of 0.28 yuan per catty (0.56 yuan per kilogram). Two hundred million catties (100 million kilograms) were brought in making a loss of 61.05 million yuan. On this one item alone losses incurred amounted to 7.8 per cent. Shipping in 300 million catties (150 million kilograms) is equivalent to throwing away 23.4 million catties of grain (11.7 million kilograms) or 11.466 million yuan; shipping in 400 million catties (200 million kilograms) is like throwing away 31.2 million catties (15.6 million kilograms) of grain, or 15.288 million yuan! Commodity grain requirements in the entire region were 290 million catties (145 million kilograms) in 1984. It was planned to ship in 300 million catties (150 million kilograms) and subsidise the deficit to the tune of 8.4 million yuan. The following year (1985) shipments of 400 million catties (200 million kilograms) were planned, with predicted losses of 110 million yuan.

The increased scale of capital construction means that commodity grain requirements will rise sharply in years to come and the amount of grain shipped in by the central authorities will also show a corresponding expansion. We will not get very far going down this road.

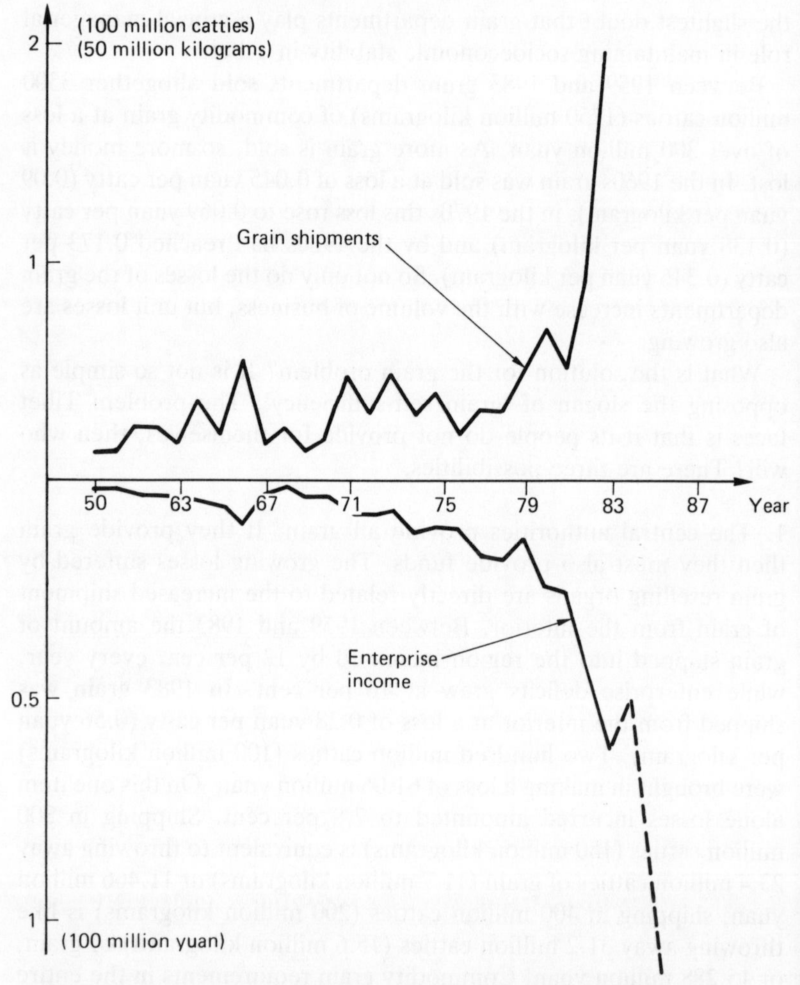

Figure 5.3 Grain shipments into Tibet and income in state-run grain enterprises (Base-line at financial forecast for 1984/5)

Note: Planned shipments are 300 million catties (150 million kilograms) for 1984 and 400 million catties (200 million kilograms) for 1985.

As well as the huge losses the problem lies in freight capacity. In 1983 freight capacity for goods and materials entering the region was 193 200 tons. Shipping in 200 million catties (100 million kilograms) of grain already takes up more than half of the total capacity. If this were to be raised to 400 million catties (200 million kilograms) even the entire existing freight capacity would be insufficient.

2. On-the-spot grain purchases. Despite severe natural disasters average annual output of grain remained at over 900 million catties (450 million kilograms) between 1980 and 1983. For the agricultural population that is 771 catties (385.5 kilograms) per capita. If the level of per capita distribution can be kept down to 600 catties (300 kilograms), then 200 million catties (100 million kilograms) can be released for marketing. This would basically take care of the supply of commodity grain for the existing pastoral and urban populations in the entire region. In terms of market grain prices the average of 0.48 yuan per catty (0.96 yuan per kilogram), based on the 20 market prices we collected, is cheaper than the average grain price in the interior of 0.49 to 0.53 yuan per catty (0.98 to 1.06 yuan per kilogram). If on-the-spot grain purchases can be made at 0.48 yuan per catty (0.96 yuan per kilogram), leaving the market price unchanged then, calculating from the marketed volume of 1983, the deficit could have been reduced by around 14 million yuan.

The extent of fluctuation in grain prices in Tibet due to local and seasonal variation is within 160 per cent. If well organised the cost of grain purchases can be reduced even further. The problem is that this requires an extremely high level of business motivation on the part of grain departments, which is just not possible under the present system of reimbursement for all expenditure.

3. Expand grain imports. In 1983 grain departments imported 4.2 million catties (2.1 million kilograms) of grain from Nepal. Border exchange prices were 0.325 yuan per catty (0.65 yuan per kilogram) for wheat flour and 0.375 yuan per catty (0.75 yuan per kilogram) for rice. Nepal is at present eager to sign long-term contracts with China for the export of 20–30 million catties (10–15 million kilograms) of grain at an average price of 0.325 yuan per catty (0.65 yuan per kilogram). At the trading post of Gyirong grain is locally traded at 0.30 yuan per catty (0.60 yuan per kilogram). Taking Shigatse as the destination, the price of imported grain is only about 70 per cent that of grain shipped in from the interior. What is more it saves greatly on freight capacity (Shigatse is 1520 km from Golmud in Qinghai Province and 486 km from the trading post of Zhangmu on the Sino-Nepalese border).

In addition, there has long been a tradition of trade in salt and grain. The lakes of Tibet are a rich source of salt and traditionally hundreds of thousands of catties are traded every year with Nepal. Nepal wants to import 50 000 tons of lake salt every year. If this can be arranged then it will bring in 50 million catties (25 million kilograms) of grain in exchange. Lake salt now sells for 0.144 yuan per catty (0.288 yuan per kilogram) at the border. At an exchange rate of two catties (kilograms) of salt to one catty (kilogram) of grain, this converts into a grain price of only 0.29 yuan per catty (0.58 yuan per kilogram). However, this too is impossible under the present system.

What is the solution for the grain problem? We believe that a long-term policy should be formulated with on-the-spot purchases as the basic source of supply, supplemented by shipments from the interior and the expansion of imports. There are three reasons for this. Firstly, even if there were spare freight capacity and even if it were profitable shipping in grain from the interior would still be undesirable. The opportunity cost of grain transportation is too high; if food is shipped in then goods of greater value for a commodity economy cannot be brought in, particularly those commodities that once brought in continually increase in value and which are able to change backward methods of production and open up local resources. Secondly, even if Tibet remains primarily pastoral, it cannot rely on grazing alone to modernise animal husbandry. Shipping in large amounts of grain to be sold cheaply can only have the negative effect of inhibiting the impetus for local grain production. Thirdly, on-the-spot purchases can raise the commodity rate locally in the countryside, stimulate exchange and promote the switch from a natural economy to a commodity economy.

However, in order to implement this policy, there must be a thorough-going reform of grain departments. At present, grain departments in all areas claim to support fluctuating market prices, but at the autonomous regional level nothing has been done except for preparing to gradually raise purchase prices (even after the rise they will still be about 20 per cent below the market price). In reality they still depend upon grain transfers from the central authorities, with every locality bringing in whatever it can (strictly speaking, this is however much the people want to sell). If this situation does not change, the grain supply is bound to depend more and more on provision by the central authorities, and grain departments at all levels will simply become administrative organs for allocating and transferring grain from the authorities to the grassroots.

Two Proposals for Reform

Grain shipped in by the central authorities will be maintained at 300 million catties (150 million kilograms), and there will be a ceiling of 84 million yuan for the subsidy. Loss subsidies in proportion to grain shipment quotas are to be allocated to all levels in accordance with the fixed supply of commodity grain. All organs dealing with grain below county level may be transferred to individual management through tender and may fulfil their undertakings through imports, local purchases or bringing in state grain at cost. They will be responsible for their own profits and losses. New increases in commodity grain demand by society will be subject to market prices: if grain comes in at a higher cost it will be sold at a higher price. Relief grain will no longer be accompanied by subsidies and will be directly distributed by government departments. With losses contained, this measure may enable grain enterprises to buy in cheaper grain from a number of sources rather than the more expensive shipped in grain.

The disadvantages are: 1) It will be hard to put a ceiling on loss subsidies in severely understaffed localities. 2) The existing below-cost purchase and sales prices and loss subsidies are retained, and the 300 million catties (150 million kilograms) of grain shipped in each year continue to take up 78 per cent of existing freight capacity, creating a highly irrational freight structure. 3) With the loss subsidy as a backstop, the monopoly of existing grain departments is strengthened and trade in grain among the people is curbed. Nevertheless, this could still be the first step towards reform.

In an alternative scenario the role of the regional grain bureau will remain unchanged. It will be responsible for shipping grain in from the interior and for the wholesale allocation of the shipped grain to local grain enterprises at supply and demand prices. All grain departments below regional level may be tendered out to individual management, with purchase and marketing prices fluctuating according to market forces. Each enterprise will be responsible for its own profits and losses, with no subsidies. No enterprise will be subordinate to another. Relief grain will be distributed by government departments. Grain shipped in and stored by the regional bureau may be used to regulate the market price and ensure that is never too low so as to ruin the farmers or too high so as to affect the urban population. In this way the macroscopic situation can never get out of control. This measure can solve the contradictions mentioned above, but seeing as it affects the welfare of the urban and pastoral population, it should be considered within the overall reform of the relevant departments. The implementation of this measure can be scheduled after the results of the first measures have been examined.

Eliminating the grain subsidy is not an insurmountable difficulty. At present grain is sold at 0.21 yuan per catty (0.42 yuan per kilogram). If the subsidy is removed, the price will rise by more than 100 per cent. But if the state purchase price of wool is also allowed to float, the price of grain will not overly affect the pastoral population. In 1983 87.16 million catties (43.58 million kilograms) of grain were sold in pastoral areas at a loss of 23.53 million yuan compared with the market price. But with the price of wool freed herders can increase their income by 18 million yuan. This plus income from meat, leather and livestock, even at existing state purchase prices and quantities, would more than offset the increase in the price of grain. So allowing the grain price to follow market forces will have a greater impact on the 0.28 million strong urban population. Calculating from the amount supplied in 1983, the increase in spending on grain by urban residents would be 32.4 million yuan, equivalent to 115 yuan per person annually or 9 yuan per person per month. This is only just over half of the 1983 grain department deficit. Even allowing a greater margin for error, there would still be enough to distribute in the form of grain subsidies.

Commerce

Retail and wholesale enterprises of the state-run (and collective: quasi state-run) system account for around 90 per cent of the total retail sales volume in the whole of Tibet, and are in an overwhelmingly advantageous position. In the light of the analysis of the prospects for trade in rural areas given in the previous chapter, it is certain that the pre-eminent position of state-run commerce will remain unchanged in the short term.

In 1983 Tibet's state-run commercial system suffered a loss of 9.55 million yuan. The estimated deficit for 1984 is 25 million yuan. The situation of 'more business, greater losses' seems already to be an irreversible trend. In the entire region's commercial system profits

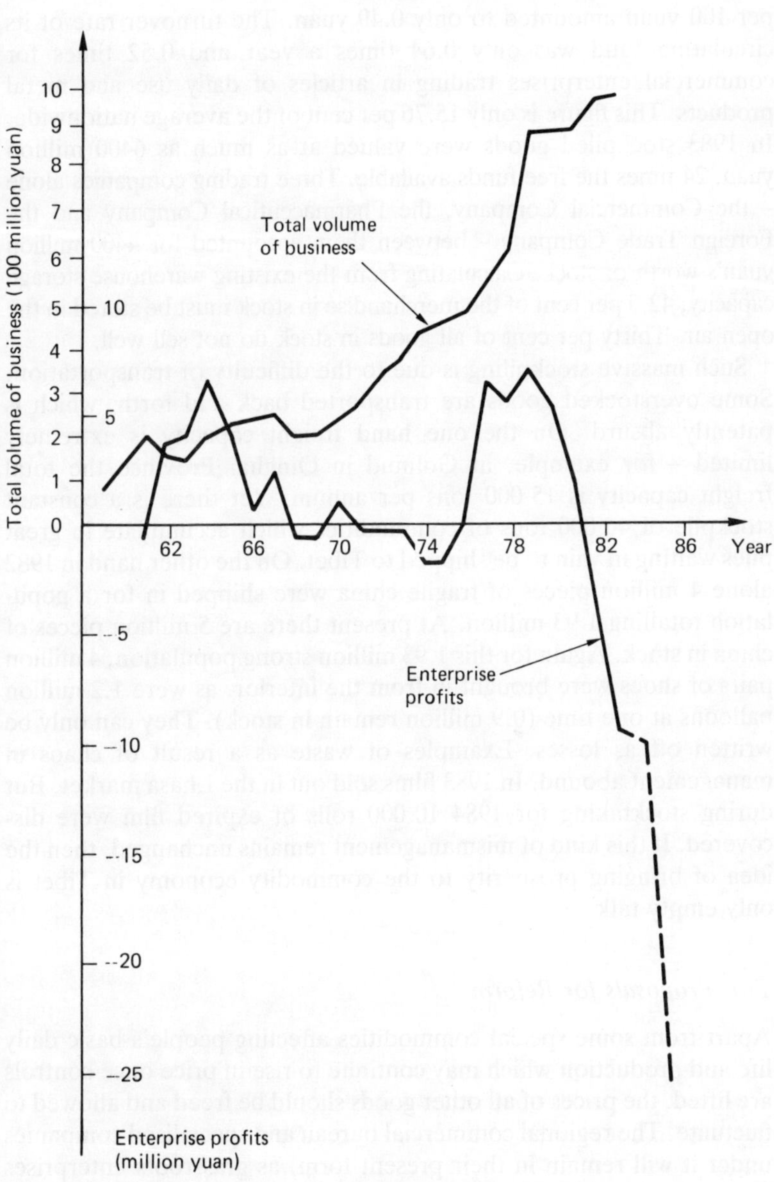

Figure 5.4 Total volume of business in state-run commerce and commercial enterprise profits (dotted lines based on forecasts for 1984 and 1985)

per 100 yuan amounted to only 0.49 yuan. The turnover rate of its circulating fund was only 0.64 times a year and 0.52 times for commercial enterprises trading in articles of daily use and metal products. This figure is only 15.76 per cent of the average nationwide. In 1983 stockpiled goods were valued at as much as 6400 million yuan, 24 times the free funds available. Three trading companies alone – the Commercial Company, the Pharmaceutical Company and the Foreign Trade Company – between them accounted for 4400 million yuan's worth of stock. Calculating from the existing warehouse storage capacity, 42.5 per cent of the merchandise in stock must be stored in the open air. Thirty per cent of all goods in stock do not sell well.

Such massive stockpiling is due to the difficulty of transportation. Some overstocked goods are transported back and forth, which is patently absurd. On the one hand freight capacity is extremely limited – for example, in Golmud in Qinghai Province the total freight capacity is 15 000 tons per annum. Yet there is a constant stockpile of 40 000 tons of commodities which accumulate in great piles waiting in vain to be shipped to Tibet. On the other hand in 1982 alone 4 million pieces of fragile china were shipped in for a population totalling 1.93 million. At present there are 5 million pieces of china in stock. Again for this 1.93 million strong population, 4 million pairs of shoes were brought in from the interior, as were 1.2 million balloons at one time (0.9 million remain in stock). They can only be written off as losses. Examples of waste as a result of chaos in management abound. In 1983 films sold out in the Lhasa market. But during stocktaking for 1984 10 000 rolls of expired film were discovered. If this kind of mismanagement remains unchanged, then the idea of bringing prosperity to the commodity economy in Tibet is only empty talk.

Two Proposals for Reform

Apart from some special commodities affecting people's basic daily life and production which may continue to rise in price once controls are lifted, the prices of all other goods should be freed and allowed to fluctuate. The regional commercial bureau and specialised companies under it will remain in their present form, as grassroots enterprises are unfamiliar with the channels for purchases from the interior (mainly the Ministry of Trade, various trade fairs and the three major producer cities of Beijing, Tianjin and Shanghai). However, they will mainly deal with wholesale business. Management in all commercial enterprises below county level should be put out to tender and made responsible for their own profits and losses, personnel and wages. Special commodities are to be handled by special government organised stores. As an interim measure, these stores will be allowed to handle a wider range of merchandise at the beginning, such as tea, petroleum, chemical fertiliser and building materials.

Few commodities are in short supply at present, except for tea and meat which are sold at a loss of 1.5 million yuan per annum. Therefore, we can be optimistic about the overall degree of fluctuation once prices are freed, and over 30 per cent of overstocked goods can be sold at reduced prices.

This proposal can only be an interim measure. Once all enterprises below the regional level are responsible for their own profits and losses, and have no commitments to the regional trade deficit, at least the transportation of overstocked goods will be greatly reduced and popular non-governmental exchange will be rapidly activated. However, although this proposal imposes some constraints on trade at the regional level, it will not be able to wipe out losses resulting from large-scale random imports as in the case of the china mentioned above. Nor will it be able to eliminate the massive wastage in the so-called 'commodities relating to the national economy and the welfare of the people'. At present wastage of cement in Tibet is as high as 30 per cent, and despite the serious shortage of cement it is readily available to anyone who wants to build a house. Losses and pilfering of glass and other building materials are even more serious. In the case of petroleum, which is of vital importance, wastage is at its height. The market prices of diesel oil, petrol and engine oil are even lower than the rationed prices of the petroleum companies. For petroleum, supplies of which are severely restricted, there is even a 'buyer's market'. Whenever a privately owned tractor stops by the roadside, crowds of drivers from state-run companies try to sell off their petroleum vouchers which have been purchased by their companies. In addition, allowing special stores to sell goods in short supply when other enterprises have been opened up is bound to lead to the emergence of a black market which will deny consumers any of the benefits of subsidised low prices. Admittedly, compensatory measures such as issuing coupons for goods in short supply and subsidised commodities can be adopted, but considering their limited scope and complexities of administration these are not long-term solutions.

A second proposal is that following changes in the market the number of commodities handled by special stores will be reduced one by one and the various specialised companies will be detached, so as to gradually realise the transformation of wholesale organisations into individually managed enterprises. Special stores will be abolished apart from those handling a tiny number of vital goods and materials and the entire commercial system will be turned into enterprises, leaving administration to be handled by the government, which will not concern itself with the running of businesses.

Transportation

Tibet's present freight capacity is almost 100 per cent in the hands of the state-run system. This state of affairs in the transportation system cannot continue.

Tibet is the only region in the whole country without rail transportation and which is totally reliant on road transportation. It is also the only region in which road transportation incurs losses. During the twenty years between 1965 and 1985 total freight capacity reached nearly 7 million tons with losses totalling 300 million yuan, averaging a loss of 46.86 yuan per ton. In 1983 losses amounted to 24.82 million yuan, and in 1984 a 68 million yuan deficit was forecast. The more goods that are carried and the further they are transported, the greater the losses. Judging from these figures the primary problem for transportation in Tibet, just as for grain and commerce, is not to increase personnel, enlarge the transportation network or expand business.

The massive losses in the transportation sector have to do with objective factors such as unreasonably low prices, oxygen deficiency on the high plateau and poor road conditions. Yet the main reason for the deficit is poor management. Judging from the reports of two companies directly under the transportation bureau, the situation in the state-run transportation system in Tibet is characterised by the 'one high' and the 'three lows':

1. Highest costs: in 1983 the cost per thousand ton-kilometres was 175 per cent of the national average for petrol-run vehicles, making this the most expensive in the country; while the per unit consumption of both diesel oil and petrol was 1.5 times the national average.
2. Lowest vehicle operation rate: in last place nationwide, this was 40 per cent in 1983 or 56 per cent of the national average.
3. Lowest number of vehicles in good condition: in 1983 the pro-

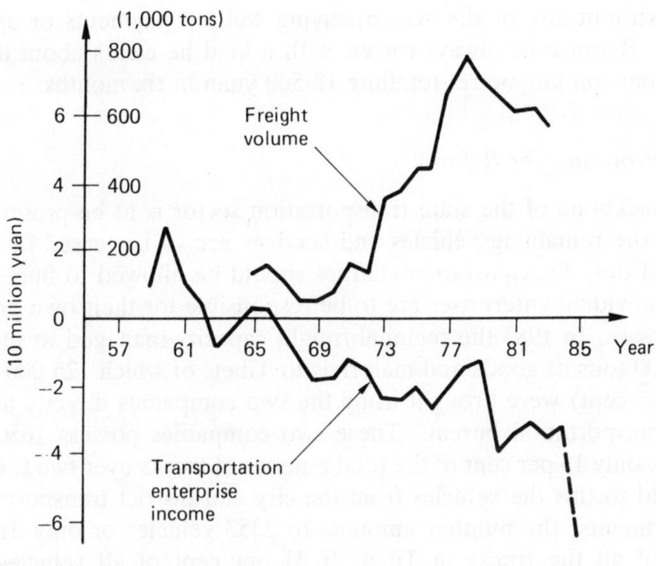

Figure 5.5 Freight volume and transportation revenue in Tibet (dashed line based on forecasts for 1984 and 1985)

portion was 60.3 per cent or 69 per cent of the national average.

4. Lowest annual tonnage per vehicle: in 1983 Tibet ranked last in the combined transportation rate for vehicles and trailers, which at 26 155 tons/km was 67 per cent of the national average.

Transportation is the artery for invigorating commodity exchange. But given a situation in which the more goods that are carried and the further they are transported the greater the losses, there is no incentive for transportation departments to do anything other than carry out the plan laid down by the government administration. Without radical change in this situation, reform in the grain and trade sectors is again only empty talk. However, is Tibet's transportation system doomed to losses? Not according to our investigations. The best evidence of this is in the emergence of rural specialised transportation households as this example shows. In the state-run system the proportion of unloaded vehicles on the road is as high as 60 per cent. Xiraowangjie of Chengguan Town, Lhasa bought a truck from the production brigade at the beginning of 1984. He drives the truck 25 days a month and he never travels unloaded. His customers are mainly state-run institutions who pay him the same state stipulated rate without any of the accompanying welfare payments or allowances. Because he always travels with a load he clears about 0.125 yuan per ton-kilometre, totalling 12 500 yuan in six months.

Two Proposals for Reform

The backbone of the state transportation sector is to be preserved, while the remaining vehicles and services are to be leased or contracted out. Transportation charges should be allowed to fluctuate, and individual enterprises are to be responsible for their own profits and losses. In 1983 the regional freight capacity managed to ship in 190 000 tons of goods and materials to Tibet, of which 125 000 tons (65 per cent) were brought in by the two companies directly under the transportation bureau. These two companies possess 1650 vehicles, only 15 per cent of the total number of trucks over two tons. If we add to this the vehicles from the city and district transportation departments, the number amounts to 3353 vehicles or only 31 per cent of all the trucks in Tibet. If 31 per cent of all vehicles are retained, then 91 per cent of the freight shipped in will be guaranteed. The remaining 70 per cent of trucks should be leased or contracted out, which will have no great repercussions. This proposal may be adopted as an interim measure. Its advantage is that transportation at the grassroots level can be greatly stimulated. However, a disadvantage is that there is bound to be intense competition over petrol, spare parts and sources of freight between the two systems, in which the state sector will have a clear advantage.

After assessing the results of the first stage of the reform, the second proposal is to release the truck fleets under the regional transportation bureau and city and district transportation departments level by level, leaving only a very small section of vital freight capacity. Once the city and district fleets have been released, regional level fleets will still retain control of 65 per cent of freight capacity even though they possess only 15 per cent of all vehicles. The final aim is to transform all transportation departments into enterprises. In principle, administrative departments should relinquish all vehicles which can be used for transportation. Deployment of vehicles will be mainly controlled by the market. Government institutions should also go through the market if they need vehicles, although requisition will be allowed under special circumstances.

Freeing transportation prices will not be as terrible as some people fear. Although people everywhere complain about the shortage of means of transportation, the prices charged by individual operators are not much higher than that stipulated by the state. Some specialised households charge the same as the state for their trucks. Freight costs from Lhasa to the Zhangmu trading post for wool, renowned for its marketability, are only 0.45 yuan per ton-kilometre by privately-owned truck and 0.36 yuan per ton-kilometre by state-owned truck. If we ignore the wages, welfare and additional income elements of state-employed drivers, the prices charged by private operators are only 25 per cent higher. In 1960 transportation department earned 270 million yuan. Freight costs at that time were higher than they are now, but the amount charged was only 0.26 to 0.42 yuan per ton-kilometre. Even if the freight price includes all losses (including losses incurred through poor management), it will only rise by 0.006 yuan per ton-kilometre.

Credit Cooperatives

Finance is the catalyst or lubricant for a commodity economy. Despite the shortage of funds in Tibet, credit cooperatives are still failing to fulfil their role of promoting the turnover of funds. In 1983 loans worth 2500 million yuan were made in the rural system throughout the region which, at 714 yuan per household, was quite a sum. But actual credit amounted to only 26.55 million yuan in total. Shigatse prefecture boasts the highest rate of lending, but loans amount to only 8.5 million yuan out of a credit fund of 41.19 million yuan. With the utilisation rate of funds at only 0.6 times per annum, this is virtually dead money.

The most acute problem of this slow turnover is that loans are interest-free. The banking system only encourages rolling base savings, while credit cooperatives are reimbursed by the Agricultural Bank for the 3.3 per cent interest on any interest-free loans they make, although reimbursement is withheld until the loan is repaid. This 3.3 per cent interest rate is even lower than the 3.6 per cent rate of interest earned by ordinary deposits. In this way the Agricultural Bank reimburses the credit cooperatives free of charge and the credit cooperatives make no profit on loans. There is no incentive for the bank to encourage credit cooperatives to make loans, and they for their part would rather deposit the money in the Agricultural Bank where it will earn a higher rate of interest. Loans are an unattractive proposition. Consequently, credit cooperatives do not make loans but only deposit funds. Even funds allocated by higher levels are deposited in the Agricultural Bank. Over half the deposits held by the Dingri county credit cooperatives consist of funds allocated from above. Popular opinion has it that credit cooperatives are 'happy with deposits but hard on loans'. Loans are refused unless there is really no alternative.

As a result this has a counter effect on people's willingness to make deposits. In 1983 rural commune members held deposits of 16.82 yuan per capita, only 36 per cent of the national average and ranking last but one in the country as a whole. What is more, due to the cancellation of several overdue loans some people see no difference between bank loans and government relief funds, and so defaults on repayment occur on more and more loans. Consequently credit cooperatives find it difficult to recover their money, which further dampens their enthusiasm for lending. The situation has been such for so long that it has now become a vicious circle. The underlying cause is that credit cooperatives do not make money. While people continue to default on repayment, the credit cooperatives become less and less willing to make loans. Since the credit cooperatives only deposit funds but give no credit, people are less willing to make deposits even if they have the money. Finally, the function of credit cooperatives to promote the turnover of funds is weakened.

The problems of low coverage, poor quality of personnel and chaotic management in the credit cooperative network are all much more serious than in the commercial sector. Each credit cooperative serves an average area of 2588.5 square kilometres, while every employee is expected to cover 1078.1 square kilometres. In Shigatse prefecture there are 97 credit cooperatives with an average staffing level of 2.7 persons. Frequently the accountant also serves as the cashier. Almost none of the employees have even finished primary school. In 1983 30.16 per cent of credit cooperatives in the entire region incurred losses, and the degree of accountant and cashier error was respectively 5.7 times and 15.3 times that fixed by the bank.

Funds are one of the most active elements in a commodity economy. If funds are not actively used there can be no active commodity economy. For the purposes of stimulating Tibet's economy and breaking the stagnation of the natural economy, a key role will be played by accelerating the turnover of funds. That is why the reform of financial departments is so crucial.

Two Proposals for Reform

The management of all credit cooperatives should be leased or put out to tender, and they should become individually responsible for their own profits and losses. Interest rates for deposits and loans should float within a restricted range. Reserve funds will be stipulated by the Agricultural Bank, which at the same time will free the trust business and encourage the flow of funds. Initially the flow of funds within the rural economy will be subject to market readjustment. Later, credit cooperatives will be allowed to establish direct relations with the various specialised banks in order to gradually enlarge the scope of the reform of the financial system. This proposal deals with the question of how to channel loans into areas of greatest need, and solves the problems of chaotic management and the 'one big pot' system in credit cooperatives. However, fluctuation in credit cooperative interest rates may result in the banks competing for deposits or in remote regions being unable to afford high-interest loans.

In the present banking system credit cooperatives are furthest from the 'one big pot' centre, and to a certain extent are responsible for their own profits and losses. It is highly likely that they will form the breakthrough point for the transformation of banks into enterprises. But looking at the situation in the long term, the functions currently performed by credit cooperatives are more complex than those of other specialised banks. Acting as branches they are the 'tentacles' of the Agricultural Bank. Credit cooperatives are also responsible for industrial and commercial loans in rural areas, with similar responsibilities to commercial banks in urban areas. Moreover, they also act as community deposit banks and financial mutual-aid institutions in small communities in order to meet the possible needs of local residents and depositors. Therefore, the proposal for reform discussed above is only tentative. In implementing this proposal, there should certainly be conscious guidance in separating the functions of credit cooperatives, including those performed within each cooperative. Meanwhile the reform of the specialised banks must be pushed ahead.

Along with the separation of the different functions of the credit cooperatives, we propose that in the Agricultural Bank, Construction Bank and Industrial and Commercial Bank interest rates should gradually be allowed to fluctuate relatively freely while business should be organised along enterprise lines. The Agricultural Bank and the Construction Bank can lead the way in this reform. When appropriate credit cooperatives can then be divided up and subordinated to the various banks. Until then, the Agricultural Bank and local financial departments can meet the urgent needs of individual and enterprise customers through special loans or reduced interest.

The reform of the departments mentioned above can be seen as the keypoint of the reform, and are to be given primary consideration. There should be overall coordination in the implementation and promotion of the reform. If carried out in a simplistic, isolated manner in separate departments, then it is likely to get bogged down in individual details and the loss of impetus may affect the whole situation. The precondition for reform is floating prices (including interest, the cost of funds). Once the grain price is floated, wages have to float. Once wages float, the cost of all products (including service 'products' such as trade and transportation) will change too. Once transport costs float, the prices of all transported commodities will also float. This is even more true in price reform in the commercial sector. Once the cost of funds is altered, all institutions in need of funds will be affected. Even with the reform of credit cooperatives, this will come as a big shock to supply and marketing cooperatives and grassroots enterprises. Hence, any individual action taken by any department may have ramifications (even disastrous ones) for the interests of related departments. That is why it is necessary to carry out full investigations and accurately calculate the range of potential price fluctuations and the level of tolerance in society.

5.5 'TIME AND PLACE' REFORM STRATEGY[1]

The above-mentioned interrelated proposals for reform in several crucial areas form a massive operation amounting to a rebirth. This will undoubtedly arouse profound repercussions and a violent social response within the overall socioeconomic system and the entire sphere of social activity. Not only will the all-round reform touch upon every individual's material interests, but social standing, value judgments, self-esteem and many other aspects of social life will also be affected. A certain degree of chaos will be difficult to avoid.

Historical transformation on such a large scale is bound to involve the initiative and imagination of millions of invididuals. No mere technical project, it cannot proceed without some element of social, economic and even political risk. We can say that the greater the scope of the reform's action the more deeply it involves social life, and the greater the expected economic and social benefits thus the greater the risks will be. It is impossible to avoid mistakes however well the reform project is designed and however carefully the investigation is carried out. Reform is an historical process of constant innovation and not constructed on past experience. We cannot hope to create history in a comprehensive and precise manner on the basis of experience already gained. Nor is it possible to predict at every step the likely direction and impact of measures in the process of reform. Human society is a 'super complex system' in the cybernetic sense, of which the most salient feature is that it is irreversible, unrepeatable. Yet the tragedy of human thinking lies in the fact that people can use only the known, that is their knowledge of the past, to grasp the future, that which has not yet happened and which will happen only once.

In the course of this historical transformation it is one thing to conduct careful investigations and meticulous studies, but it is quite another matter to deal with the high level of uncertainty to create enough room for manoeuvre for policy making. Therefore, in order to allow the reform to be carried out more safely and to avoid the potential dangers of rash large-scale measures for reform, it is necessary to draw up a time and place reform strategy which makes use of the great difference between backward regions and the hinterland, poor roads and transportation, the relative separation and isolation of regions and slower communications. Its guiding principle will be to break down the 'super complex system' by areas and by levels, dealing with the easier and more urgent while leaving out the more difficult and less urgent, and dividing up areas to select breakthrough points. Keeping to Tibet as our example, there are six areas to concentrate on. The city of Lhasa has a relatively high economic level and reform there could produce quick results and rapidly create material conditions conducive to reform in other areas. However, Lhasa is also the home of the regional party committee and is where the urban population and government organs are concentrated. Reform will be difficult as there will inevitably be a certain degree of chaos and the strong response from society will be hard to quell.

The two prefectures of Nagqu and Ngari have backward economies and unsophisticated economic relations. Successful reform would be easy to achieve there. However, the two regions are mainly engaged in animal husbandry, an undiversified economic activity. In the short term the potential for economic development is limited. Even the experience gained from the success of the reform there would not be applicable to other regions due to the unsophisticated nature of the economic relations involved. Moreover, the economic benefit achieved by the success of the reform would be unable to reverse the decline of the region as a whole.

The Chamdo and Shannan (Lhoka) prefectures have combined agricultural-pastoral economies with well-developed traditional trade, industry and handicrafts, and are rich in natural resources. They would make excellent pilot zones for experiments in reform of the economic structure. However, Chamdo prefecture lies next to Sichuan Province, and reform there would soon affect the interior and so the complex relations (for example commodity circulation as a result of different price systems) between areas undergoing reform and other areas would have to be dealt with immediately. Shannan (Lhoka) prefecture is close to a politically sensitive border region over which there is some controversy, and so discretion and security must be considered in any reform.

Shigatse prefecture stands at present second in the region in terms of fixed capital funds and assets. Its economy comprises industry, agriculture and animal husbandry, and 17 out of the 27 traditional foreign trading posts are situated within its borders. The region has a long history of foreign trade and is rich in tourist attractions. The economic relations of the 'one big pot' system are fairly lax, it has a developed economy and greater potential for opening to the outside world. It also presents fewer political risks. Therefore, this prefecture can be selected as a breakthrough point.

Within the focal area for reform a smaller 'special zone', such as the Zhangmu trading post, should be selected for initial price deregulation and the transfer of enterprises by contract or leasing so that they become responsible for their own profits and losses. As experience is gained reform can be steadily extended to other areas.

As for reform measures, we must consider formulating a series of linked schemes. At every stage responses must be quickly collected and a further assessment made (including an evaluation of the social situation) in order to make readjustments for the next step and to form a feedback system. In spatial terms we can consider applying reform measures of varying intensities in different areas in a series of steps. For instance, when the whole region or some parts of it are undergoing the first step in reform, the focal area for reform will be embarking on the second step and the smaller special zone will be starting on the third step. The first step, now being implemented in the whole region or some parts of it, will be a step which has already proved successful in the latter two areas. In this way, step by step, area by area, we can expect to achieve the greatest success at the least cost.

The leading body for reform at the regional level in the focal area of reform should be composed of able cadres. At the same time a powerful 'think tank' for policy study and the design of reform measures should be set up so as to maintain coordination and speedy, up-to-the-minute communication between the area undergoing reform and the region as a whole, and also to sum up experience in a timely fashion for readjusting the policies. Meanwhile, attention must be paid to the selection and training of cadres for reform in the course of the reform so as to facilitate its application throughout the entire region.

Reform of the economic system is the exploration of future uncertainty. During this process there must be material conditions to support the reform, a new economic theory to provide energetic guidance for the reform and a new body of cadres to implement the reform.

However, reform in China is being realised on a foundation of backwardness and poverty and the model we are creating cannot be completed *a priori* through logical inference. We have to create the material conditions for reform through reform, create our particular economic model and theory through reform, and train a new body of cadres through reform of the cadre system. Herein lies the paradox of circular logic. Without a strong material basis reform cannot be successfully implemented, yet if there is no reform the material conditions for reform can never emerge. Without the guidance of a reform theory reform cannot be conducted smoothly, but the creation of a new theory of reform is dependent on the practice of reform. Without a new cadre body, the best cadre system is only a piece of paper, yet without the new cadre system a new cadre body can never be formed.

How are we to escape from this circular logic and achieve reform at the least cost? The proposal we give above may offer a solution – gradually progressing step by step and area by area, selecting focal areas as breakthrough points so as to avoid all-round repercussions and at the same time creating material conditions to support the reform, originating reform experience and training a new cadre body. Starting from this proposal, with the powerful support of state financial and material strength, we should select some backward regions with better resources and higher economic potential, and in which there is less risk of repercussions on the whole social, economic and political fabric when reform is launched, and implement an all-round thorough-going reform so as to create the experience, cadres and material conditions for reform in other areas. This model may also be of some strategic significance for the reform of the economic system in the nation as a whole.

6 A Hundred Enterprises at the Ready, One to Take the Lead

In terms of economic growth, the backwardness of backward regions is exhibited in the overall underdevelopment of industry, agriculture, transport and communications, commerce and the catering and service industries. Also in terms of economic growth, the end result of boosting the economy should be the comprehensive invigoration of all these sectors. This much is clear. What we need to address now are the intrinsic organic links which hold between the different sectors. Industrial growth cannot be divorced from the development of agriculture or transport and communications, neither can the growth of the infrastructure be separated from the expansion of manufacturing and production, and vice versa. In the transition from economic backwardness to economic invigoration, we need to select a 'leading' sector which, through its intrinsic organic links with other sectors, will direct the development of all other sectors and consequently activate the national economy overall. This is generally known as selecting the orientation of the economy.

At an early stage it was the development of the textile industry in England which provided the impulse for the emergence of the capitalist productive forces which were to dominate the world. In post-war Japan a strategy of industrial renovation managed to boost the economy with shining results in just a few decades. Growth in the motor industry promoted the development of the processing and oil industries, which accordingly spurred on the motor industry. This curious mechanism of mutual pacing, with industries constantly closing the gap and overtaking each other in development, has aroused intense interest among Western developmental economists.

Several questions need to be decided. First, which should take precedence – the import or the export sector? Given China's well-known advantage of an 'unlimited supply of labour', Lewis proposes reliance on the export of primary products to provide the capital accumulation necessary for industrialisation. Prebisch and Singer, on the other hand, argue according to 'conditions of trade' that concentration on the export of primary products should be avoided and the outflow of profits and purchasing power prevented through a strategy of 'import substitution'. Yet another view is put forward by Balassa, Yang Shujin and others who believe that exportation on a wide scale, and of manufactured goods in particular, will act as a dynamo for economic development.

Secondly, which should come first – the infrastructure or production sectors? According to Rosenstein-Rodan (early period), infrastructure requirements generally have a lengthy gestation period and moreover call for massive capital injection with a high capital-returns rate. From this he concludes that the infrastruture sector should be given developmental priority and the direct production sector subsequently established on this base. The theory of 'unbalanced growth' proposed by Hirschman in *The Strategy of Economic Development* maintains that too much emphasis on the development of the infrastructure may result in production being left behind, causing a concomitant waste of resources and slowdown in the rate of growth. In order to guarantee a market, Hirschman proposes that sectors producing goods directly required by the consumer should be developed first of all, followed by sectors satisfying indirect demand on the principle of 'backward linkage'.

Strong opposition has provoked a new scholarly division. The view taken by Nurkse, Chenery, Tinbergen and Rosenstein-Rodan (later period) is that all sectors of the economy should be developed in concert, with the crucial proviso that there be a reasonable degree of mutual support between sectors. Indeed, Kuznets' statistical analysis of collected 'equitable proportions' won him the Nobel Prize. But research and discussion still continue. The fact remains that under this or that theory or model, some underdeveloped countries have surged forward while others have fallen ever further back.

Here, we neither intend nor are able to provide an overall evaluation of all these different theories. We merely wish to observe that in selecting a leading sector or development strategy in backward regions it all comes down to the same old question: *who* is doing the developing?

Developmental economists emphasise the *economic* links between different sectors of the economy, whether they be 'forward-linking' (in which the thrust comes from infrastructure development) or 'back-linking' (in which production for direct consumption takes priority, and leads on to the development of other indirect sectors). These economic relations all presuppose a social system in which an impetus to develop these kinds of economic links already exists, and which is able to utilise them. In reality, however, were it possible for such a social system to be established, development in developing countries would long since have ceased to warrant such unremitting efforts. The problem of backward regions is precisely one of how to create a socioeconomic system in the region in which there is an impetus to develop economic links and which is able to utilise these links.

Looking at the problem from the point of view of developed countries, selection of the leading sector should take as its starting point the task of making economic man's economic activity more economic. From the viewpoint of a developing nation or backward region, however, the problem is one of how to teach natural man – who, as a producer with a tendency towards developing the natural economy, cannot be as enterprising as the commodity producers of developed countries – to plan and organise his life and production in the same way as economic man in developed countries; and moreover to select and exploit resources in accordance with the principles of a commodity economy. Rather than trying to specify the economic links between different sectors of the economy, we ought at this point to gear sectoral priorities and strategies for development primarily towards deciding the growth of different sectors of the economy, and towards promoting a rise in the quality of human resources and speeding up the degree of social development.

The same reasoning lies behind our analysis of the reform of the economic structure: only when sectoral guiding principles or development strategies are closely integrated with the intrinsic laws of backwardness in backward regions can there be any real hope of solving the difficulties of backward regions.

6.1 GOALS AND LIMITATIONS

Viewing economic development as a natural historical process, the links between different sectors of the economy exhibit an objective, necessary logic. Whatever the demand it will be met by the appropriate supply, and vice versa. However, the history of mankind has never ruled out human subjective activity and continuous choice. From what we know of the laws of economics, the choice of economic orientation is a powerful lever to promote and speed up economic growth. Growth in which different sectors of the economy pace each other is a dynamic process of constant change resulting from the demand for change concomitant with economic development. This dynamic process involves never-ending selection of a sector to act as leader of the economy or, in simple terms, a singular pursuit of two economic goals:

1. *Capital accumulation* At any given time, the sector earmarked for prioritised development is the one that gives the highest returns on the lowest investment and hence most effectively realises capital accumulation and most swiftly empowers the forces of progress and development through the economy as a whole.
2. *Sectoral linkage* At any given time, the sector of the economy selected for prioritised development is the one which most effectively promotes and directs the development of other sectors, whether through 'backward linkage' or 'forward-linkage', and which most rapidly effects the most efficient exploitation and utilisation of the widest range of natural resources.

These two goals are of particularly crucial significance to poverty-stricken regions completely lacking any development. The right choice of economic orientation not only has an effect on the speed of economic development and rate of income growth, but at the same time plays a decisive role in the shift from the vicious circle of a natural economy to the flourishing growth of a commodity economy. Looking at the natural resources utilised in backward regions discussed above, development in these areas does not have to contend with the usual severe resource limitations which confront most economies. On the contrary, many developmental economists conclude from progressively decreasing capital returns and steadily increasing exploitation and production costs that the marginal profits which accrue from the all-round development of the economy in a region with a low degree of exploitation are far, far higher that those obtained in areas with high level or excessive exploitation.

The reasoning behind this is very simple; a highly developed region taps its resources more intensively, while in the dimension of time the rising demand for new and increased investment to maintain output levels results in a higher capital-production rate. Regions with a low degree of resource exploitation are by comparison, potential above-quota profit makers. Clearly, there is a contradiction between this line of argument and the fact that developed regions continue to develop while backward regions fall further behind. This is because

Table 6.1 Average transportation distances in ten provinces and regions (1983)

Province/region	*Av. distance (km)*
Tibet	867
Xinjiang	212
Qinghai	172
Yunnan	130
Guizhou	72
Ningxia	75
Guangxi	48
Inner Mongolia	43
Jiangsu	35
Nationwide	42

although backward regions do not suffer from severe limitations on natural resources in their development, yet they are faced with other, harsher restrictions of a distinctive nature:

1. *Poor quality of human resources* This has already been discussed above so here we will only stress that the development of any and every sector of the economy in backward regions must take into consideration the fact that the region's local inhabitants living within a natural economy lack a sense of commodity exchange.
2. *Transport and communications difficulties* An account of this also appears above, and here we want only to reiterate that the development of any and every sector of the economy in backward regions must face the inescapable fact of high transportation costs. Poor transportation conditions, vast distances and scattered populations mean that the average transportation distance per unit is much greater than in the developed provinces. To take an example, Table 6.1 shows the distances covered in major haulage runs in backward regions.

A comparison of the eight backward regions with Jiangsu Province reveals that in transporting by road the same unit-weight of exchange, Inner Mongolia, Guangxi, Ningxia, Guizhou, Yunnan, Qinghai, Xinjiang and Tibet have to pay out respective haulage costs of at least 1.23, 1.37, 2.14, 2.05, 3.71, 4.91, 6.06 and 24.77 times that paid by Jiangsu. We say 'at least' because distance is only one factor in the composition of haulage costs. With the mountains and valleys, detours and lack of roads in backward regions, there is a huge disparity between average transportation distance and actual transport costs.

If we compare for instance Guizhou and Shandong, their average transportation distances are 72 kilometres and 68 kilometres respectively (a ratio of 1.06). Actual haulage costs, however, stand at 190 yuan per thousand ton-kilometres and 110 yuan per thousand ton-kilometres respectively, so that Guizhou's transport costs are 1.73 times those of Shandong. Bearing this ratio in mind, if we turn to Tibet which has no railways and so relies totally on the road system, and add on the costs of high altitude oxygen deficiency, fuel and spare parts, the restrictions placed on commodity exchange by transportation difficulties are even more evident. High transport costs are equivalent to an 'exchange tax' levied on commodity exchange irrespective of place in proportion to distance. As well as being one reason for the lack of contacts between backward regions and the outside world, this 'tax' is also largely responsible for the lackadaisical state of economic exchange within backward regions themselves.

Enterprise in the producer can be a source of impetus for the creation of commodity exchange and production, while transportation is the indispensible medium through which material exchange quality of human resources takes place. Neither of these limitations – quality of human resources and transportation – can be got round by any sector of the economy. It is clearly absurd to expect to achieve the two objectives of capital accumulation and sectoral linkage by placing hope in some strategy that does not involve exchange and hence does not require the tranportation sector.

Admittedly, these two limitations can be reduced through the development of cultural and educational sectors, and through road maintenance and vehicle purchases, but despite the favourable conditions for development in all sectors of the economy which would result from these measures, they cannot in themselves, at least at present, generate capital accumulation and forge effective sectoral links, and so must be excluded from the pool of potential candidates for leading sector. Thus, as a prerequisite for correct choice of orientation of the economy in backward regions, a potential leading sector ought to have the power to transform the quality of human resources to the greatest degree, and to overcome transportation difficulties. The ability to transmute the first restriction in particular should be of prime consideration when selecting a leading sector in backward regions.

6.2 IMPORTS CREATE MORE IMPORTS

In *Post-Industrial Society* Daniel Bell depicts the history of human progress as 'pre-industrial society', 'industrial society' and 'post-industrial society'. 'Pre-industrial society relied on a primitive labour force, investing its initial resources from the natural world.' 'Industrial society was organised around an axis of production and machinery for the purpose of creating commodities.' Whatever angle you look at it from, the growth of modern industry has been the fundamental force behind progress from feudal society to both capitalism and socialism. The major characteristic of backwardness in backward regions with respect to productive forces is the weak and undeveloped state of industry. In a general sense, devoting major efforts to the development of industry is absolutely the right choice, and for over thirty years this has been the line of thought which has directed growth. All hopes for economic invigoration in backward regions have been placed on a development strategy which puts modern industry first.

A number of backward regions are richly endowed with natural resources for the development of industry (see Chapter 2) and so resources present no obvious obstacle to the implementation of this strategy, be it 'back-linking' or 'forward-linking'. Nevertheless, the outlook today after thirty or so years of unremitting effort is far from bright. The all-out development of modern industry and the question of whether or not modern industry can actually arise at any given stage in the economic development of backward regions are, unfortunately, two quite separate issues.

Looking at Table 6.2, in state-owned industrial enterprises with separate accounting the profit and tax realised on every 100 yuan's net worth of fixed assets, expressed as a percentage of the national average, is 49 per cent, 39 per cent, 16 per cent and 37 per cent in Xinjiang, Guizhou, Qinghai and Inner Mongolia respectively. Profit and tax realised on every 100 yuan of capital stands at 89 per cent, 74 per cent, 29 per cent and 31 per cent respectively.[1] The output value per 100 yuan of the original value of fixed assets in these regions is 62 per cent, 72 per cent, 39 per cent and 63 per cent respectively, while profit realised per 100 yuan gross value of industrial output is 53 per cent, 62 per cent, 29 per cent and 102 per cent respectively. In the regions of Xinjiang, Guizhou and Qinghai, the sales revenue derived from every 100 yuan of capital is 91 per cent, 69 per cent and 46 per cent respectively, with circulating capital per 100 yuan gross industrial

Table 6.2 Major financial indicators in state-owned industrial enterprises with separate accounting

Unit: yuan					1982
Region	*Nationwide*	*Xinjiang*	*Guizhou*	*Qinghai*	*Inner Mongolia*
Profit and tax realised per 100 yuan fixed assets net value	33.4	16.53	12.97	5.27	12.49
Profit and tax realised per 100 yuan capital	13.7	12.25	10.15	4.03	4.26
Value of output realised per 100 yuan fixed assets original value	95.0	58.53	68.63	36.99	60.99
Sales revenue realised per 100 yuan capital	75.4	68.62	51.75	34.35	–
Profit realised per 100 yuan gross value of industrial output	14.4	7.65	8.96	4.16	14.66
Circulating capital per 100 yuan gross value of industrial output	29.7	34.74	46.22	62.35	–

output value standing at 117 per cent, 156 per cent and 210 per cent respectively. With this level of economic performance, it is clearly impossible to attain the desired objective of swift capital accumulation.

In circumstances such as these, where industrial enterprises as a whole are uneconomic, neither 'forward' nor 'back-linking' between the different sectors of the economy can give rise to a healthy, self-propagating mechanism. Of all the backward regions and provinces Guizhou has a relatively well-developed machining industry, but even so after thirty years or more of unstinting efforts it still lags far behind the national average in terms of profitability. Table 6.3 shows that active 'back-linking' would be hard to put into effect since

Table 6.3 Profitability in the machining industry in Guizhou and nationwide (average) (1982)

	National	*Guizhou*	*Guizhou/nationwide (%)*
Average capital/output value rate (yuan/100 yuan)	88.9	33.1	37.2
Per capita profit and tax (yuan/person)	2158	584	27.1
Circulating capital turnover rate (days)	290	439.9	151.4
Steel utilisation rate (%)	68	51.7	76.0
Productivity (yuan/capita)	13400	4255	31.8

the processing industry itself is in difficulties. Would then it be feasible to promote 'forward-linkages' between different sectors of the economy by tapping the abundant mineral resources, improving management and technology, and expanding mining and construction, primary industries which do not require a high quality labour force? The answer is that it would prove just as difficult. As an example, Guizhou with the third largest coal deposits in China ought to maintain high technical standards, but in fact the situation in the complete reverse: all Guizhou's technical norms fall far below the national average, as can be seen in Table 6.4.

To take another example, Guizhou has abundant limestone reserves with at present over 43 quarries possessing reserves of over 875 million tons which are known suppliers of material for concrete mixing. Guizhou has in addition huge coal reserves which provide an assured energy supply. However low profitability has shackled progress in these areas. In 1980 an average 200.3 kilograms of coal was required to produce one ton of concrete locally, equivalent to 121 per cent the national average amount required. The labour/output rate for total labour and materials was an annual 44.54 tons per capita, a mere 55 per cent of the national average, while 74 per cent of all output was up to standard, a figure 10.13 per cent lower than the national average, and losses had soared to 55.56 per cent or 30.87 per cent above the national average. If concrete cannot be produced economically, then brick making is out of the question. Coal consumption in brick kilns at county level or above stands at 1.04 tons per 10 000 bricks for the country as a whole, and at 1.57 tons per

Table 6.4 Technical norms in the coal industry – a comparison between Guizhou and the national average (1983)

Major Technical Norms	*Unit*	*Guizhou*	*National*	*Guizhou/Nat (%)*
1) *Quality*				
Commodity coal loss	%	21.88	20.91	105
Proportion of waste in commodity coal	%	0.86	0.45	191
Clean coal loss	%	12.47	10.32	121
Rate of recovery of clean coal	%	42.73	52.49	81
2) *Productivity*				
Overall productivity for unprocessed coal	tons/capita	0.587	0.873	67
Extraction efficiency rate	tons/capita	2.992	4.094	73
Excavation efficiency rate	tons/capita	0.091	0.113	81
3) *Materials Consumption*				
Pit props per unprocessed coal output	cubic m/ 10,000 tons	150.27	90.9	165
Dynamite per unprocessed coal output	kg/10,000 tons	3375	3117	108
Av. monthly coal face extraction output	tons/month	8110	10908	74

10 000 bricks in Guizhou, which is over half as much again as the rest of China. Even so, the supply of bricks in the province cannot keep pace with demand, and the Guiyang region alone has to spend an extra 5 million yuan or more annually on importing 100 million bricks from the provinces of Sichuan, Hunan and so on.

It is evident that poor quality of human resources is seriously hampering the growth of modern industry in backward regions. From our investigations into almost the entire range of sectors including the mining, construction, electronics industries, textile and other light industries, as well as the agricultural sideline processing industry, we have seen that aside from a few exceptional quotas of one or two ethnic minority products, in terms of economic profitability almost all industries and products rank far below the national average, let alone China's advanced levels. The poor quality of human resources is one of the fundamental reasons behind this low profitability.

If we look at the figures for numbers of scientific and technical personnel, the 1982 national average was 62 scientific and technical workers per 10 000 population. In Guizhou, however, the figure was 49, putting the province in 21st place nationwide. Although high-grade talent made up 1 per cent of the total scientific and technical workforce in China as a whole, in Guizhou this group formed only 0.49 per cent, leaving the province in 19th place. Moreover, middle-grade scientific and technical workers made up 19 per cent of the total nationwide, but in Guizhou they comprised only 12.7 per cent, whereas low-grade personnel in this category formed 80 per cent of the total in China as a whole and 86.8 per cent in Guizhou. In the country as a whole, 45 per cent of the scientific and technical workforce are graduates, of which research students comprise 0.36 per cent. The figures for Guizhou, however, are 41 per cent and 0.15 per cent respectively. If we look at the proportion of engineers and technicians in the workforce of state industrial sectors in Guizhou, the figures are less than 2 per cent in the mining and construction industries, 1.82 per cent in light industry (including a mere 1.6 per cent in textiles, clothing, shoes, paper making, cultural and educational supplies) and only 1.19 per cent in the catering sector.

Leaving aside the restrictions on growth imposed by the poor quality of human resources, it is clear that problems in transportation and communications have also set tremendous limits on the development of modern industry in backward regions. For instance, in machining enterprises in Guizhou Province, inconvenient communications mean that fuel consumption per unit output value is 29 times higher than the national average. Some primary products have to travel great distances to processing centres, often adding transport costs of over 30 per cent of the product price. In this way products which were originally second-rate and highly-priced have an additional massive transport cost slapped on top which predictably affects their profitability and competitiveness.

In reality, despite the present low economic benefits of industrial sectors in backward regions, transport costs are kept down by state subsidies. The losses of the state-subsidised transportation sector and the ensuing below-cost pricing etc in grain purchase and marketing mean that industry's real production costs are spread out over the

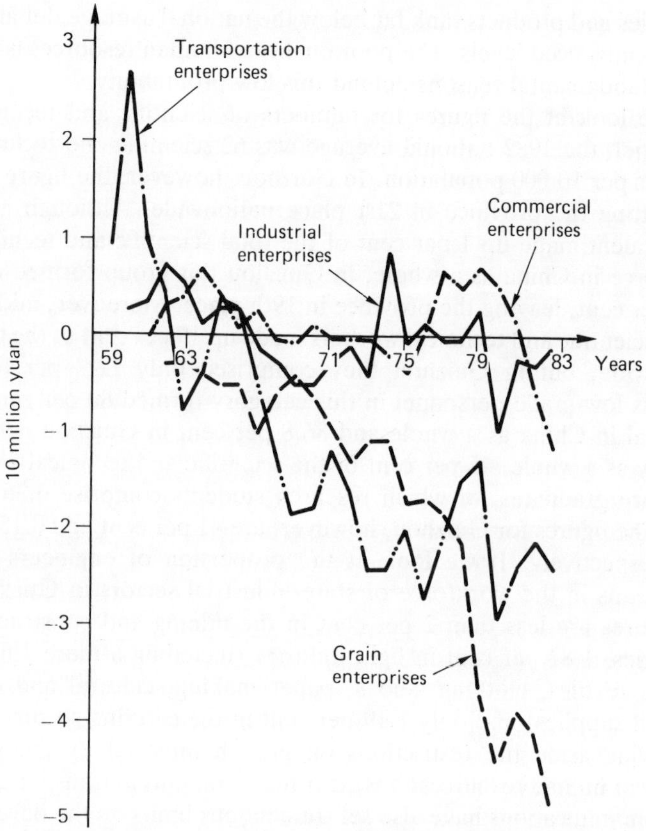

Figure 6.1 Revenues of industrial enterprises and the transportation, commercial and grain sectors in Tibet

grain, commercial and transportation sectors. The effects are shown in Figure 6.1. In Tibet losses in the commercial, grain and transportation sectors amounted to 75.37 million yuan in 1983. This was sustained in return for a 1.96 million yuan deficit in industrial enterprises and a trifling 12.32 million yuan's worth of industrial products, equivalent to a mere 9.5 per cent of GVIO, 1.8 per cent of GVIAO, or 16 per cent of the combined commercial, grain and transportation service sectors' deficit. But facilitating the purchase of industrial products does not necessarily mean that they will sell well. This, then, is the cost of the industrial strategy for development.

To stimulate backward regions there needs to be an expansion in advanced productive forces. In today's society backward regions cannot themselves spontaneously bring about this development. Imposed 'implants' which transcend natural historical progression should therefore be very significant in invigorating the economy of backward regions. So where do the problems arise? According to the distinguished scholar Schumacher, when the level of advanced industrial technology (this includes the corresponding level of management and the requisite degree of social advancement) is too far above the socioeconomic base of backward regions, the result is 'indigestion'. In answer to this, he suggests that 'social and economic problems require the development of intermediate technology'. Intermediate technology is a concept worthy of note. In Guizhou, for instance, of the 7526 industrial enterprises in existence in 1983, 148 were large or medium-scale, and the remaining 98 per cent were 'small is beautiful' small-scale businesses, 20 per cent of which were collectively run. The techniques employed by these small-scale enterprises were advanced in some cases and traditional in others, but for the most part might be best described as the 'intermediate technology' suggested by Schumacher. Thus it can be seen that we can only partially ascribe the setback to the industrial strategy for development to the factor of imported quotas of engineers and technicians. Even so, where Schumacher hits the nail on the head is in the light he throws upon a simple but elusive fact: the problem of 'identity' between the 'implanted' advanced productive forces and the socioeconomic base of backward regions.

In deciding which sector of the economy is to receive the initial 'implant', the problem is not one of whether the techniques employed in modern industry are advanced, but of what sort of relationship exists between the development of a given sector and the degree of social development together with the transformation in quality of human resources in the region. The links in this relationship are not directly economic sectoral links but are primarily links between the sector and changes in the way of life and concept of value of the local inhabitants. In a general sense this means that the more advanced the techniques, the greater the conflict there will be between them and local modes of production in backward regions. But whether the technology is advanced or 'intermediate', if the result of its implementation – the product – is not acceptable to local ways of thinking, then making the technology more advanced or, alternatively, more 'applicable' will still fail to generate a positive response from the local inhabitants of backward regions.

During our investigations in Tibet we often came across brand-new tractors left out exposed to all weathers simply for want of a few spare parts. Or that is how it appeared ostensibly – that there were hitches in the servicing system. But at a deeper level, the local people saw tractors as unnecessary embellishments without which production could continue just the same. A number of industrial goods such as thermos flasks, Mao caps, bicycles and watches have to differing extents been nominally accepted by a proportion of urban dwellers in backward regions, but for the large majority these sorts of commodities which can only be obtained through cash exchange are still far from becoming 'necessities' such as tea has become. Much of the population in backward regions are not only able to do without watches or bicycles, but can also go without vegetables, poultry, fish and even wheat, as in Tibet. The traditional way of life prolongs the traditional modes of production, and moreover sustains traditional concepts of value and leads to contentment with the traditional way. When people are satisfied with the traditional natural economy, there is no demand for commodities that are solely available through exchange, and consequently the initiative engendered by exchange vanishes in backward regions with a strong bias towards a natural economy.

Both 'latent' and 'implant' development of any sector of the economy presupposes a transformation in the lifestyles and concepts of value of the indigenous people. Unless the local inhabitants can be persuaded to shift from a way of life that has no need of exchange to one that does, and one that moreover produces for exchange, organising production and selecting techniques for tapping resources more economically in order to increase exchange, then it will be extremely difficult to realise capital accumulation and create effective sectoral linkages, whichever sector of the economy is developed first. For the inhabitants of backward regions undergoing the shift away from a natural economy towards a commodity economy, the economic logic is straightforward: *only with the transformation of the existing state of self-sufficiency* can there be enterprise activity and education geared towards production for exchange, and a guarantee of business accounting practice which will generate an impulse towards greater profitability, which in turn will develop into a demand for non-traditional techniques of exploitation. There is little point in discussing whether the technology should be advanced or appropriate before this logical transformation has been carried through. Equally, neither can the indigenous socioeconomic system respond positively to industrial techniques which bear little or no relation to this process of transformation before it is completed.

We cannot claim that introducing modern industry via the 'implantation' technique has absolutely no impact on the lifestyles and concepts of value of the local inhabitants. On the contrary, the influx of a large body of 'immigrants' has brought new learning and culture; and the growth in numbers of indigenous urban dwellers has brought about a fundamental change in the way of life and concepts of value of a considerable proportion of them. This is precisely where hopes for the invigoration of the economies of backward regions lie today. But in terms of selecting a leading sector of the economy, the industrial strategy for development is not the only, and most certainly not the best, choice for stimulating socioeconomic development in backward regions. Quite the reverse, 'implants' of modern industry do not come into direct contact with the lifestyle, customs and values of the indigenous people to any great extent. The local socioeconomic system is quite naturally oblivious to the growth of modern industry: go on and expand primary product exports in order to increase accumulation, we don't need cash; go on and develop processed and finished goods in order to raise living standards, technology and management standards aren't up to scratch, and moreover once the goods have been manufactured no-one will buy them. Unable to obtain a positive response from the indigenous socioeconomic system, economic sectoral links are forced to turn back on themselves for feedback, creating a closed system which transcends local realities. Therefore, regrettably, the entire industrial strategy for development evolves into a vicious circle of 'imports creating more imports'.

The introduction of advanced techniques by no means ends with the purchase of machinery and equipment. To function the equipment needs power, spare parts and materials, and technicians and skilled management are also required. To meet these conditions in backward regions of low-level exploitation which are almost totally unprepared both mentally and materially, we need to keep importing power generators, raw materials, processing equipment and spare part repair equipment, as well as the technical and management know-how required to run these back-up systems. The personnel thus brought in from developed regions cannot be expected to live on the local fare of *tsampa* (roasted barley flour) and raw meat. They need good housing, hospitals, cinemas and schools for their children. Hence in order to make use of the initial equipment, new personnel and machinery have to be continuously brought in, which in turn require the successive construction of buildings and other facilities.

Figure 6.2 is a diagrammatic model of the 'imports create more imports' situation engendered by the backward regions' indigestion when faced with advanced modes of production and imposed 'implants' of modern industry. Living as they do within a self-sufficient natural economy, the vast majority of inhabitants of backward regions have no great desires or demands, nor do they possess the urge to make money or exchange goods. In circumstances such as these, modern enterprises and departments, called the 'implant economy' by developmental economists, are like Martians visiting Earth. Not only do they speak a different language but their whole system of values is completely different. Equipment A requires the importation of a whole support system of power, raw materials, spare parts and transportation (Equipment B, C, D and E) which in turn require a whole set of service systems B_2, C_2, D_2 and E_2 which have to be continuously brought in. This indeed strains the interpretation of the principles behind economic sectoral linkages and provides clear proof that the 'great push forward theory' is inseparable from demand as Rosenstein-Rodan has observed.

Through this process of linked importation the original aim of the import is often gradually obscured. While everyone is busy installing equipment B_3, B_4, B_5 etc, who is likely to remember that all this is to enable Machinery A to function? While the huge imported workforce are clamouring for food, who is going to care whether or not the equipment is functioning properly? The import mechanisms of 'the greater the blood transfusion, the worse the anaemia' and of 'external capital' buying in 'external goods' are encompassed in this import chaining mechanism. Given that the indigenous population are completely divorced from advanced modes of production, the result will be that every single item related to the machinery and equipment will be imported, from spare parts, raw materials, concrete, grain and personnel right down to the tables, chairs and crockery.

The negative response of backward regions makes progress difficult for the isolated force of modern industry.

> Because society does not fulfil all its functions, enterprises find themselves in a position of total isolation, cut off from any help. They are forced to take on social functions which eat away at their accepted economic functions in order to maintain normal production, and this is one of the major reasons behind the falling

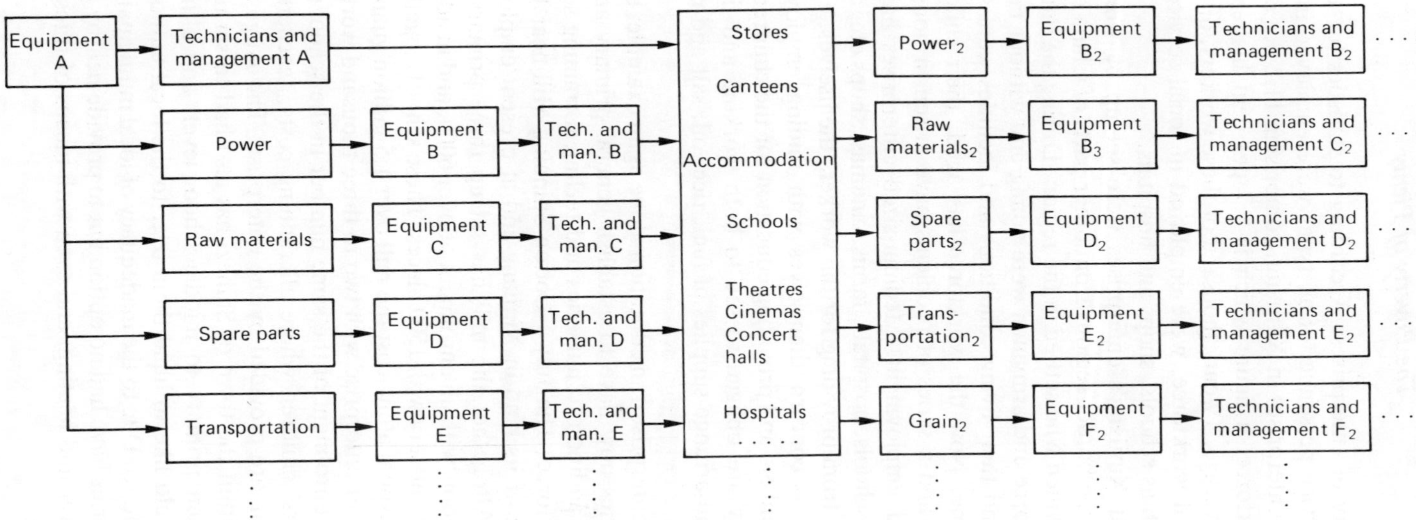

Figure 6.2 The 'imports create more imports' mechanism in backward regions

profitability of enterprises. According to statistics for 1981, over 45 000 service personnel of all types were employed in state-run industrial enterprises in Xinjiang, comprising 11.2 per cent of the total workforce, a figure which is 1.7 per cent higher than the national average. Twenty thousand of these workers, or 5 per cent of the total workforce, were employed in social service organisations such as schools, shops and hospitals.

Many of Xinjiang's enterprises were set up by workers who moved to the border regions from other parts of China or demobilised armymen who settled in the region. During the initial phase, the workforce and armymen were young and without family obligations, and their living conditions and facilities were spartan in the extreme. Now the workforce has aged, their children have grown up and a series of problems have arisen in housing, education and employment. Medium-sized enterprises have set up their own schools, hospitals, farms, cinemas, shops etc, and moreover aside from providing for the workers themselves, enterprises have had to concern themselves with finding employment for family members and providing education for the children. What is more, they are obliged to see to both working and living conditions, and arrange supplies of fuel, rice, oil, salt and non-staple foodstuffs.

Taking enterprise-run education alone as an example, businesses and factories now have to establish general primary and middle schools in addition to nurseries and technical training schools for their workforce. The July 1 Cotton Spinning Mill near Urumqi is the largest of its kind in Xinjiang and at present employs 11 600 workers. Altogether the mill has set up three primary and two middle schools with an enrolment of over 6000, and in addition has organised a nursery with 1500 places. These schools together with a 200-bed hospital alone cost the mill over 1.5 million yuan a year to run. Another enterprise with two to three thousand workers has a staggering enrolment of the same number in the school set up for the workers' children where all running costs, teachers' salaries and housing are provided by the enterprise. The August 1 Sugar Factory within the town of Shihezi has also had to set up general schools from primary to middle school level, and although the factory would like to hand them over to the local authorities it is unable to do so. Due to the inadequacy of local municipal facilities, some factories have had no option but to provide nearby units with water, power and heating, and even with means of transportation and employment opportunities for the children of their workers.

The expansion of the societal role of enterprises inevitably leads to shrinkage of economic functions and a drop in profitability. Another aspect of this problem is that when society fails to fulfil all its functions, enterprises are unable to obtain the external services they require through horizontal channels, and are forced instead to seek assistance via vertical channels. An enterprise which is handicapped by its societal role requires greater assistance from above, and this serves to progressively inhibit the growth of horizontal links within the social organism creating instead a number of separate, unrelated vertical systems where every level from top to bottom controls the one below, and where every level from bottom to top depends on the one above, where the individual is dependent upon the enterprise which in turn is dependent upon its affiliated departments. Within the context of an indigenous economy originally inclined to be exclusive, this means that a number of new closed systems emerge and that already established trades, professions and industries are unable to combine into an integrated production force, thus exacerbating the difficulties of opening to the outside. This is not all: if society does not fulfil all its functions the inevitable result is raised investment costs, lowered investment returns, and increasing restriction on capital flow, which makes it difficult to effect deep and lasting growth. The task of economic development is not simply to start up direct production projects but also to vigorously expand the function of society within the region. Traditional strategies have failed precisely because they have missed this point, focussing solely on individual production growth at the expense of integrated development within the region, and in their eagerness for instant success and quick returns have landed themselves in a situation of 'more haste, less speed'. Not only has a rise in profitability failed to materialise, but deep and lasting development has been held back by shortcomings in the functions of society.[2]

It is commonly held that the advent of modern enterprises and organisations ought to provide a seed-bed for advanced production methods, and should through dissemination enable these advanced methods to gradually penetrate the rest of the region. However, a parallel can be drawn with what has happened in many developing nations following the introduction of modern enterprises and organisations where a diametric opposition has rapidly arisen between city and countryside, creating a 'dual structure'. In exactly the same way modern enterprises and organisations which have been transferred into backward regions from developed countries or regions have utterly failed both in their system of organisation and product composition to arouse a positive response in terms of local social and economic demand. Consequently they have, in the end, been reduced to so many individual, autonomous closed systems operating on a natural economy foundation and relying on 'blood transfusions' from the external world to sustain themselves.

Leaving aside for the moment difficulties in transport and communications, the most fundamental limitation is still the poor quality of human resources. This does not only mean that at present poor management and inadequate technical personnel in modern industry result in a poor economic performance. At a more serious level it also means that the people who live within the natural economy of the vast backward regions require neither commodities manufactured by modern industries nor the up-to-date culture and education brought in alongside these industries, but remain materially and spiritually content with their old way of life. It is precisely this basic limitation which transforms the capital accumulation of the industrial strategy for development into a huge, spiralling deficit, and which causes the sectoral linkage of modern industries to evolve into a vicious circle of 'imports creating more imports'. Moreover, as a consequence, compelled by straitened financial circumstances and aid restrictions, the hoped-for 'disseminator effect' bursts forth with an exclusive, xenophobic instinct quite contrary to its original intention, which erects and strengthens barriers that ordinary people have no way of overcoming such as residency controls, commodity and grain regulations etc, and contains 'modernisation' in weak and isolated pockets within backward regions with the intention of protecting central government financial subsidies from encroachment by the indigenous population.

6.3 UNDIVERSIFIED EXPLOITATION AT A SUPERFICIAL LEVEL

Traditional agriculture and animal husbandry make up a much bigger proportion of the economy in China's backward regions than in the country as a whole, as Table 6.5 shows. Given that almost all the provinces and regions in the table are grain importers, the development of agriculture and animal husbandry must not be neglected in

Table 6.5 Gross value of agricultural and animal husbandry output as a percentage of GVIAO (1983)

Region	*Gross value of agricultural & animal husbandry output as percentage of GVIAO*
Tibet	81
Qinghai	39
Ningxia	35
Xinjiang	43
Inner Mongolia	41
Yunnan	44
Guizhou	46
Guangxi	47
Nationwide	32

view of their contribution to output value. In addition agriculture and animal husbandry provide a guaranteed stabilising force for society. In the long term, a unilateral stress on industrialisation will simply create a serious imbalance in the national economy, while advancing the industrial strategy for development in backward regions will incur even heavier costs. Critics of the industrial strategy are returning to the general slogan of 'agriculture and animal husbandry as the base' as an economic development strategy for these regions. Following criticism of the 'leftist' guiding principle in production of 'take grain as the key link', the four backward regions of Tibet, Qinghai, Xinjiang and Inner Mongolia have placed greater hopes on the development of animal husbandry. At a time when the problems of inadequate food and clothing still affect a considerable proportion of the population in these areas, this development strategy which emphasises agriculture and animal husbandry evidently requires no demonstration of its practical necessity.

A closer examination, however, reveals that within the forseeable future it will be difficult to base the invigoration of the economy in backward regions on a development strategy which stresses the primacy of agriculture and animal husbandry.

1 Transportation Limitations

The current low value content of agricultural and livestock products makes it difficult to overcome the obstacle posed by transportation. Insufficient cold storage and processing capacity in the Xi prefecture of Inner Mongolia means that every year over 250 000 head of livestock have to be transported live, herded some of the way, to places such as Beijing and Tianjin (they are transported by train from Zhangjiakou), Hailar, Urumqi, Jining and Chifeng for processing. These great distances take their toll in the form of tremendous carcass weight loss while other expenses are also considerable. If we take Dongwu banner, the closest to Hailar, as an example, the cost of delivering a live sheep to Hailar can be broken down as follows: herding costs on the overland route from Dongwu banner = 1.70 yuan per head, train transportation costs = 6.00 yuan per head, weight loss en route = 8–9 catties (4–4.5 kilograms) per head. Cattle driving costs are ten times those of sheep, and sustained weight loss is also greater.[3] Xinjiang is world famous for its fruit, and its Hami melons and grapes are especially popular on the world market. With the train journey down to Hong Kong taking eleven days minimum, only semi-ripe fruit can be picked, and moreover transport costs are very high. On the local Xinjiang market Hami melons are priced at 0.26 yuan per catty (0.52 yuan per kg) on average, but once transported down to Shenzhen they fetch 0.99 yuan per catty (1.98 yuan per kg), 2.8 times the local price. The local purchase price per head of cattle is an average 284 yuan which rises to 503 yuan with total costs when transported down to Shenzhen, thus doubling the export price. In this way, long-distance transportation turns Xinjiang's advantage into disadvantage.[4]

2 Limited Market

China is a vast agricultural nation where over 80 per cent of the population is concentrated on the land. At present there is a relative surplus of agricultural produce and so, handicapped by their high transport costs, conventional farm and livestock products from outlying backward regions have difficulties in penetrating the domestic market (this excludes special products available nowhere else such as yaks). Xinjiang, the second biggest livestock producer, has now dropped back to 24th place nationwide as meat supplier to the domestic market. The resultant stockpiling causes its own problems. By the end of 1983 there were 109 million kilograms of cotton in storage, equivalent to almost two years of sales. Sugar stocks stood at 49 600 tons, or eleven months' sales. As for cotton cloth, there were 60 million metres in storage, and it is estimated that in 1984 stockpiles will reach 100 million metres, or almost a year's worth of sales.[5] In

Inner Mongolia 20 million catties (10 million kilograms) of fine spinning wool alone were stockpiled in 1983, and it is estimated that in 1984 farmers and herdsmen will want to sell to the state another 38 million catties (19 million kilograms) at the very minimum. The government arranged to transfer 31 million catties (15.5 million kilograms) out of the region, but by the end of July only 17 million catties (8.5 million kilograms) had been shifted. Eighty per cent of the stockpiled wool was stored in the open air at the mercy of the weather and pests.[6] In a situation where self-sufficiency is the dominant economic force, these stockpiled goods which everyone is able to produce for themselves are hardly going to achieve extensive sales.

China's agricultural tradition goes back several thousand years. In this most traditional of sectors, short of giving full play to certain resource monopoly factors, to expect a boost to the economy of backward regions as well as success in overcoming transportation limitations and market barriers is as good as asking the local inhabitants to organise traditional production more efficiently and economically than elsewhere in China. This is something which in the short term is impossible to achieve. Market and transportation restrictions are obstacles which directly affect the *exchange* rather than the production of farm and livestock products. And it is in the sphere of exchange that the local inhabitants possess the least attributes. Even if advanced production techniques are introduced, an increase in the *volume* of farm and livestock products will by no means entail a rise in exchange activity nor yet heightened commodity enterprise attributes amongst the indigenous populations in backward regions.

In thirty or so years, while the value of output in Tibet has quadrupled the commodity rate has not risen at all. The facts speak for themselves: the emergence of exchange activity is not decided by the quantity of products, but hinges upon the development of social relations. Production volume may in a general sense determine the degree of prosperity, but it in no way directly implies the transformation of economic relations. It seems over-simplistic and out-of-date to summarise historical progress, and particularly the changes in socioeconomic relations, as an increase in product volume, and to believe that it only requires a surplus of goods to bring about exchange and hence naturally the transformation of production relations. We are faced with the facts of the long stagnation of the natural economy in backward regions and of a good deal of 'prosperous stagnation' in these regions. Moreover, despite several thousand years of major efforts in agriculture and animal husbandry in China a commodity economy has never fully developed. If we accept that the evolution of a commodity economy is a selective process in which people's subjective initiative is given rein, then the choice of traditional agriculture and animal husbandry as the launching point for boosting the economy of backward regions will most likely result in the progressive atrophy of existing commodity economy relations, impeded by transport and market restrictions. For these reasons it is hard to see that this is a wise choice.

Production in backward regions has unconsciously been oriented towards agriculture and animal husbandry over the past several thousand years. The flourishing commodity economy in the countryside in central and coastal parts of China has in recent years given rise to a popular misconception. Many are of the opinion that simply freeing rural accumulation from the financial burden of industry, raising the prices of agricultural products and once again emphasising agriculture as the base will result in a thriving and vigorous overall rural economy. This view ignores the fundamental reason behind the transformation of central and coastal China's rural economy, namely that by reorganising socioeconomic relations the responsibility system released the latent forces of the commodity economy which had long been brewing.

In backward regions where the quality of human resources still remains basically unchanged, if industrial development were to be halted because of the accompanying mounting deficit, it would admittedly stop the rise in financial subsidies. And supposing industry were to be abrogated, then the deficit might perhaps be eliminated and a balance obtained between revenue and expenditure. Moreover raising farm product prices might also restore a certain harmony and balance through recuperation. But the extreme debility of local commodity entrepreneurial impulse means that in abandoning the one-sided development of industry, relaxing controls and once again emphasising the primacy of agriculture and animal husbandry, it is quite possible that we might escape from the slippery slope of industrial deficit only to find ourselves in the quagmire of what has been called the 'low-level equilibrium trap', caught in the old vicious circle of apathy and sapped vitality.

Agriculture and animal husbandry are the breeding grounds of poverty and backwardness in undeveloped regions. The social fabric of these modes of production is much more primitive than elsewhere in China. In terms of the relation between human production and natural resources, modern modes of production are characterised by multilateral, highly stratified exploitation and multiple utilisation of natural resources. The former is expressed as the *extent* and the latter as the *intensiveness* of resource exploitation. One aspect of the evolution of modes of production is evident in the growing extent of resource utilisation, namely that previously disregarded material is gradually transformed into a precious resource through the development of exploitation techniques. The other aspect is manifested in the increase in intensiveness of exploitation, that is, the multiple utilisation of multiple aspects of the same resource. (It is hard to keep these two aspects separate in practice.)

If we take as an example early plant gathering production methods, in terms of extent of resource utilisation they were extremely limited and also, in terms of utilisation intensiveness, simple and undiversified. The discovery of fire turned animals into a hunting resource, and the bones of the animals thus caught were used to make both tools and ornaments, providing an instance of multiple utilisation. In agricultural civilisation the gradual expansion of crop varieties shows the growth in extent of utilisation, while the use of such techniques as ploughing and fertilising reflects a rise in the intensiveness of land resource utilisation. Industrial civilisation opened up the earth with mining, and hitherto unknown metals were smelted. Biological engineering, too, produced man-made varieties and strains of plants and animals, as well as opening up the possibility of factory farming. Clearly, extent and intensiveness of resource utilisation show a high degree of overlap.

The use of these two indicators to differentiate between modes of production at different periods reveals the distinct characteristic that the more primitive the mode of production, the more superficial and limited the extent of resource utilisation, and the less intensively it is carried out.

China's traditional agricultural mode of production is known as the 'horizontal expansionist' mode of production because its major feature is that the area under cultivation has expanded (this includes double cropping) under population pressure. In this way it is distinguished from the all-embracing modern mode of production with its multilateral, highly stratified exploitation. In terms of extent and intensiveness of natural resource utilisation, agricultural and pastoral modes of production in backward regions possess the same basic properties as the traditional mode of production elsewhere in China, but at a lower, more primitive level. These modes of production represent a type of 'over-superficial horizontal expansionism'. Farmers and herders in Qinghai, Tibet, Inner Mongolia and Xinjiang make use of extremely primitive methods of resource exploitation, and within the domains of traditional agriculture and animal husbandry, their needs are moreover highly uniform and exhibit virtually no stratification. An example is the basic subsistence level of their food and clothing.

During this period of 'horizontal expansionism', long before the introduction of industrial civilisation, almost anything that flew, swam or crawled was fit for the pot in the eyes of the Cantonese. This enriched the extent of natural resource utilisation and at the same time resulted in highly stratified intensive exploitation which moreover brought about the continuing reorganisation of modern agriculture. In Tibet, on the other hand, even today, many years after the introduction of industrial civilisation, the indigenous people still neither eat vegetables or fish nor raise poultry. In Yamdok Tso Lake alone natural fish stocks stand at 200 to 300 catties (100 to 150 kg) but are left untouched while the local inhabitants live on *tsampa* (roasted barley flour) and a very limited variety of meat products. The slices of meat hacked off a sheep's carcass left hanging up to cure are considered a delicacy. They are eaten raw, with not even the addition of salt. There is absolutely no demand for pots or pans, bowls or utensils, or any condiments such as oil, salt, soy sauce or vinegar. Although natural conditions in Tibet are suited to wheat, often giving more than double the yield of highland barley, the indigenous population cannot benefit from this as they have neither the equipment for cooking wheat nor the culinary techniques other than roasting grain. Even though the authorities ordered the wide-scale planting of wheat, which resulted in a tremendous leap in grain production, in the end they had no option but to allow a return to growing barley.

In this situation, despite the fact that backward regions are often vast and sparsely populated with a much lower density of population than elsewhere in China, yet utilisation of resources remains over-superficial and undiversified, and non-intensive. Moreover, because of the prevalent 'over-superficial horizontal expansionist' mode of production, the unit area of land required to support the population is much greater than elsewhere in China. Thus in trying to solve basic subsistence problems, the formation of an ecologically destructive vicious circle is much more marked than in rural areas in other parts of China.

Livestock raising and other pastoral activities make up about 60 per cent of GVAO in Tibet, forming the basis of the agricultural economy. At present, pressure of population has already caused a sharp expansion in stock numbers and overgrazing is having a serious deleterious effect on the grasslands. Figures from surveys in thirteen counties show that on average overstocking is as high as 17 per cent. Years of depredations from overstocking, grazing competition and human activity have led to a critical deterioration of pastureland. Desertified areas already exceed by one-third the area of viable grassland. If we break down further this area of viable grassland, remaining top-grade pasture (grass yields of around 250 catties per mu (approximately 188 kilograms per hectare)) account for only 7 per cent, middle-grade pastures (grass yields of 80 catties per mu – 60 kilograms per hectare) make up about 40 per cent, while pastures yielding a mere 20 catties or so per mu (15 kilograms per hectare) now comprise 53 per cent. To give some idea of what this means, a single sheep thus requires an average 34 mu (2.38 hectares) of pastureland to provide adequate grazing.

In Qinghai the situation is the same. Immediately following Liberation there was an average livestock population density of one sheep per 32 mu (2.24 hectares), but this has now dropped to 12 mu (0.84 hectare), and in the Qinghai Lake region where stocks are concentrated it has fallen to 10 mu (0.07 hectare) or less in some counties and communes. Overstocking has led to a serious degeneration of the grasslands, and throughout the province desert areas have already increased 32 per cent from 89.55 million mu (7 268 500 hectares) to 118.5 million mu (8 295 000 hectares). In the initial period after 1949, grass in the model pastures of Qinghai's principal pastureland grew to an average height of 20 centimetres, with an overall coverage of 75 to 90 per cent. Today, the grass grows to a maximum height of only 10 centimetres, while overall coverage has dropped considerably and grass yields are estimated to have fallen by approximately 50 per cent. The acute contradiction between stock and grassland has reduced Qinghai's entire stock population to a state of semi-starvation, with both a high mortality rate and a widescale drop in the numbers and quality of the surviving animals. In the same period, the average weight of a sheep has fallen from over 20 kilograms in 1949 to a mere 16 kilograms today. These factors alone mean that every year the province as a whole suffers livestock carcass losses of 1000 million catties (500 million kilograms). The degeneration of pastures and accompanying stock losses are day by day becoming more critical. In the last dozen years or so, annual spring stock losses have amounted to an average one million plus or 5 per cent of total livestock numbers, while lambing/calving/foaling losses have reached two million head.[7]

On Xinjiang's vast stretches of grassland the pastoral population has doubled between 1965 and 1983, while sheep carcass weights have fallen from an average 19.5 kilograms in 1966 to 13 kilograms in 1983. In the region as a whole, wilderness pastures make up a staggering 65 per cent, and waterless pastures comprise 27 per cent, which leaves only 2 per cent of viable pastureland. Grave overstocking has meant that on average every year some seven million standard livestock have no assured winter and spring grazing, and close on two million animals die of hunger and cold, a figure equivalent to the total number of livestock sold to the state every year. The mortality rate among full-grown livestock is about 10 per cent in a normal year, but can rise as high as 16.4 per cent. Xinjiang's annual livestock losses make up half the national total. Since 1949 livestock losses have totalled 63.37 million, exceeding by 34.7 per cent the total marketable livestock supply for the same period. One result of this 'flourishing' state of animal husbandry is that in 1982 the per capita supply of meat in the second largest meat-producing region in China was just 21.5 catties (10.75 kilograms), or only 80 per cent of the national average for the same year.[8]

The situation in Inner Mongolia is largely similar. Soil erosion and water loss affect 200 008 000 mu (over 14 million hectares) in the region as a whole, or 15.7 per cent of the total land area. Affected banners and counties number 53, eight of which are key soil erosion areas in the middle reaches of the former course of the Yellow River, comprising an affected area of 31.5 million mu (2.405 million hectares) which discharges up to 180 million tons of mud and sand into the Yellow River every year. Of the 80 million mu (5.6 million hectares) under cultivation in the entire region, 16 million mu (1.12 million hectares) are seriously affected by water loss and soil and wind erosion, while alkaline and salt land in urgent need of improvement amounts to over 10 million mu (42 million hectares) in the region as a whole, equivalent to 34 per cent of the total land area. Of this figure, the area affected by desertification has expanded to 150 million mu (10.5 million hectares) in under five decades and continues to grow at a rate of 5 million mu (350 000 hectares) per year. Sixty-seven of the region's total of 88 banners and counties suffer sandstorm damage. Desertification and degeneration of the grasslands have resulted in falling production levels per unit area. We can deduce that grass yields in pastures over the region as a whole have dropped to 40 to 60 per cent across the board.[9] In these circumstances, overstocking had already topped 33 per cent in 1983 throughout the region, while total stock mortalities amounted to 58.7 million head between 1958 and 1979, 6.4 million more than the number of livestock sold to the state within the same period.

The 'low-level equilibrium trap' is a factual explanation for the decline in animal husbandry in the west of China and for the continued destruction of forests to open up wasteland in Yunnan and Guizhou. Far from being a simple case of stagnation, it is rather a dynamic vicious circle of environmental destruction and consolidated backwardness and poverty. Within this vicious circle, the potential progressive shrinking of existing relations of commodity exchange brings about the gradual retreat of the entire economy into the closed, fixed state of a natural economy. In addition, the increasingly strained relationship between man and nature leads to a worsening ecological situation and the destruction of natural resources. From either point of view, subjective or objective, this vicious circle increasingly restricts people's efforts to break out of the cycle, escape from the 'over-superficial horizontal expansionist' mode of production, and realise three-dimensional highly stratified exploitation. Carried out badly, the development strategy which emphasises agriculture and animal husbandry is equivalent to a negative investment in the latent forces within both material resources and the quality of human resources for the development of backward regions.

6.4 INFORMATION AND THE ECONOMY

A review of the analysis given above reveals that neither of the two development strategies – industrial or agricultural/pastoral – can fulfil the two fundamental targets in formulating the orientation of the economy, namely 1) rapid capital accumulation and 2) the appropriate development of other sectors of the economy. This is summarised in Table 6.6.

Looking first at the second aim – promoting the appropriate development of other sectors of the economy – the industrial strategy unfortunately transforms the internal relations of modern industry into a vicious cycle of 'imports creating more imports', and at the same time is quite unable through the development of modern

Table 6.6 Industrial and agricultural strategies for development

Economic orientation	*Capital accumulation*	*Sectoral linkage*
Industry	enormous deficit	'imports create more imports' vicious circle
Agriculture/animal husbandry	low-level equilibrium	vicious circle of environmental destruction

industry to halt the vicious circle of continued environmental destruction by the rural population. Turning next to the financial target of capital accumulation, the 'low-level equilibrium' of the agricultural strategy does not lead to frequent huge deficits of the industrial strategy, (leaving aside relief aid in times of disaster), but because of its incompatability with cash and exchange there is nevertheless no prospect either of achieving rolling capital accumulation.

In the light of these two specific targets and limitations, a non-traditional input is required when selecting a leading sector in the economy of backward regions. As well as realising capital accumulation and encouraging the development of other sectors, the correct choice must also be able to transform the quality of human resources to the greatest extent and overcome transport and communication difficulties. Both the industrial and agricultural strategies for development present feasible and realistic programmes with regard to natural resource advantages, but their failure to satisfy the four accompanying requirements described above means that all their efforts are wasted, to be compared with the labours of Sisyphus.

The question is: must we first tackle the huge deficit, develop education, science, health and culture, carry out road maintenance work and vehicle purchases, raise the quality of human resources, and improve transport conditions *before* we can consider developing sectors of the economy in backward regions? The 'Infrastructure First?' section in Chapter 4 has already refuted this line of thought. So where does the solution lie? We have to seek a novel and path-breaking way out of the situation.

Transformation of Lifestyle

In selecting the orientation of the economy in backward regions it is fundamentally recognised that any transformation of the quality of human resources begins with change in the indigenous population's way of life and not initially in production methods.

In *The Economics of Developing Nations* the British scholar Professor Myint makes an important point: farmers in a natural economy are only really able to fully utilise 'technological opportunities' and raise levels of work and output *after* tapping 'market opportunities' to the full and turning all or most of self-sufficiency production over to exchange use. Over the past few decades immense effort has been put into introducing advanced production techniques into backward regions – this has been the major component of the 'blood transfusions' – but at the same time the staggering fact is that the local people themselves have been indifferent or oblivious to this technology brought in at such cost. We conclude that what backward regions lack first and foremost are not advanced production techniques but commodity relations of fair exchange. Only when commodity exchange relations have become widespread throughout a society can there be cost accounting within the production process and a demand for technology brought about by the need to economise. This topic has been dealt with above.

Another theme similarly addressed above is that a rise in output and increase in commodity surplus are material preconditions for exchange, but are a long way from being in themselves exchange. Following the implementation of the rural responsibility system when the compulsory state unified purchase and supply system was abolished, the general reluctance to sell in backward regions and the typical cases found everywhere of richly-endowed self-sufficiency demonstrate that exchange is not a function of commodity surplus.

In the final analysis, it is the expectations of raised living standards of the local inhabitants which will provide the impetus towards exchange of a societal nature. Our tenet of the poor quality of human resources is supported by the fact that due to limited knowledge of the outside world the indigenous people have extremely low expectations of consumption or standards of living, and consequently they do not strive for higher living standards and lack any impetus towards new forms of economic activity. Two co-existing curves for production potential occur in backward regions (see Figure 6.3). The *Z* curve represents the realisation of key production factors according to the rules of combination in a natural economy, while the *W* curve represents the realisation of key production factors according to the rules of combination in a commodity economy. The *Z* curve shows the existing state of affairs, while the *W* curve represents the situation

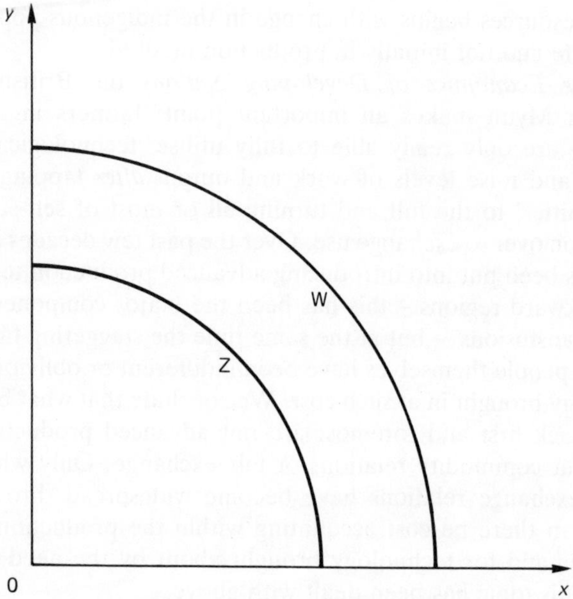

Figure 6.3 Co-existing curves for production potential in backward regions

in developed regions and the theoretically possible situation in backward regions. Friction is inevitable as the *Z* curve shifts towards the *W* curve; as the tranquil way of life in which no outside help is required for any activity is transformed, through commodity exchange and the adoption of new technology, into a hectic lifestyle, unpredictable and constantly changing, in which nothing can be achieved in isolation.

Far from being subjective motive forces for the shift from the *Z* curve to the *W* curve, the low cultural and technical levels and transport limitations are right now nothing but objective obstacles to the transition. The impetus for change will stem only from the indigenous population's discontent with the present way of life and the people's desire to seek a new lifestyle. The greater this desire the greater the contradiction when the traditional mode of production cannot fulfil living standard expectations, and the higher the chances that people will take the plunge into a commodity economy. In circumstances where the Tibetans eat neither poultry nor fish (and so, naturally, do not raise them) and even have no use for oil, salt, vinegar and soy sauce, it is difficult to imagine how they might engage in exchange and exactly what they might exchange.

The debate throughout the history of mankind over whether supply creates demand or whether demand creates supply is a 'which came first: the chicken or the egg?' kind of question. But at certain points in the course of history it is true to say that both production potential curves have co-existed in backward regions. At these times, the impetus behind the shift from the real *Z* curve to the equally real *W* curve can only be explained with recourse to the fundamental aim of human economic activity. At the present point in time, what is needed first and foremost is not the introduction of techniques to raise output but information on different ways of life which will fan this impetus into flame – and this is what should be given primary consideration when selecting the orientation of the economy in backward regions. More important than the choice of either industrial or agricultural strategies is to consider the problem from the angle of production orientation. Thus not only has administration and management in a general sense been impeded by poor quality human resources, but in addition there is a lack of impetus at a fundamental level connecting advanced techniques and changes in the local people's way of life in backward regions. As long as the inhabitants of these regions cling to their self-sufficient ownership of livestock that are never sold, or to their wealth which consists in the consumption of a few hundred kilograms of yak butter every year, then it is apparent that they can in no way appreciate production techniques designed for exchange. Thus, *the transformation of the local way of life is a prerequisite for any change in modes of production.*

Overcoming Transport Limitations

Exchange is a function of transportation; without transportation there can be no exchange. The limitations imposed by transport difficulties in backward regions are heavy shackles on the total amount and rate of commodity exchange. This implies that any development of a sector of the economy has to take on board the burden of a 'transport tax' which is much more expensive than in developed regions, with the result that despite growth (starting further down the scale than in developed regions) the backward region still remains uncompetitive. However, it does not mean that any development in backward regions is doomed to failure, because this is only part of the problem. The real problem lies in *what* is transported.

High-cost transportation stems from transporting bricks. Every year, Guizhou Province has to 'import' around 160 million bricks, requiring 8000 freight cars in rail transportation alone. High-cost transportation stems from transporting mining waste. Guizhou exports phosphate-bearing rock with a P_2O_5 grade material content of as high as 30 per cent, which nevertheless leaves a remaining 70 per cent of wasted labour. Leaving aside manufactured goods for direct export, if post-selection P_2O_5 grade material rose to even 50 per cent, the annual phosphate freight capacity could increase from the current 1.8 million tons to 3 million tons. Without the need for any extra transportation, capacity could go up by 67 per cent and at the same time the unit transport costs for phosphate would fall. If the reform of the economic structure can as far as possible bring a halt to this blind importation and the totally pointless shunting around of unsaleable goods in Tibet, then the right choice for the orientation of the economy ought to be able to overcome the limitations posed by transport and communications difficulties.

According to the theory of control, any exchange activity brought about through transportation and communication is the result of three different types of 'flow'.[10] The first is 'material flow' where the turnover volume of goods is expressed in tons per kilometre, that is, x tons of goods flow y kilometres from Point A to Point B. The value of this 'flow' is expressed as the cost of transportation. Clearly, the greater the distance the higher the cost of transportation regardless of the kind of goods. The second type is 'value flow' where value is transferred from Point A to Point B by means of 'material flow' (through tons-kilometre transportation). It is important to note this distinction where the cost of transportation and commodity value are treated as two separate entities. The third type is 'information flow' and like 'information' it is an expression that is hard to define. For the purposes of our analysis, let us define it as the realisation of information transmission through the flow of material and value from Point A to Point B. This realisation of 'information transmission' is the same as common knowledge, and indicates the change of state from ignorance and doubt to knowledge and certainty.

That the crux of all problems lies in the transport and communications limitations on commodity exchange is true only in an *average* sense. Under comparatively similar transport conditions, different commodities possess material, value and information contents in varying proportions. As every exchange transaction conducted through transportation involves identical processes for identical items, the relations between the three different 'contents' can therefore only be shown by their relative proportions (of material, value and information content). Hence, the same quantity of goods may possess dissimilar value and information contents, and by the same token equal units of value or information content may be realised in different quantities of goods. In financial terms, only when the value content exceeds the cost of transportation will the goods be unequivocally considered worth transporting. But in terms of information gain, that is to say with transportation costs and realisable value all being equal, the greater the information content the richer and hence the more worthwhile the goods. If we take an example of three loads transported over the same distance, the realisable value of a truckload of grain cannot begin to cover the cost of transportation, and as for information content it is virtually impossible to taste the difference between Chinese or foreign imported grain and local-grown grain of the same variety. Transportation costs for a truckload of diamonds, on the other hand, represent the merest fraction of its realisable gross value, but again diamonds are not much better than grain in terms of information transmission, seeing as local and imported diamonds differ only in size. Turning now to our third load – a truck full of colour TVs – although its realisable value is much lower than that of the diamonds, yet in bringing in a source of information its information transmission is vastly superior to either of the other two loads.

This is not all. As regards the actual physical quantity of any one item needed to satisfy consumer demand, it is frequently the case that a commodity's consumer life (that is, the number of times it can be used – the fewer times an item can be used, the shorter its consumer life) is directly proportional to its value and information content. Hence commodities with low value and information content entail a greater material consumer demand while placing a concomitant greater burden on transport capacity. For instance, many backward regions employ thousands of kilometres of road and thousands upon thousands of vehicles (that is, tons-kilometres) to transport grain, but still complain that their freight capacity falls short of consumer demand. But when we consider that an equivalent value in diamonds

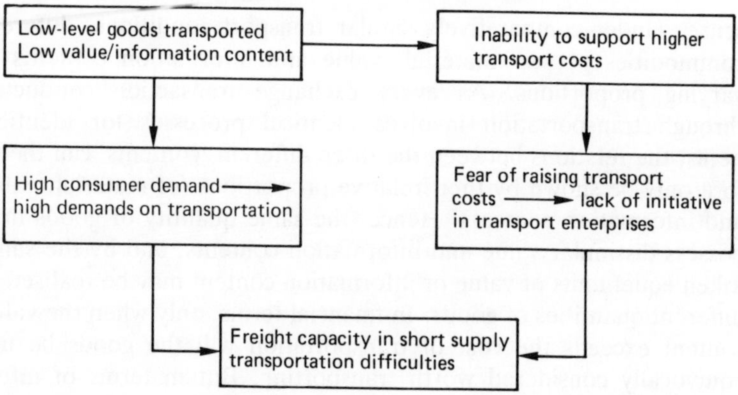

Figure 6.4 Results of transporting an excess of low-levels goods

could be brought in in someone's pocket, then it is likely that the roads and vehicles currently in use would be far in excess of requirements.

We can see from the foregoing that poorly developed transport and communications restrict commodity exchange solely on the level of material flow. The 'transport tax' is levied on the quantity of material flow alone. On the levels of value and information content it is entirely feasible that the right choice of a leading sector for the orientation of the economy can overcome the limitations of transport conditions. Over 50 per cent of Tibet's freight capacity is given over to bringing in grain which possesses virtually zero information content and moreover is sold at below cost, while much of the remaining transport capacity is taken up with 'importing' construction materials such as bricks, tiles, mortar and stone. Far too many low-level goods are being carried which is the root cause behind scarce freight capacity as well as the artificially low transportation charges and the inability of transport and communications to develop. The logical relations are shown in Figure 6.4.

Apart from road maintenance and vehicle replacement, and aside from raising transport enterprises' initiative to carry more goods faster, one much-neglected solution to the problem of freight capacity in backward regions is to carry more high-level goods and develop the high value/information content sector of the economy. It is worth noting that the value of a commodity is generally proportional to its information content in exchange between the border regions and the rest of China. When backward regions follow suit in producing goods already available in eastern and central China, the additional high costs of transportation make these goods uncompetitive even if they are on a par with existing Chinese goods in variety of design, size, colour, quality and standards. By way of contrast, local handicrafts with ethnic minority regional features can sometimes fetch relatively high prices even though they do not match up to standards elsewhere in China precisely because they possess a special information content that no other Chinese product has. This applies to both 'exports' and 'imports'.

Tales abound of profiteers and sharp tricksters from the border regions, and within the limits of what the local inhabitants find acceptable goods which are scarce in the region will always fetch a higher price. Thus in selecting the economic orientation of the backward regions' economy, special attention should be paid to sectors with high information content whose distinctive products differ from those produced elsewhere in China.

Priority development of high information content sectors will be able to overcome the severe limitations on the economic development of backward regions. Through the increased value resulting from high information content this strategy can escape the restrictive costs of transportation and utilise this high information content to assail the traditional way of life, gradually transform the quality of human resources and initiate reforms in lifestyle and related economic development. An outstanding example of this type of sector is the tourism industry.

As regards resources, backward regions are ideally equipped for tourism. The legendary Tianshan Mountains of Xinjiang, the rolling grasslands of Inner Mongolia, Qinghai Lake and the nearby Ta'ersi Monastery, tropical Xishuangbanna and the hot springs of Yunnan, Guizhou's great waterfalls and caves, and the mountain and river scenery of Guilin in Guangxi Province are all tourist attractions famed the world over. The region richest in tourist attractions is Tibet, paradoxically also the most poverty-stricken. Perched on the 'roof of the world', Tibet has a reputation as a land of mystery with magnificent scenery, a multitude of snowy peaks and vast forests, abounding in places of historical interest. All this together with the attraction of a unique and age-old art and culture make Tibet all in all a place where conditions and customs are quite out of the ordinary. Tibet attracts droves of visitors from both China and abroad who pour in prepared to brave all hardships.

Tourism is a typical case of information consumption. Prices depend more on the information that can be provided by a tourist spot (that is, its desirability) than on the investment costs of services and facilities. Even the most luxurious hotel will not break even if it is sited in an uninteresting place. By way of contrast, in places where accomodation, transport and communications, food and services are all far below the levels of developed regions elsewhere in China, a high 'tourist information content' can create the astounding situation prevailing in Tibet where, with the plane ticket at double the price, tourism is twice as expensive per person as the national average and yet the demand from tourists cannot be met. Between 1980 and 1983 6300 overseas mountaineers and tourists visited Tibet, and not counting the income of the transportation sector and sports organisations, the tourist industry alone turned in 8.33 million yuan in both convertible and non-convertible currency with a profit of 5.32 million yuan. Whereas most other sectors of the economy in the region as a whole failed to break even, the direct profit rate of the tourist industry was as high as 64 per cent, with each employee remitting an average 30 000 yuan every year. While in terms of profitability other sectors of the economy are in bottom place nationwide, the tourism industry is, by itself, the sole bearing branch, ranking first throughout the entire country.

The development of tourism in Tibet has tremendous potential. In 1983 China as a whole received only 3 per cent of the world's international tourists, and of this figure only 1.8 per cent visited Tibet. At the same time Nepal, which is only a tenth of the size of Tibet and has far less to offer in the way of scenic spots, places of historical interest and fascinating local conditions and customs, received 114 times as many tourists as Tibet, with tourism earnings 27 times higher than in Tibet. The problem is not that Tibet lacks Nepal's attraction for tourists. On the contrary, large numbers of would-be tourist 'information seekers' who are prepared to pay dearly to visit Tibet are turned away due to limited tourist facilities.

There can be no doubt at all that for a considerable time now tourism has been a seller's market in Tibet. Tourism department projections for Tibet from 1984 to 2000 show that once tourism has reached the level in Nepal we can expect accumulated earnings of 2100 million yuan at the very least, which would bring in a net profit of 1100 million yuan, even calculating from the national average 51 per cent net profit rate for tourism in 1983. The extra 6000 beds that would be required during this period, not counting the previously loss-making guest houses and hotels which would be mobilised, will require a mere 300 to 400 million yuan total investment outlay on new construction. Tourism itself is well able to realise 'money making money'. The initial period apart, no outside investment will be necessary. If we commit ourselves to the restructuring of the economy, if we mobilise loss-making guest houses, hotels and local community-use buildings, if we make use of 'tons-kilometre' freight capacity to bring in people rather than grain, bricks and tiles or mining waste, and if, under conditions of surplus accumulation, pooling resources leads to public capital accumulation and turnover, then tourism will gradually become more and more profitable and this process of 'money makes money' capital accumulation will progressively gather speed.

People are a prime source of information, possessing the greatest information load as measured in tons-kilometre. As well as paying for previously unvalued 'tourist information', the people thus transported in bring with them free of charge a lot of new information for the inhabitants of backward regions. The tourists' eating habits, clothing and jewellery, how they treat people, their appearance and behaviour may become the objects of wonder, admiration and emulation by the local people. The American army of occupation which stayed on in Japan after the end of the Second World War brought about tremendous changes in the Japanese lifestyle and patterns of consumption, known as the 'chewing gum effect'. This effect of example is highly significant. The consumption patterns of the indigenous population in backward regions can, through emulation and learning, become enriched thus resulting in production for exchange, and from this there emerges the possibility of transforming modes of production. The modern culture and information brought in by tourists from developed regions has, in effect, a similar impact to the personnel from developed regions brought in to backward regions by the industrial strategy for development, and can be a tremendous impetus for change in lifestyles, patterns of consumption and concepts of value among the local inhabitants. The difference is that information comes free with the tourists who at the same time are contributing enormous amounts to capital accumulation for the economic development of backward regions, while the personnel from developed regions are brought in at the cost of huge deficits in the backward region's finances.

The vast influx of visitors to backward regions not only brings with it modern culture and information creating something similar to the 'chewing gum effect', but in addition directly creates a new demand for 'tertiary industry' products and services in backward regions, such as the catering and service sectors, ethnic handicrafts and so forth. Foreign tourists visiting Tibet are quite content with ordinary transport to go sightseeing while horse-riding, boating in yakskin coracles, hunting and dressing up in Tibetan costumes all have great appeal. Visitors also enjoy Tibetan cuisine and appreciate Tibetan culture, music and dance, and at the same time they are keen to purchase as souvenirs such ethnic minority commodities as Tibetan robes, boots, hats, cloaks, seating cushions (traditional woven wool items), wooden bowls, steels, Buddha figurines, pagodas and *tangkas* (Buddhist hangings). During our talks with representatives from Tibet's tourism departments, one point often raised was that foreign tourists were prepared to change vast amounts of foreign currency into yuan in order to buy cheap, worthless local souvenirs. On top of this, the arrival of tourists in large numbers can directly stimulate normal consumer demand in backward regions which at present barely exists, and so encourage market gardening, fish and poultry farming and related food processing industries (the produce of which Tibetans neither consume nor produce), as well as improve housing, related facilities and service levels. Thus it is possible that development in service sectors will be spurred on by tourism and gradually spread out from here, creating sectoral linkages (see Figure 6.5).

As a model of a high information content sector, tourism is able to both overcome the limitations posed by transportation difficulties and achieve the most rapid capital accumulation, while at the same time it can maximally raise the quality of human resources and create expanding sectoral linkages. All this means that tourism may well be a favoured choice for orientation of the economy in backward regions (see Table 6.7).

Conclusion

Invigorating the economy of backward regions can be represented as the attainment and surpassing of a series of economic goals. Achieving this depends not on the goals themselves but on the methods employed. Of fundamental importance is a rise in the quality of human resources. Changes in lifestyle are a precondition for changes in methods of production.

One special characteristic of information exchange is that it is not bound by time or space. Maximum information exchange is a basic

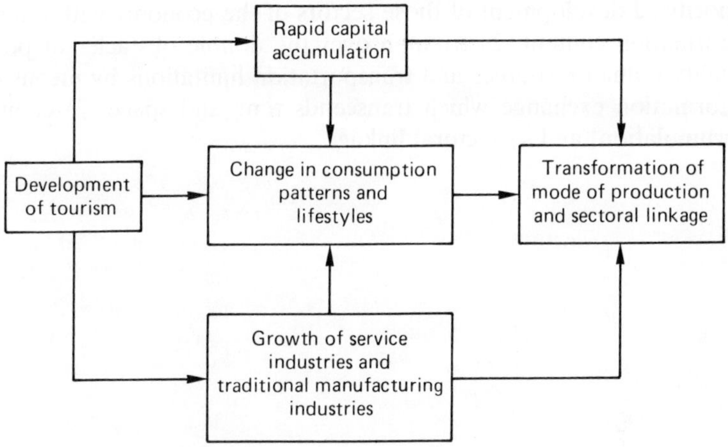

Figure 6.5 The function of tourism

Table 6.7 A comparison of three sectors of the economy

	Industry	*Agriculture animal husbandry*	*Tourism*
1) Capital accumulation capacity	low	medium	high
2) Sectoral linkage capacity	medium	low	high
3) Limitations posed by poor quality of human resources	high	medium	low
4) Limitations posed by transportation difficulties	medium	high	low
Material content	medium	high	low
Value content	medium	low	high
Information content	medium	low	high

condition for stimulating the economy of backward regions both from the point of view of overcoming transportation limitations as well as from the standpoint of transforming the way of life in backward regions.

The transportation and manufacture of low-level goods in backward regions needs to be upgraded towards a higher-level economic structure. The fundamental indicator of a high-level economic structure is its information content. The basic principles behind the selection of economic orientation in backward regions should be 1) prioritised development of those sectors of the economy with a high information content; 2) triumph over the double obstacles of poor quality human resources and transportation limitations by means of information exchange which transcends time and space; 3) capital accumulation, and 4) sectoral linkage.

7 An Open Conclusion

The difficulties we encountered in writing this book were due to the fact that logically speaking what we were describing was not a complete, closed system. We have considered some matters in sufficient depth, but there are still a number of things we would like to have mentioned but were unable to do justice to which remain to be covered. We leave the reader to reflect on the following ideas.

7.1 STRENGTHENING THE ROLE OF GOVERNMENT

Reforming the 'one big pot' economic management system in no way signals the collapse of the government's leadership of the economy and, similarly, weakening administrative command style business management entails no diminution of the government's powers of intervention in the economy. On the contrary, according to the analysis presented above in the section 'Two-way Initiative' in Chapter 3, in backward regions where the quality of human resources is poor the greater the wish to speed up economic development and catch up with advanced areas, the less likely it is that this will be achieved by simply 'relaxing controls', seeing reform as washing one's hands of the whole business and letting things drift. It would be extremely dangerous to approach the present reform in this manner, especially in the case of the reform and development of backward regions.

Previously in the unified economic management system there were no separate interests, no separate interest groups or representatives and no differences in quality between people. All behaviour was geared towards one direction – solely to follow the lead of the planned economy. Without the stimulation of immediate interests, people did whatever they were told to do no matter how skilled or educated they were. The will of the government at this time was the will of the entire economic system, and the monolithic functions of organised state undertakings were the functions of the entire economic system. Once controls were relaxed and 'to each according to his work' was brought in as a measure to stimulate the economy, differences in quality between those in charge of enterprises inevitably became apparent in their different understandings of 'work' and 'reward', and their dissimilar measures for attaining different kinds of prosperity.

What was most striking was that relaxing controls in backward regions and developed areas released two kinds of impetus working in different directions, one leading to the development of the natural economy and the other to the development of the commodity economy. In developed areas, because the foresight and qualities for conducting commodity business do exist among those in charge of enterprises, recognising the personal economic interests of those involved is in itself to be regarded as encouraging the development of the commodity economy. Thus, given the space for invigoration, those running businesses who have long been constrained by the 'one big pot' system can without too much effort speedily bring about the realignment of production factors in accordance with commodity economy business principles. Yet they also find themselves in ever deeper conflict overall as spontaneous self-organisation emerges within the social and economic spheres with all those as yet unreformed government functions such as the systems of pricing, commerce, transportation and finance, as well as the personnel systems for workers and cadres, the residency administration system and so on. In the reform of the superstructure the reform and readjustment of the structure of government functions is primarily manifested by the pre-existing organisational system continuously adapting itself to suit the development of the commodity economy according to changing requirements.

In the light of this, there is a certain objective basis for thinking along the lines of the 'impact reflex' and continuing to relax controls. However, relaxing controls in backward regions, where the 'bound' object is merely seen as the quality of enterprises within the natural economy, results in producer enthusiasm being linked with economic interests associated with the natural economy mode of production. Thus, 'to each according to his work' approves rewards obtained through work which destroys the natural environment. For the inhabitants of backward regions who are able only to realign production factors in accordance with natural economy business principles, there is simply no room for boosting commodity business management. As a result, when controls are relaxed in these regions, those in charge of enterprises lack the hoped-for vitality. Furthermore, not only is a serious all-round clash unable to develop between these people and the former economic control functions of the state as in developed areas but, on the contrary, there is a retreat into a primitive state of affairs where people remain isolated from even their nearest neighbours. Far from being close, the invigorated economic system and the superstructure display a tendency towards moving ever further apart. Even after the reform of the state-run system in the cities, if there is no active response from the government organisational system, then this tendency may well still occur to some extent.

To put it simply, what the state organisational system needs to do in developed regions is to constantly adapt itself to the requirements of the commodity economy as self-organisation grows. It makes no difference whether the government itself initiates or passively accepts this adjustment; this historically developing impetus has its basis in the commodity economy impulse which has built up in society.

Although backward regions encounter much less difficulty in the initial breakthrough than developed regions, nevertheless without a spontaneous commodity economy impetus it is a far more complex matter for backward regions to truly attain the goal of economic prosperity. The argument that the potential force for developing a commodity economy in backward regions lies in the urban state-run system, is only tenable in a comparative sense once the socioeconomic system in backward regions has become independent.

If we take educational levels as an example, virtually the entire educated and competent population in Gyantse county, Tibet, is concentrated in the county's highly articulated superstructure, and educational levels amongst urban residents are several times higher than among the rural population. Hence, if we want to readjust commodity exchange relations throughout society, we have no alternative but to shift our attention from the countryside to the cities and to the structural reform of the urban state-run system. However, looking at the situation nationwide, the educational levels of the urban population in Gyantse county cannot be compared with those in developed regions, and furthermore still fall well below the national average. In circumstances such as these, even when structural reform of the urban state-run system is completed in backward regions, we cannot be sure that the productive factors with the potential for realignment in accordance with commodity economy business principles, then in the hands of the urban inhabitants of backward regions, will be combined in the best way possible under ordinary conditions of commodity management. Even less can we be sure that these productive factors will not be combined in the worst possible way, to the point where they are quite simply left separate (which would be tantamount to not using them) or form a negative or destructive combination. Thinking of the chaotic mismanagement of Tibet's Nyingchi Textile Mill, who can guarantee that the mill will not halt production and close once the reform is implemented, thus causing the textile industry to revert to the developmental level of handicraft workshops?

In terms of absolute value, reform – particularly reform of the urban state-run system – must be sharply distinguished from the simple 'freeing' of the rural responsibility system in that it should extensively mobilise the latent forces for commodity economy development in backward regions. Reform will undoubtedly stimulate the vitality for economic development in backward regions at its very roots, and is the only way to change the face of backwardness in these regions. At the same time reform is a crucial step. The first breakthrough in the rate of reform in backward regions may result in greatly accelerated economic growth, and may also result in the experience of reform in backward regions becoming something for other regions to draw on in their own reform. However, we must not forget that reform in developed areas and even in China as a whole is proceeding at an ever-increasing pace. The above analysis of the 'one big pot' system and the major latent forces for commodity economy development also holds for developed provinces in the interior. If the reform of the urban state-run system succeeds in successive developed provinces or even in China as a whole, then the even greater latent commodity economy forces of developed areas which have been constrained by the urban state-run system will be brought into play on a massive scale. What then will the prospects be for the backwardness of backward regions and the comparative gap existing between them and developed areas? We know from the past that it was precisely in backward regions that the rural responsibility system reform was first introduced.

The more backward a region, the less hope there is for economic prosperity. To place hopes on the spontaneous, natural formation of a commodity economy all the more requires a government with a high degree of awareness, which will wisely and systematically guide the economy of the entire region on to the commodity economy path. It is crucial to study governmental functions, reform government structure, and strengthen the government's functions of administration and of encouraging the commodity economy in order to make up for deficiencies in commodity economy impetus in backward regions. This is a question of vital importance which has not been adequately dealt with in this book.

7.2 BRINGING IN AND UTILISING SKILLED PERSONNEL

In the case of backward regions where the quality of human resources is low, importing and tapping skills is of paramount importance. However, the vast backward regions are now facing nothing less than a serious brain drain. Once again it is the 'Matthew effect': the fewer talented people there are, the less able a region is to hold on to its skills or to bring them in from outside.

There are two aspects to this loss of talent: the mechanical and invisible brain drains. The mechanical brain drain results from the movement of talented people out of the region and is so well known that it needs no further explanation. What people are less well acquainted with is the invisible brain drain. Due to backwardness, it is difficult for research and work carried out in backward regions in the fields of science, technology, education and culture to gain recognition as leading work in these fields in the country as a whole or to be accepted as setting standards. Because developed regions are developed, their research and work in the above fields not surprisingly is seen as the dominant trend and becomes the publicly recognised standard. Is there anyone who does not wish to rise to the top in his or her field? Is there anyone keen to make a mark in some high level discussion who settles instead for what are considered second or third-rate topics? There are a few people of this sort. So, even if there are talented people who do not leave the backward regions for whatever reason (for example, administrative measures), the problems and fields that they deal with, the topics and aspects that they are researching into, the achievements and contributions that they make are often not geared towards the needs of backward regions but instead serve and are of use only to the developed areas. This authority extends even to the public announcements of achievements, which more often than not are made in developed areas. This is what is meant by the invisible brain drain. Although in the physical sense talented people remain in backward regions, their mental energies have gone out to developed areas where they contribute to the further development of these regions.

The inability to attract skills is part of the same problem. Life and work in backward regions is undoubtedly much tougher than life in developed areas. Economic and living conditions are poor and there are numerous social difficulties, such as the separation of family members, children's education, provision for the elderly and so on. But it is working conditions and the possibility for personal development that are the greatest cause for disappointment. Ignoring the isolation from exchange of information and the dearth of cultural activities and looking only at specialised and technical conditions, any specialist who works in backward regions for a few years falls behind in his or her field.

Clearly there is a heavy price to pay for living in backward regions, especially for those people who have moved there from developed areas. If a lot is invested then future rewards will be high. Thus, if people are going to want to live under poor conditions in backward regions, then opportunities in these regions must be increased, especially those relating to raising personal income and satisfying individual social requirements. People's requirements are many-faceted: economic requirements are one aspect and apart from this there are non-economic requirements such as improving one's social standing, pursuing ideals, displaying one's abilities and catering to one's interests. These two types of requirements are both extremely important. In a certain sense the second type is even slightly more important in people's eyes, as our investigations showed. If the opportunities for satisfying people's economic and non-economic requirements are increased, then people will be willing to make a greater personal sacrifice. However, in both backward regions and developed areas alike there is a 'one big pot' system awaiting reform, and so the degree of socialisation and commoditisation in daily life and production is much lower than in developed regions, while labour and sectoral divisions as well as social stratification are underdeveloped. On top of this working conditions are poor. So, compared to developed areas, there are certainly no more and possibly even fewer opportunities for increasing personal incomes and satisfying individual social requirements. That is to say, a higher price has to be paid for living and working in backward regions and not only will it be impossible to meet all requirements adequately, but opportunities may even be missed. Are there likely to be many takers for such an offer?

Therefore new skills must be brought in, existing talent must be retained and the brain drain must be reduced. These are all crucial for determining whether or not backward regions can create and increase the above-mentioned opportunities for talented people. This requires reform, particularly in the employment, personnel and wages systems, and in the financial and social security systems. As we have pointed out above, the loosely-knit nature of the socioeconomic structure in backward regions has a certain advantage for reform. This point can be positively utilised to take greater steps forward in the reform than in developed areas, promote the formation of a labour market, develop circulation among the people, strengthen the market element in social and economic life and in this way increase the opportunities for people to increase their incomes and improve their social standing.

7.3 NEW TOWNS FROM SCRATCH

Urbanisation is another serious problem in the development of backward regions. Like the majority of problems facing China, the difficulties are compounded with reform and development. On the development side alone the problem of urbanisation is fairly straightforward, but with the addition of the reform element it becomes much more complicated. Thus, we are confronted with the dilemma of where to start. Should we focus on the reform and development of existing towns or should we change the face of these regions and construct new towns from scratch?

We are inclined towards the latter option. The final stage of reform is the formation of a socioeconomic structure advantageous to long-term development and modernisation, which amounts to a wholesale restructuring of the relations and interests existing between individuals and between individuals and social organisations. We will not discuss the natural obstacles encountered in the development of existing towns with regard to the environment, ecology and the construction of public facilities, but look solely at interpersonal relations, the distribution of interests, and the situation regarding institutions, which are quite complex enough. Shielded by the 'one big pot' system, urban residents have more to gain than the peasants. This difference is even more apparent in backward regions which enjoy vast state subsidies, with 'external funds' buying in 'external goods'. Compared to the countryside there are more interest groups in urban areas, they are more complex and exhibit more uniformity. Due to historical and political factors, this aspect is more exaggerated in backward regions, particularly so in the system whereby interests are distributed under the 'one big pot' system in complete harmony with the requirements and adaptability of 'natural man'. This in turn results in the increased rigidity of the interest distribution set-up in backward regions. Under the onslaught of commodity production, these disparities might seem of minor importance, but unfortunately it is precisely this impetus which is lacking in backward regions.

Thus in one respect backward regions have a low degree of social integration, creating a loophole to be taken advantage of, while in another respect there is insufficient commodity production impetus to reform the situation regarding interests and social relations in existing towns, making it difficult to proceed with urban reform. We propose skirting the problem by creating separate areas and building new towns from scratch, making them into 'special reform zones'. The model for building new towns from scratch is the Shekou industrial zone in the Shenzhen Special Economic Zone. Its greatest significance lies in the fact that a brand-new structure encompassing organisations, institutions and individuals has emerged right within the socioeconomic system in this 'new town' (although it has not yet been perfected).

In reality, Shekou is to date an export processing zone which has attracted foreign funds, technology and skills. 'New towns' in backward regions should become 'reform pilot zones', attracting funds, technology and skills from developed regions, not that foreign countries are to be excluded. In building 'new towns' the market will be utilised to a greater extent, and urban development corporations will be set up by the government to organise the construction of basic facilities, formulate long-term development plans, invite tenders from outside and sell plots of land and residency permits. Special policies will be formulated for legal persons coming to the 'new towns' to develop them and run businesses (particularly in aspects concerning personnel and financial administration), making the 'new towns' attractive to skills and funds from developed regions by providing numerous opportunities. By breaking the bounds of the different systems of ownership and by breaking down the distinctions between cadres and workers, anyone (including farmers) will be able to become a citizen of the 'new towns', working at a job he or she can do with the sole proviso that he or she accords with the demands. According to the principle of efficiency, steps must be taken to harmonise the relations between enterprise, state and citizen; try to devise a new enterprise system; determine the role of the government, and formulate measures for indirect control by the state; set up a new system of social welfare and social security to deal with enterprise bankruptcy and unemployment; implement both social and economic development and seek methods of social administration that are both efficient and democratic. Whether or not promoting urban reform locally results in overall reform, we believe that building new towns from scratch will nevertheless promote local growth by attracting skills and funds, and can achieve much more notable results than remoulding existing towns while at the same time being much easier to handle.

The degree of social integration is low in backward regions; there are few towns in their sparsely populated vast area and everywhere resources are left untapped. All these are advantageous for building new towns from scratch. However, we do not intend our proposal to be restricted to backward regions alone. It can also be applied to developed areas which also have problems in urban reform and restructuring the urban layout.

'New towns' amount to totally new socioeconomic systems. Our interest in putting forward this highly cursory proposal is with the aim of extending the scope of choice and not of dismissing the experiments in reform and development already being carried out in existing towns – this too is an option.

7.4 NATIONALISM AND RELIGION

Throughout the undeveloped border regions there exists another important problem, that posed by the issues of nationality and religion. A fresh appraisal of these issues from the angle of social and economic development (which is not simply a 'resist and conquer' approach) shows that they are extremely important to invigorating the economy of backward regions.

Fundamentally, the development of national minority regions depends on the enterprising spirit and efforts of the local national minority inhabitants. The desire for national improvement is a force which will not hinder but in fact invigorate national minority regions. Those intellectuals, cadres and young members of the workforce now in backward regions who are relatively well-educated and receptive to new lifestyles and innovative production methods, and who moreover have the latent qualities appropriate for a commodity economy, are often precisely the most ardent nationalists. Relatively knowledgeable about the outside world they are deeply aware of the very real national 'inequality' which stems from their backwardness, and this is what inspires their national zeal. As reformists who also combine aspects of tradition and change they are an essential human resource for reform and modernisation. These outstanding social elements are a major force for invigorating the economy, and any attempt to attack or suppress national consciousness simply attacks and suppresses initiative and the desire for national improvement.

Encouraging a healthy desire for national improvement and excellence depends crucially on the treatment of indigenous traditional national minority culture. The importance of preserving and developing this culture takes first place in national consciousness, and it is this which gives rise to the desire to achieve real equality with other nationalities (and especially with the Han Chinese). This is at the heart of the nationality issue, while such questions as financial and material aid, the proportion of national minority cadres and so forth form the surface layer. The two should be clearly distinguished and the central point must not be lost amidst a welter of superficial problems. Money alone cannot buy solidarity among nationalities. If national minority culture is not given due attention national feeling will be seriously damaged and increasing the provision of money and jobs will offer no solution. Effort expended on preserving and encouraging national minority culture and better use of initiative will allow a wider range of options in resolving a whole range of problems such as emancipation and making full use of national consciousness, financial and material assistance, the national minority composition of the cadre body and the influx of personnel from the hinterland. Thus less expenditure and more effort will promote social stability, development and reform.

Analysis of the facts demonstrates clearly that fears of national minority culture delaying social progress, destroying solidarity among nationalities and undermining China's unity are entirely unfounded. Seeing the development and modernisation of national minority regions in terms of Sinification will, however, have precisely this result.

Religion plays a considerable role in the fundamental activities of several national minority societies, and in some cultures it is inseparable from such areas of cultural heritage as philosophy, history, language, literature, art, architecture, medicine, astronomy, the calendar and so forth. Hence, for some national minorities, religious repression cannot go hand-in-hand with championing national minority culture and preserving its normal social functioning.

In these national minority regions today, religion is no longer the mainstay of the old order but has become something which can be made use of. To give an example, when the household responsibility system was introduced a number of lamas and imams urged the local people to carry out the Party's rural policies. Religion can be separated into rational deliberation and formalised blind superstition. The former is largely the source of the positive impact of religion such as the development of national culture and meeting people's needs, while the negative effects, such as superstition, extravagance, fatalism and other pernicious concepts, are mainly confined to the latter. Experience proves that the more religion is repressed the more pronounced such aspects as blind worship and superstition become. On the other hand, promotion of unity between nationalities, social stability and social development can be achieved through respecting national minority cultural traditions, recognising religion and making use of its positive side. On this basis, it is quite possible that the negative aspects of religion will gradually diminish and disappear through religious reform.

We have carried out a number of investigations on precisely this question in religious and cultural circles in Tibet, and can state with certainty that there is already an existing social basis and demand for religious reform in Tibet, which moreover has received the support of a section of the religious upper strata. Religious reform, however, cannot spontaneously come about in an atmosphere of religious repression. Repression leads only to increased religious solidarity and rigid adherence to established doctrine for fear that traditional religious practices will be lost. If, however, controls are relaxed and freedom of belief allowed, with the growth of a commodity economy, a rise in social demand and increased debate between different religious sects, religious reform could be achieved. Reformation has already taken place once in the history of Tibetan Buddhism and precedents do exist for religious change and the growth of sects under the influence of other nationalities. A commodity economy is a powerful force, and in the trading posts of Zhangmu and Yadong where commercial activity has become commonplace the negative influence of traditional religion has already all but disappeared. We believe that given these premises, at the same time as successfully invigorating the economy, together with our national minority compatriots we will be able to accomplish an historic religious reformation and cultural renaissance.

7.5 TWO CHILDREN ARGUE OVER THE SUN

Travelling eastwards, Confucius came across two children quarrelling and asked them what their dispute was over.

The first child said, 'I say that the sun is closer when it rises, and farther away at midday'. The second child believed that the sun was farther away when it rose, and closer at midday.

Said the first child, 'The sun when it rises is the size of a cartwheel, but by midday it is as small as a plate. Isn't this because distant things are small and near things are large?'

Said the second child, 'At sunrise it is very cold, while at midday it is burning hot. Isn't this because near things are hot and distant things are cold?'

Confucius could not decide which of the children was right. The children laughed and said, 'Who is more knowledgeable than you?'[1]

Notes and References

2 Contradictory Reality

1. Huang Zhenggen, 'The First Peasant Aircraft Owner', *Fortnightly Chats*, (*Ban Yue Tan*) 1984, no. 9.
2. Dai Qing, 'Beijing Suburbs Peasant Cheng Xiuzhi Celebrates Her Purchase Of A Piano' *Guangming Daily* (*Guangming Ribao*) 17 February 1984.
3. 'Earning to Spend, Spending to Earn', *Chinese Youth* (*Zhongguo Qingnian Bao*) 13 December 1984.
4. 'The Peasants of Talinpo Hold A Gourmet Cookery Competition', *Henan Daily* (*Henan Ribao*) 11 December 1984.
5. 'The Families of Xingfu Village Undergo A Tremendous Change in Consumer Spending', *Liaoning Daily* (*Liaoning Ribao*) 3 December 1984.
6. Yang Zhilong, '100,000 Yuan Shi Zhimin: A Bold Pioneer In Family Prosperity', *People's Daily* (*Renmin Ribao*) 28 September 1984.
7. Lu Xueyi and Wang Xiaoqiang, 'The Initial and Future Development of the Household Responsibility System', *Agricultural Economy Series* (*Nongye Jingji Congkan*) 1981, no. 2.
8. Ji Xiaoming, 'An Investigation into the Pastoral Economy of Xinjiang', *Economic Development Strategies for Backward Regions* (*Luohou Diqu Jingji Fazhan Zhanlue*), State Council Rural Development Research Centre mimeograph.
9. Bai Nanfeng and Wang Xiaoqiang, 'Human and Social Structure and the Development of the Social System: A Look at the Development Problems in Backward Regions with Reference to Guizhou', *Economic Development Strategies for Backward Regions* (*Luohou Diqu Jingji Fazhan Zhanlue*), State Council Rural Development Research Centre mimeograph.

3 The Intrinsic Determinant of Backwardness

1. Wang Xiaoqiang and Bai Nansheng, 'Changing Trends in the Development of the Rural Commodity Economy – An Investigation into the Small Commodity Production and Marketing Base of Wenzhou, Zhejiang', *People's Daily* (*Renmin Ribao*) 13 November 1983.
2. *People's Daily* (*Renmin Ribao*) 24 June 1985.
3. Zhang Shaojie *et al.*, 'An Investigation into the Economy of the Xishuangbanna Region', *Economic Development Strategies for Backward Regions* (*Luohou Diqu Jingji Fazhan Zhanlue*), State Council Rural Development Research Centre mimeograph.
4. Sun Fangming *et al.*, 'Socioeconomic Development in Backward Regions', *Economic Development Strategies for Backward Regions* (*Luohou Diqu Jingji Fazhan Zhanlue*), State Council Rural Development Research Centre mimeograph.

4 The Way Out?

1. From *The Book of Master Guan.*
2. Shi Zhengyi, 'View Problems of Economic Development Strategy in Minority Regions From the Strategic Perspective', in *Nationality Economic Research* (*Minzu Jingjixue Yanjiu*) vol 2 (Ningxia People's Publishing House, 1984) p. 41.
3. Candidates had entered teaching after 1966; had been teaching for less than 25 years; were under the age of 49 (men) or 44 (women).
4. Reform of socioeconomic relations has a greater impact on the entrepreneurial spirit than such infrastructural factors as education, access to information or the development of transport and communications. This has been validated by our survey described in Chapter 3 – see especially Table 3.3.
5. Wang Baoliang and Li Tianqi, 'A Preliminary Strategy for Economic Development in Minority Nationality Regions in Qinghai Province', in *Nationality Economic Research* (*Minzu Jingjixue Yanjiu*) vol 2 (Ningxia People's Publishing House 1984) p. 195.
6. Cao Yuanzheng, 'Investigations and Reflections on Problems of Development in Animal Husbandry in Pastoral Areas of Qinghai Province' *Economic Development Strategies for Backward Regions* (*Luohou Diqu Jingji Fazhan Zhanlue*), State Council Rural Development Research Centre mimeograph.

5 Reform

1. For this concept, see Wang Xiaoqiang, 'Take the Countryside as the Breakthrough Point and Implement a Three-Dimensional Development Strategy in Separate Regions' in *Rural Economy and Society* (*Nongcun. Jingji. Shehui*), State Council Rural Development Research Centre, vol. 3 (Knowledge Press, 1985).

6 A Hundred Enterprises at the Ready, One to Take the Lead

1. These and the following figures are expressed as percentages of the national average.
2. Zhang Xiaoguang and Lu Mai, 'An Inquiry into the Strategy for Economic Development in Xinjiang', *Economic Development Strategies for Backward Regions* (*Luohou Diqu Jingji Fazhan Zhanlue*), State Council Rural Development Research Centre mimeograph.
3. Li Bing, 'Stimulate the Transportation of Livestock Products and Promote the Development of Animal Husbandry – Report of a Survey on Problems in Transporting Livestock Products in Inner Mongolia', *Economic Development Strategies for Backward Regions* (*Luohou Diqu Jingji Fazhan Zhanlue*), State Council Rural Development Research Centre mimeograph.
4. Gu Jinsi, 'Expand Jiangsu-Style Trade to Promote the Economic Development of Xinjiang – An Investigation into the Emphasis in Xinjiang's Strategy of Opening to the Outside World', *Economic Development*

Strategies for Backward Regions (*Luohou Diqu Jingji Fazhan Zhanlue*), State Council Rural Development Research Centre mimeograph.

5. Zhang Xiaoguang and Lu Mai, *op. cit.*
6. Li Bing, *op. cit.*
7. Cao Yuanzheng, *op. cit.*
8. Ji Xiaoming, *op. cit.*
9. Ah Xingxia, 'The Economic Development of the Inner Mongolian Autonomous Region Since the Third Plenum, and Suggestions for Future Economic Growth' in *Nationality Economic Research* (*Minzu Jingjixue Yanjiu*), vol 2 (Ningxia People's Publishing House 1984) p. 80.
10. See Bai Nansheng, 'A Trial Investigation of Form of Distribution from the Angle of Information Flow', *Economic Studies* (*Jingji Yanjiu*) 1983, no. 5.

7 An Open Conclusion

1. From *Liezi*, 'Tang Wen'.

Index